# Caring for a child with autism

This book donated by:
*Autism Advocates of Indiana, Inc.*
www.AutismIndiana.4T.com

With Funds raised at:
*The 2001 "Answers for Autism" Walk*

For more information about autism and autism resources in Indiana.

*Indiana Resource Center for Autism*
(812) 855-6508   http://www.iidc.indiana.edu/irca/

*of related interest*

## Asperger's Syndrome
**A Guide for Parents and Professionals**
*Tony Attwood*
*Foreword by Lorna Wing*
ISBN 1 85302 577 1

## Pretending to be Normal
**Living with Asperger's Syndrome**
*Liane Holliday Willey*
*Foreword by Tony Attwood*
ISBN 1 85302 749 9

## Asperger Syndrome in the Family
**Redefining Normal**
*Liane Holliday Willey*
*Foreword by Pamela B. Tanguay*
ISBN 1 85302 873 8

## Diet Intervention and Autism
**Implementing the Gluten Free and Casein Free Diet for Autistic Children and Adults – A Practical Guide for Parents**
*Marilyn Le Breton*
*Foreword by Rosemary Kessick, Allergy-induced Autism (AiA)*
ISBN 1 85302 935 1

## A User Guide to the GF/CF Diet for Autism, Asperger Syndrome and AD/HD
*Luke Jackson*
*Foreword by Marilyn Le Breton*
ISBN 1 84310 055 X

## Growing Up Severely Autistic
**They Call Me Gabriel**
*Kate Rankin*
ISBN 1 85302 981 6

## Autistic Thinking
**This is the Title**
*Peter Vermeulin*
*Foreword by Francesca Happe*
ISBN 1 85302 995 5

## Asperger Syndrome, The Universe and Everything
*Kenneth Hall*
*Forewords by Ken P. Kerr and Gill Rowley*
ISBN 1 85302 930 0

## Enabling Communication in Children with Autism
*Carol Potter and Chris Wittaker*
ISBN 1 85302 956 4

# Caring for a Child with Autism
## A Practical Guide for Parents

*Martine Ives and Nell Munro*

Illustrations by Fiona Bleach

Jessica Kingsley Publishers
London and Philadelphia
Published with the National Autistic Society

First published in the United Kingdom in 2002 by
Jessica Kingsley Publishers Ltd,
116 Pentonville Road, London
N1 9JB, England
and
325 Chestnut Street,
Philadelphia PA 19106, USA.

*www.jkp.com*

**Library of Congress Cataloging in Publication Data**
Ives, Martine, 1975-
    Caring for a child with autism / Martine Ives and Nell Munro.
    p. cm.
    Includes bibliographical references and index.
    ISBN 1-85302-996-3 (pbk. : alk. paper)
    1. Autism in children. I. Munro, Nell, 1979- II. Title.

RJ506.A9 I93 2001
618.92'8982--dc21                                    2001038436

**British Library Cataloguing in Publication Data**
A CIP catalogue record for this book is available from the British Library

ISBN 1 85302 996 3

Printed and Bound in Great Britain by
Athenaeum Press, Gateshead, Tyne and Wear

*This book is dedicated to Marc and to Jack — the first to teach us about autism*

# Contents

## *Acknowledgements*

We would like to express our thanks to the following people for all their help:

- to the NAS Information Centre staff for all the books borrowed and the hours spent clogging up the library.

- to David for sharing his wisdom. For his vital pointers, advice and constructive feedback.

- to Andrew, who got it all started.

- to Edna for inspiring us.

- to Annie for her invaluable contacts, help with copyright and her good humoured assistance.

- to Fiona for her lively illustrations and ability to deliver at the eleventh hour.

- to Sylvia for providing the index.

- to all our colleagues on the Autism Helpline who do such good work everyday.

- to Lewisham and Harringay parent support groups for allowing us to eavesdrop.

- to all the parents who returned questionnaires and provided case studies.

- to everyone at the NAS who has played a part in creating this book.

- and lastly but most importantly, we'd like to thank all the people who so kindly reviewed our work and made such vital contributions. They are: Catharine Binney, Janet Corcoran, Christine Deudney, Carolann Jackson, Rosemary Kessick, Steve Lambourne, Rosalyn Lord, Joe Marshall, Eileen Munro, Greg Pasco, David Potter, Karen Reeves, Sara Truman, and Wanda Zablocki.

Naturally any mistakes or omissions remain the responsibility of the authors.

# Introduction

The aim of this book was to produce a concise, informative text which would answer many of the questions that parents of children with autism have following the diagnosis of their child. We hope that this book provides a solid introduction and it signposts parents on if they have further queries. Academic references have been kept to a minimum, and feature mainly in brackets. The emphasis has been placed on practical, useful information, rather than dense theoretical jargon. Each chapter of the book has been reviewed by both parents and professionals. We hope that the sections on behaviour and therapies can be consulted time and time again as new questions arise. Case studies are provided throughout so readers can see how theory transfers to real life. We are very grateful to the parents who invited us to join their support meetings for an evening, and shared ideas and stories with us.

We have referred to 'children with autism' throughout this book; however, we intend this to include all children on the autistic spectrum.

We hope you find this book useful. If you have any comments or suggestions for later editions, send correspondence to Jessica Kingsley Publishers.

*Chapter 1*

# Explaining autism

Much has been written on the subject of autism. An in-depth description could easily consume this whole book. This section concentrates on summarising the main features and explaining commonly-used terms; the basics that any interested parent needs to know. The chances are that if you are reading these words, you are concerned about your own child. Perhaps your child has already been diagnosed, or maybe you are waiting for an assessment. For some of you, this book may be a starting point to see if the term 'autism' applies to your child. Whatever stage you are at, a clear understanding of the condition enables you to make informed decisions for your son or daughter. A parent is the most useful resource a child can have.

## What is the autistic spectrum?
The concept of the autistic spectrum was developed to describe a range of individuals – children and adults of varying ability levels – who display particular difficulties in some or all of the following areas:

- communication
- social interaction
- imagination

These areas are commonly referred to as 'the triad of impairments'.

Due to the range of the autistic spectrum, the people placed within it may sometimes appear quite different to each other. Professionals often refer to an individual's 'level of functioning' to indicate to what extent they are affected by their autism. Some individuals may be low functioning, meaning they are profoundly affected and clearly display the difficulties of the triad. Others may be very able and functioning at such a high level that, without knowing them well, it is hard to see any evidence of a disability at all. So the autistic spectrum encompasses people functioning at a low level, people functioning at a high level, and all the people in between. The notion of an autistic spectrum works particularly well as there are no sharp boundaries or rigid sections. This allows for the inclusion of individuals who display many of the characteristics of autism, but who do not fit neatly into diagnostic pigeon-holes.

## The triad of impairments explained

As already mentioned, the triad of impairments refers to the difficulties in communication, social interaction and imagination that people on the autistic spectrum experience. The following section will elaborate on these main features, highlighting how each area may be recognised.

## 1. Impairment of communication

Many children with autism do not understand the purpose and meaning of language, which affects their ability to communicate. For many parents, a delay or abnormality in language development is the first difficulty that alerts them to a possible problem (Howlin and Moore 1997). Babbling may be absent, or, if present, it is of a lower quality and frequency than in peers.

The language abilities of children on the autistic spectrum can vary enormously. This ranges from children who develop normally or even precociously, to children who never develop functional language. In between, there are children who use language to express basic needs but don't progress to expressing thoughts and feelings. In most cases, if functional language is going to develop, it is usually present by the time the child reaches five years of age. However, communication is more that just speech, and many nonverbal children can learn to use alternative communication systems.

## Other possible features of communication

### ECHOLALIA

Children with autism are often echolalic, which means they repeat words that they have heard parrot-fashion (sometimes immediately, sometimes with a delay) rather than create original responses or statements. The accent and tone of the original speaker may also be mimicked. On occasions, whole paragraphs the child has overheard on the radio or television may be repeated. This can sometimes mislead parents into thinking their child has more advanced language skills than she actually does.

### PRONOMINAL REVERSAL

This refers to the inability to use the word 'I' when referring to the self. Instead the child may use his own name ('Charlie wants to eat'), or another form ('He wants /you want to eat') rather than the expected 'I want to eat'.

### LANGUAGE IS USED IN INAPPROPRIATE OR UNCONVENTIONAL WAYS

The child may develop 'codes' for indicating desires – shorthand speech that only regular caregivers recognise. Sometimes the parent works out a logical association between the word and its meaning to the child (e.g. 'boots' indicates a wish to go to the park). Other codes may never be cracked by the parent, unless by luck or chance. Temple Grandin, an adult with autism, recalls shouting 'prosecution' whenever her kite fell from the sky. As a child she did not know the meaning of the word and used it simply because it sounded nice, much to the bafflement of people in earshot. Creation of new words (neologisms) is also possible. One child renamed kisses 'murs', as that was the sound she heard when people kissed. Novel and perceptive use of language can occur, e.g. calling highchairs 'baby sitters', or steam 'hot rain'.

PROBLEMS USING AND PROCESSING NONVERBAL COMMUNICATION

Speech accounts for only a small part of communication. Most of us pick up signals from body language, facial expressions, choice of vocabulary, voice tone and emphasis. A child with autism doesn't recognise the value of these cues and clues. This can lead to reliance on the literal meaning of words, without considering the delivery, intonation or social context that envelopes language. As well as not processing the nonverbal communication available from others, the child displays fewer of these signals herself, e.g. facial expression appears blank or unusually serious, speech is delivered in monotone.

MISSING THE IMPLICIT INSTRUCTIONS AND REQUESTS WITHIN SPEECH

Speech may be regarded simply as an exchange of facts. Therefore a child asked 'Do you know what the capital of France is?' might reply 'Yes' without elaborating to reveal the answer. 'Go and ask mum if she wants tea' may result in the child finding mum, asking the question, but not realising that the answer needs to be delivered back.

PROBLEMS WITH SPEECH THAT IS NOT LITERAL

Sarcasm does not register, words are taken at face value, even if the speaker's tone indicates the very opposite. Therefore, misunderstandings can occur:

| | |
|---|---|
| **Dad:** | 'Alex, this is the last time I'm going to tell you to pick up your clothes.' |
| **Alex:** | *(with a sigh of relief)* 'That's good, Dad, because I hate [it] when you tell me that.' (Gilpin 1993, p.63) |

Sayings like 'the cat has got her tongue' and 'keep your eye on the ball' are taken seriously if left unexplained. One teacher who jokingly told her pupil with autism to 'get lost' eventually found the missing child several miles away. Jokes beyond the simple or obvious are not understood. Slapstick comedy found in cartoons or television shows like *Mr Bean* may appeal, as can humorous exaggeration and word play (such as puns).

DIFFICULTY SAYING THE RIGHT THING, IN THE RIGHT PLACE, AT THE RIGHT TIME

Some children may inadvertently offend people around them. There is often no recognition of the social hierarchy that exists, or, in the words of Asperger (1944), there is no 'regard for differences in age, social rank or common courtesies' (p.81). There are countless stories of children approaching 'elders', strangers and authority figures with unbridled curiosity. One elderly lady with white hair and protruding teeth, was politely asked, 'Excuse me, but are you a rabbit?' (Howlin 1997, p.39). Even when social niceties are taught and apparently understood, social exchanges can fall short of the intended mark. This is aptly demonstrated by the student who tried to compliment a girl by saying, ' I like the way your hair falls over your eyes, it reminds me of a dog.'

PEDANTIC AND OVERLY FORMAL SPEECH

This tendency can make the child appear advanced for their age. One mother asked her nine-year-old child how she spent her lunchtime and was told, 'I meandered around the playground perimeter and took some air.' In some cases hyperlexia is evident, where the child has a reading age beyond their peers, but has trouble comprehending the individual meanings of the words used. Once hyperlexia is recognised, the child can be helped to learn the semantics of the words she is already using.

Suggestions for how to communicate more effectively with your child can be found in Chapter 6 'Moving forward after diagnosis'.

## 2. Impairment of social interaction

From early infancy some children with autism do not recognise humans as distinctly important. As a result they do not engage in the same manner with caregivers, or appear to receive the normal rewards from social exchanges. Kanner (1943) described this as an 'inability to relate themselves in the ordinary way to people and situations' (p.41).

Wing and Gould (1979) defined this inability further, in terms of three main subgroups of social impairment:

(i)   A child in the *aloof* group does not participate in social interaction, and is often described as being 'in a world of their own'. These children are happy to spend large periods of time alone. Communication, if present, is limited to obtaining basic needs. Being with others is not a motivating factor:

> I spent a great deal of time alone in my bedroom and was happiest when the door was closed and I was by myself. I cannot remember ever thinking about where my mother, father, brother and sister were, they did not seem to concern me. I think this was because I did not for a time realise that they were people and that people are supposed to be more important than objects. (Jolliffe 1992, p.12)

(ii)  Children within the *passive* group do not actively search for social interaction. However, when they are included in activities, they will accept this and even show pleasure. A passive child rarely makes demands on his caregivers. Peers may play with these children as if they were giant dolls (the patient to be nursed, the pupil to be taught). Clara Claiborne Park (1990) describes the passivity of her daughter in *The Siege*:

> What is one to think, feel and do when confronted by a 2-year-old – one's own – who makes no exploration or approach, who expresses neither hostility nor anger, and who wants for nothing? (p.88)

(iii) The third group is made up of children who make social approaches in a manner best described as *active but odd*. These children display a desire to be involved with peers, but lack the social skills to engage appropriately. Donna Williams, an adult with autism, provides a real life anecdote:

> I did not know how to make friends, so I would stand there calling this girl every four-letter word I knew... Eventually this girl would take to her feet and chase me for several blocks. I'd always go away and I'd be back the next day to do

it again. One day she caught me. She was about to 'smash my face in', when she decided to ask me why I had tormented her so persistently for so long. 'I wanted to be your friend,' I blurted out furiously. (Williams 1993, p.29)

(iv)   Later, Wing added a fourth category to describe the social impairment found in the most able adolescents and adults. Individuals falling into this group display 'an *inappropriately stilted and formal manner of interaction* with family and friends as well as strangers' (author's italics). An example is the son who addresses his parents as 'Mr and Mrs Jones'.

Not all children slot neatly into one of these four groups. Parents may be able to recognise aspects of some or all of these categories in their child, at different times.

## 3. Impairment of imagination

The term 'imagination', as it is used here, can be confusing. It should not be taken as a complete absence of imagination. Problems in this third area can be shown in a variety of ways:

### Rigidity in thinking

The child may try to see the world as a black-and-white place with no grey in between (e.g. people are either bad or good). Rules and regulations provide a comforting structure and are strictly followed. The many exceptions to rules that crop up in life cause confusion. Wendy Lawson, an adult with autism, has remarked that she was in her forties before she realised that people were allowed to change their minds. Related to this rigidity is a difficulty in coping with change and a marked preference for sameness.

### Problems with abstract concepts

Some children develop a good level of concrete language, but cannot grasp abstract concepts. Sentences that follow a clear path of reasoning are understood, but the child is lost when the conversation veers off in unexpected directions.

### Difficulty in accepting what might happen in the future

The ability to plan for the future is affected. Problems are displayed in thinking ahead to the possible, but not yet definite. The child is unnerved by life's uncertainties, and becomes stressed worrying about what may or may not happen.

> Life is such a struggle; indecision over things that other people refer to as trivial results in an awful lot of inner distress. For instance, if somebody at home says, 'We may go shopping tomorrow,' or if somebody says, 'We will see what happens,' they do not seem to realise that the uncertainty causes a lot of inner distress, and that I constantly labour, in a cognitive sense, over what may or may not occur. (Jolliffe 1992, p.16)

Related to this is an inability to see the consequences of an action. Therefore a child who is just about to throw her ball against a window may be unable to appreciate the possible results, i.e. she may not be aware that the window could break or that the owner of the window will be angry.

### Impairment in imagination shown through play

Normally, play is a natural, enjoyable activity. Through play, children explore new concepts, develop new ideas and progress to higher levels of understanding. Parents watching their child with autism will notice distinct differences.

### Limited scope

Long periods may be spent playing with one particular toy. The pattern of play may appear mechanical, with the child following the same motions and actions each time (e.g. spinning the wheels on a truck).

### Difficulty playing with peers

Approaches from other children may be refused, passively tolerated or responded to inappropriately. For some children, these advances will be seen as unwelcome intrusions and they may respond with distress or anger. There may be no initiation from the child with autism to begin play. If play with others occurs, the child with autism may insist on certain rules. If these rules are broken, play inevitably stops.

### Love of rough-and-tumble play

The majority of children with autism gain obvious pleasure from physical play with a parent.

### Inability to engage in make-believe/pretend play

Activities that depend on the child pretending (e.g. cowboys and Indians), or using objects in a novel, original way (e.g. using a box as a car or a banana as a telephone) are not common, or, if present, are limited. If a playmate models pretend play, the child with autism may incorporate the game into her own repertoire, but she is likely to follow it in a rigid, unchanging manner. Similarly, the child may join in with a recognised action (pretending to drink tea from an empty toy cup) but will not go on to spontaneously extend this play in more imaginative directions.

Some children appear to play imaginatively, but they are actually copying scenes from favourite television programmes, rather than enacting games of their own creation. More able children may enjoy creative play and show some capacity for invention and learning through role-play. Certain children may create elaborate fantasy worlds, which seems at odds with an impairment in imagination. Closer inspection of the creation may reveal the specific rules and regulations imposed by the child.

## Other associated features that can appear alongside the triad of impairments

*Repetitive behaviour patterns*

Due to the problems already highlighted in the triad, the child is encountering a lot of chaos in their world. Repetitive behaviour is a way of bringing order and predictability to an unstable, frightening world.

> Reality to an autistic person is a confusing, interacting mass of events, people, places, sounds and sights. There seem to be no clear boundaries, order or meaning to anything. A large part of my life is spent just trying to work out the pattern behind every-thing. Set routines, times, particular routes and rituals all help to get order into an unbearably chaotic life. (Jolliffe 1992, p.16)

This constant need for reliable structure, and the relief gained when the expected happens, can help explain why a child will persist in asking a question to which they already know the answer, or flicking a light switch on and off for extended periods without growing bored:

> I loved repetition. Every time I turned on a light I knew what would happen. When I flipped the switch, the light went on. It gave me a wonderful feeling of security because it was exactly the same each time. (Barron and Barron 1992, p.20).

*Special interests*

These preoccupations are more pervasive and obsessional in nature than with normal hobbies or fads. Some children become attached to cartoon characters and insist on watching endless video replays. Other children verbalise their interest, and would happily talk all day about whatever fascinates them. The pleasure the 'audience' gains from these extended monologues is not a consideration. Collecting objects or brands is also popular, but as Asperger (1944) notes, 'The children accu-mulate things merely in order to possess them, not to make something of them, to play with them or to modify them' (p.82).

Interests vary from the weird to the wonderful. From sock marks left on ankles to the conservation of the countryside, from serial killers to sunsets – the interest is usually highly specific to the individual. Digby Tantam (1995) recalls one man who memorised the addresses of juvenile courts but was 'bored to tears' by details of other courts.

The energy and motivation that special interests generate can be put to good use. Obsessions can be used to motivate learning, and in some cases can form the foundation for a career. Temple Grandin's fascination with cattle chutes as a child and her subsequent career in livestock handling design provide a clear example.

### Sensory disturbances

These are so commonly reported by people on the spectrum that certain authors have suggested that sensory disturbances are a primary deficit, rather than secondary feature (e.g. Williams 1993). Individuals may be hypersensitive (over-sensitive) or hyposensitive (under-sensitive). Any of the senses can be affected. Hypersensitivity explains the child who clamps his hands over his ears every time the phone rings, or who refuses to eat certain textures of food.

Hyposensitivity is displayed in the child oblivious to temperature, or with a high pain threshold. This should not be confused with cases where a serious illness or injury goes undetected due to the child's inability to communicate his discomfort. Abnormal responses to pain are also noted by some parents: a child who bangs her head repeatedly against the wall may giggle rather than cry. Some children do engage in self-injurious behaviours (e.g. eye-poking, hand-biting) but seem oblivious to any pain. In sharp contrast the same child may find hair washing and brushing unbearable and certain textures and materials against the skin insufferable. The child may shy away from gentle maternal embraces but scream with delight during rough-and-tumble play. Tremendous variations exist between people; an individual can show a mixed profile of hypersensitivity in certain areas, contrasting with hyposensitivity in others.

Difficulty filtering out unnecessary sounds is a common problem. The listener may find it hard to attend to noteworthy details (e.g. listening to a speaker's voice when there is background noise).

Conversely, one feature in the environment may be focused on, to the exclusion of all else:

> When left alone, I would often space out and become hypnotised. I could sit for hours on the beach watching sand dribbling through my fingers. Each grain was different, and I was like a scientist studying the grains under a microscope. As I scrutinized their shapes and contours, I went into a trance which cut me off from the sights and sounds around me. (Grandin 1995, p.44)

This may also happen in the child's dealings with people, where a part is focused on rather than the whole:

> When the book was taken away from him, he struggled with the hand that held it, without looking at the *person* who had taken the book… When the *Reader's Digest* was taken from him and thrown on the floor and a foot placed over it, he tried to remove the foot as if it were another detached and interfering object, again with no concern for the *person* to whom the foot belonged. (Kanner 1943, p.35)

Some senses appear to be used in a different way. The senses of smell and taste may be used to inspect new objects and even people. Temple Grandin recounts how, when younger, she used to smell the people she met, much as a dog would. Young children may lick objects or themselves for exploration, comfort, or out of habit. Certain children experience difficulty determining where their body ends and the external world begins. The child may be amazed at the arm appearing from the end of his sleeve during dressing. One adult recalls shaking her hands as a child, to see if they were truly part of herself or whether they would fall off. This lack of sensorimotor awareness may account for some of the motor co-ordination problems displayed by children with autism.

## Self-stimulatory behaviours

Some children engage in particular behaviours (sometimes referred to as 'stimming') which produce a stimulating effect. Examples include hand-flapping, rocking, grunting, teeth-grinding and jumping from foot to foot.

> Rocking and spinning were other ways to shut out the world when I became overloaded with too much noise. Rocking made me feel calm. It was like taking an addictive drug. The more I did it, the more I wanted to do it. (Grandin 1995, pp.44–45)

Stimming usually increases when the child is excited, but in other situations can signal boredom. In stressful situations the behaviour may also increase, as a way to cope with anxiety. As a result, the appearance of these behaviours at certain times can help parents recognise their child's state of mind.

### Problems with motor skills and control

Some children on the spectrum have poor motor skills. Overall co-ordination and gross/fine motor ability can be affected. Some parents notice a general 'clumsiness', and difficulty in performing specific tasks (e.g. doing up buttons or riding a bike). Left – right, back – front may be muddled up by the child. In some cases a child could be diagnosed with dyspraxia.

### Savant skills

A savant or 'splinter' skill is an isolated area in which an individual excels, often in stark contrast to their overall level of functioning. It is estimated that 10 per cent of people on the autistic spectrum possess a savant skill, a similar figure to that found in the wider population. These talents commonly fall in the areas of art, music, mathematics and memory feats. Due to Hollywood interest in the savant skills found in autism (most famously *Rain Man*), a popular myth is that these talents are an integral part of the condition.

## Incidence rates

Many parents are interested to know just how many individuals are affected by autism. The National Autistic Society (NAS) currently estimates that 91 in every 10,000 people are on the autistic spectrum. This means that in the UK over 500,000 people are affected by autism, ranging from the profoundly disabled to the extremely able. These figures are based on a number of different pieces of research (e.g. Lotter 1966; Wing and Gould 1979; Gillberg *et al.* 1986).

People with an average or high ability level (i.e. IQ 70 or above) account for the majority of this total figure. Approximately 71 people in every 10,000 (Elhers and Gillberg 1993) will have Asperger syndrome or be placed at the high functioning end of the autistic spectrum.

Interest in prevalence has been stimulated in recent years by the Measles, Mumps and Rubella (MMR) vaccine debate. As a response to research published by Andrew Wakefield, the Department of Health commissioned a study (Taylor *et al.* 1999) to establish whether rates of autism had increased since 1988 (when the vaccine was introduced). The results showed that there had indeed been a sharp rise in incidence over the previous decade. Experts are divided as to whether this indicates an increase in the number of cases (due to MMR or not), improvements in diagnosis, or a widening of the definition of the autistic spectrum.

## Gender bias on the autistic spectrum

Far more boys than girls are affected by autism. This is not that unusual, as behaviour disorders and learning difficulties are generally more common in males than females. The ratio of boys and girls affected varies along the autistic spectrum. It is estimated that for every one girl with Kanner's autism there will be four boys with the condition. Figures show a tendency for girls to be more severely affected than boys, with a lower average IQ (Lord and Schopler 1985).

David Skuse (2000) offers one explanation into the gender bias found in autism. His 'imprinted – X liability threshold model' suggests that fathers pass on an activated 'feminine intuition' gene (on the X chromosome) to daughters. Boys, however, inherit an X chromosome from their mothers, but the feminine intuition gene is switched off. This means that girls are programmed to pick up socially appropriate behaviour, whereas boys have to learn these social skills. The idea of an imprinting mechanism responsible for turning protective genes on and off could explain why more boys than girls are affected by autism.

Some authors believe that girls on the autistic spectrum are under-diagnosed. Kopp and Gillberg (1992) suggest that an 'overreliance on the male prototype of autism' has led to girls' remaining unidentified. Affected girls may not display the domineering and sometimes aggressive qualities found in boys. Gillberg and Rastam (1992) examined potential links between autism and disorders like anorexia nervosa. One possibility is that in a subgroup of girls a label of anorexia nervosa, obsessive compulsive disorder, paranoid disorder or conduct disorder could actually reflect an underlying autistic spectrum disorder. This complements the explanation that girls have a passive, less overt expression of autism.

The gender bias becomes more pronounced for Asperger syndrome, with one girl affected for every nine boys. Once again this figure may reflect the high functioning females slipping through the diagnosis net. Attwood (1998) remarks that girls with Asperger syndrome seem more able to imitate peers and have more social play skills than the boys do. Therefore diagnosis is more common in boys because their problems are more difficult to ignore or dismiss – they stand out as odd. The girls are more likely to be seen as immature, but as they are not disruptive they are often left to 'suffer in silence' (Attwood 1998, p.152). Despite this, as a result of their chameleon-like ability, girls often have a better long-term prognosis than boys do.

## Movement along the autistic spectrum

It has been noted that someone's placing on the spectrum can change over time. Therefore, in certain cases, a child diagnosed at three years with Kanner's autism, when reassessed a decade later, may display characteristics associated with Asperger syndrome. This is where the value of early diagnosis and intervention really becomes apparent. Children placed in the appropriate environment, where their needs are met, can show dramatic improvements. Each child on the spectrum has room to progress, although for individuals with severely impaired language skills and additional learning difficulties, gains will be more limited.

There have been some claims by parents (Kaufman and Kaufman 1976) and professionals (Lovaas 1987) of children who have recovered from autism. As none of these reports have been successfully validated (many are anecdotal) the general consensus is that although some individuals may improve to a stage of normal, or near normal functioning, they still remain on the autistic spectrum. (See entries in Chapter 13 'Therapies and approaches' for more information.)

## The importance of personality

Everyone on the autistic spectrum is an individual. Despite the core problems that people on the spectrum share, each is unique, with a distinct personality. Similarities undoubtedly exist, but to understand each person, time must be spent understanding how their autism particularly affects them. A book can provide a good foundation but can never compare to the knowledge and experience that parents develop concerning their own child.

## Getting through the jargon

The autistic spectrum serves as a framework; however, within this, clinicians have identified certain subgroups and associated disorders. The various labels that professionals use can seem complex and confusing. The next section offers a concise explanation of the main terms you may come across.

## Different subgroups within the autistic spectrum

### Autistic Spectrum Disorder or Pervasive Developmental Disorder

Anyone placed on the autistic spectrum is said to have an autistic spectrum disorder (ASD). In some parts of the world (America in particular), the term 'pervasive developmental disorder' (PDD) is used instead. ASDs are pervasive because they affect different aspects of the individual's life. ASDs are developmental in nature because they are present throughout the individual's lifespan. This means that a child with ASD grows into an adult with ASD.

## Kanner's autism, classic autism or typical autism

These terms are used to describe an individual who is profoundly affected by their autism, and placed at the lower functioning end of the spectrum. This child may have learning difficulties (i.e. an IQ below 70) in addition to the triad of impairments. Individuals with this diagnosis are likely to have greater communication problems and a more dependent future.

## Asperger syndrome

This refers to an individual functioning at a higher level, who still displays signs of the triad of impairments, although perhaps in more subtle ways. Intelligence is usually average or above. Language could initially be delayed, but the child may quickly catch up with peers, and in some instances use vocabulary beyond his years. Speech can appear pedantic and overly formal. Difficulties with social relationships are present throughout development, but may become particularly apparent in the teenage years. Sometimes the individual has co-ordination problems, though this may be regarded as clumsiness. Walking gait can appear odd and ungainly, sports at school may pose problems, especially team games. Special interests that absorb the child are common and can range from the mundane to the bizarre. Diagnosis can be later for these more able individuals, as difficulties are not as apparent as in Kanner's autism. At the uppermost end the spectrum blends into 'normality', and some individuals may display certain traits, but never require a formal diagnosis or specialist help.

## Loners

Some people experience problems with social interaction throughout their lives, but do not have difficulty with other areas of the triad. Schooldays can be tough for these children, some of whom have special talents. While there is clear overlap with Asperger syndrome, the subtlety of social difficulties in this group has led to the separate term 'Loners' (Wolff 1995). Prognosis for loners is good; although the social impairment is always present, the majority become independent adults.

### Atypical autism or Pervasive Developmental Disorder Not Otherwise Specified (PDD-NOS)

This diagnosis may be given when a child does not display enough features for typical autism, or when the onset of autism is after three years of age. A child with atypical autism will benefit from the same interventions and strategies as another child on the spectrum. The diagnostic assessment should reveal why such a diagnosis was given. In parts of the world where the term PDD replaces ASD, the puzzling label PDD-NOS (deep breath now – Pervasive Developmental Disorder Not Otherwise Specified) may be given in place of atypical autism.

### Pathological Demand Avoidance syndrome (PDA)

This term was coined by Elizabeth Newson (1988) to describe children showing extreme avoidance behaviour when asked to comply or complete tasks. It has been argued that children with autism can display this tendency, and therefore defining a separate syndrome is unnecessary. However, supporters believe that the classification PDA allows for the diagnosis of a group of children who show far more challenging behaviours than those normally found within the autistic spectrum. To add further to this distinction, it has been recommended that children with PDA benefit from different intervention strategies to children with autism.

### Semantic Pragmatic Disorder (SPD)

This is a term used mainly by speech and language therapists to describe a child with particular problems in understanding the meaning of language and using it in the correct manner. This is a controversial diagnosis, as many children on the autistic spectrum experience these difficulties within the communication part of the triad, alongside their impairments of social interaction and imagination. It has been suggested that a child with the label SPD could also be placed on the autistic spectrum, if an assessment was widened to look at other areas (i.e. social interaction and imagination) rather than just concentrating on communication. Semantic pragmatic problems undoubtedly exist, the debate is about whether they can occur in isolation and therefore warrant a separate condition.

## Coexistence with other disabilities

Theoretically, autism could coexist with any disability. There are well-known associations between autism and certain disabilities including tuberous sclerosis, fragile X and epilepsy. Mild learning difficulties have been found in one quarter of people with autism, and half have learning difficulties of a severe nature (Wing 1995). Sensory impairments and physical disabilities can occur alongside autism. In some cases, where a child has more than one disability, underlying problems can be masked by a more overt or recognisable condition.

## Disorders associated with the autistic spectrum
### Epilepsy

It is estimated that a quarter to a third of children with learning disabilities on the autistic spectrum will experience an epileptic fit by adulthood (Wing 1996). In the wider population, onset usually occurs in childhood. For the individual on the autistic spectrum, a first fit may be experienced at any time between infancy and adult life. Onset during the early teenage years (12–14 years) is prevalent; at this time 20–30 per cent develop epilepsy. Earlier views suggested epilepsy was less common in individuals with average or above levels of ability. However, Goode, Rutter and Howlin (1994) found risk of epilepsy was not strongly associated with IQ.

### Deficits in attention, motor control and perception (DAMP)

Gillberg and Steffenburg have documented a group of children displaying DAMP syndrome (his term). As well as attention, motor control and perception difficulties, hyperactivity is also common. Gillberg and Steffenburg suggest that a substantial number of the children studied have Asperger syndrome, with a smaller number fulfilling criteria for autism.

### Fragile X syndrome

Fragile X refers to a defect in the X chromosome, which may be passed from one generation to the next. Diagnosis is by blood test. This syndrome is the most common form of an inherited learning disability, affecting more boys than girls. Problems associated with the condition include: delayed and distorted speech, attention deficits and autistic -like features (social anxiety, echolalia, poor eye contact and sensitivity to sensory stimuli). There is disagreement over the number of individuals within the autistic population affected by Fragile X syndrome. Turk and Zwink (1993) estimates that Fragile X syndrome accounts for less than 5 per cent of individuals with typical autism.

### Tuberous sclerosis (TS)

Tuberous (swellings) sclerosis (the hardening of organs or tissue) can affect all organs of the body and cause a range of difficulties including mental impairment, epilepsy and skin problems. In addition, children with TS can show autism.

### Childhood Disintegrative Disorder (CDD)

A child with CDD develops normally for the first two years; however a loss of skills follows in at least two major areas (language, play, social skills, bowel or bladder control, and motor skills). Due to the affected areas, behaviour can be similar to that of children with autism.

### Attention Deficit Hyperactivity Disorder (AD/HD)

AD/HD is diagnosed when a child shows symptoms of inattention, impulsivity and hyperactivity for a period of at least six months, before the age of 7 (criteria stated in DSM-IV). AD/HD cannot be diagnosed if it can be accounted for by an autistic spectrum disorder. That is not to say that a child cannot have both conditions. Possible causes of AD/HD appear remarkably similar to those alleged to cause autism (a combination of biological and environmental factors). Some people have suggested that the condition belongs on the autistic spectrum, as children with AD/HD can have so much in common with children with autism. However, many children with AD/HD have no inherent problem with communication or social skills. The social interaction difficulties experienced by the child with AD/HD can be linked to low self-esteem and their inability to play or work in a constructive way with peers.

## Dispelling the myths of autism

### Parents are the cause of their child's autism

At a regrettable stage in the history of autism, a lack of bonding between parent and child was believed to be the cause of the disorder. Thankfully, research and an evolution in thinking has laid this outdated notion to rest. Parents are now viewed as essential partners in enabling their child to reach full potential. Unfortunately, belief in this myth is still prevalent among some members of the public, and even some professionals.

### Autistic children are incapable of showing affection or loving others

Sadly, many parents are given the impression that caring for their child will be a thankless, unappreciated task. The image of the cold, unfeeling child who sees their parents solely as a means to fulfil basic needs is a popular yet undeserved stereotype. It is fair to say that some children on the spectrum show their affection in different ways. As always, there are individual differences – what one child enjoys, another may avoid. Some children love physical contact and are extremely generous with hugs and kisses. With other children, conventional displays of love may be scarce. Some children dislike being physically embraced, but when allowed to initiate the contact, on their terms, they show obvious pleasure. Many parents consider their children to be caring individuals, and can report clear examples of affection, delivered in their own unique way:

> One of the most touching things that Jessica ever did was to try and wipe the frown lines from my forehead. Whenever I frowned (probably too often), she would take her little hand and try to smooth my forehead. It may not be classic therapy for frowns but it always worked. (Gilpin 1993, p.67)

### Children with autism have no future

Every child on the autistic spectrum has a future. When parents are given the diagnosis for their child at a young age, it can be hard to look ahead 20 years to visualise the adults they will become. Many parents find that by the time their child has reached their fifth birthday, things have become noticeably easier. It is rare to hear of a child regressing after this age.

Every child can make progress in independence and self-care skills. Realistically, for some children, the difficulties they experience necessitate varying degrees of dependence in adulthood. More able children have a greater likelihood of gaining autonomy in their adult lives. For certain individuals living independently, holding down a job, forming friendships, and even getting married, are goals which should not be ruled out. As your child grows older, it will become easier to judge what kind of future lies ahead for them.

## Useful contacts

### 1. The National Autistic Society (NAS)
*The National Autistic Society provides a range of services for families and is the best starting point for finding out more about autism. The NAS Autism Helpline can be contacted at:*

**The NAS Autism Helpline**
393 City Road
London EC1V 1NG
*Tel:* 0870 600 8585 (Monday – Friday 10am – 4pm, calls charged at national rate)

*Fax*: 020 7833 9966
*Minicom*: 020 7903 3597
*Email*: autismhelpline@nas.org.uk
*Website*: www.nas.org.uk

### 2. The Autism Society of America (ASA)

Autism Society of America
7910 Woodmont Avenue, Suite 300
Bethesda
MD 20814-3067
USA
*Tel*: 301 657 0881
*Fax*: 301 657 0869
*Helpline*: 1 800 3AUTISM (1 800 3288476)

### 3. Asperger Syndrome Education Network of America, Inc. (ASPEN)

PO Box 2577
Jacksonville
FL 32203-2577
USA
*Tel*: 904 746 6741
*Email*: Aspen@cybermax.net
*Website*: www.asperger.org

### 4. Contact-a-Family

*This charity supports families who have children with special needs; publishes the* C-a-F
Directory *of specific and rare conditions; provides details of parent contacts and
support groups.*

**Contact-a-Family**
209–211 City Road
London EC1V 1JN
*Tel*: 020 76088700
*Fax*: 020 76088701
*Email*: info@cafamily.org.uk
*Website*: www.cafamily.org.uk

### 5. Fragile X Society

53 Winchelsea Lane

Hastings
East Sussex TN35 4LG
*Helpline:* 01424 813147
*Email:* lesleywalker@fragilex.k-web.co.uk
*Website:* www.fragilex.org.uk

### 6. National Fragile X Foundation
1441 York Street, Suite 303
Denver
CO 80206
USA
*Tel:* 303 333 6155 or 800 688 8765
*Website:* www.nfxf.org

## Suggested reading

Attwood T. (1998) *Asperger Syndrome: A Guide for Parents and Professionals.* London:
Jessica Kingsley Publishers.
*Concise and informative overviews of high functioning autism and Asperger syndrome.*

Frith U. (1989) *Autism: Explaining the Enigma.* Oxford: Blackwell.
*A fascinating historical overview of how autism was seen in the past.*

Tantam D. (1995) *A Mind of One's Own: A Guide to the Special Difficulties and Needs of the
More Able Person with Autism or Asperger Syndrome.* London: NAS.

The National Autistic Society (2000) resource list. *Autism: A Selective Guide to Book and
Videos.*
*This comprehensive list includes a section on specialist journals.*

Wing L. (1996) *The Autistic Spectrum.* London: Constable.
*A classic text and the perfect starting point for learning more about the autistic spectrum.*

*Chapter 2*

# What causes autism?

Nobody knows for sure what causes autism. Speculation abounds about possible causes. In this section the main theories are examined.

## Psychological factors

When autism was first identified as a separate syndrome, many regarded psychological factors as the primary cause. Mothers were accused of not bonding with their children, which, it was argued, resulted in the child's social withdrawal (Bettelheim 1956). This unfounded and damaging theory has long been disproven, although its influence is still felt. In countries like France it is difficult for parents to get treatment for their child unless they agree to undergo personal psychoanalysis. This is despite the fact that interaction skills do not significantly vary between groups of parents of children with autism, and parents of children not affected (Cantwell *et al.* 1979).

## Environmental factors

### Maternal rubella

A 1971 study (Chess *et al.*) showed that if the mother contracts German measles or rubella during pregnancy, there is a higher risk that her child will have autism. As almost all women are now vaccinated against rubella, this is no longer a significant consideration.

### Obstetric complications

Mothers of children with autism have been found to have a higher rate of complications during pregnancy and the birthing process (Green *et al.* 1984). A hard labour could account for brain damage which in turn could be an important factor in the child's autism. However, the obstetric complications experienced by mothers of children with autism are comparatively mild, and not the kind that usually result in brain damage to the baby (Deb *et al.* 1997). It has been suggested that a difficult birth may actually be the result of the baby not contributing to the birthing process. This explanation could indicate that the baby was damaged prior to delivery, although further damage may be sustained through birth complications. Certain authors (Rutter *et al.* 1993) have suggested that it is the baby's abnormal development whilst in the womb that prevents a normal pregnancy and delivery.

Although mothers of children with autism are more likely to experience obstetric complications, many do have straightforward pregnancies and births.

### Candida albicans

In the early 1980s, William Crook noticed similarities in symptoms between people with an overgrowth of *candida albicans* and children with autism. *Candida albicans* is a yeast that occurs naturally in the gut. Ear infections are common in children with autism, and the usual treatment is a course of antibiotics. Crook suggested that the overuse of antibiotics could lead to a disruption of normal digestive flora. 'Friendly' organisms are destroyed, whilst *candida albicans* and other fungi thrive. In some, an abundance of this yeast causes health problems. These problems can be treated with a medicine called nystatin. It was conjectured that nystatin could also benefit children with autism. Unfortunately, although some children with autism seem to have an overgrowth of *candida albicans* and benefit from this intervention, this drug does not help the majority. There is still some support for 'candida autism', and anecdotally some parents report that a low yeast diet helps their child. This is consistent with the suggestion that different subgroups of autism exist, with each group being caused by different factors.

## Diet – *leaky gut syndrome/ opioid excess theory*

In the mid 1970s an American researcher called Jak Panksepp speculated that an abnormal reaction to gluten and casein might cause autism. Gluten (found in wheat, rye, barley and oats) and casein (found in dairy products) are proteins which are broken down in the gut into short chains of amino acids called opioid peptides. In most of us, these opioid peptides are flushed through the gut. In the child with autism, the proposed 'leaky gut' (increased permeability of the gut wall) leads to the opioids leaking into the blood stream. It is suggested that the blood–brain barrier is weaker in children with autism. This would allow opioid peptides to pass through and affect the brain.

## Vaccines

In 1998 a gastroenterologist at the Royal Free Hospital in London published an important paper (Wakefield 1998). Dr Andrew Wakefield identified 12 children who had regressed and developed autism in the period following their measles, mumps and rubella (MMR) vaccination. He speculated that exposure to the triple vaccine had caused damage to both the brain and the bowel.

The Department of Health was quick to refute Wakefield's findings. It suggested that the appearance of autism shortly after the MMR vaccination was purely coincidental. The MMR vaccine is usually administered to infants aged between 12 and 15 months, the same period in which many parents first observe signs of autism. Recent research has examined whether incidence of autism has increased since the MMR vaccine program was introduced (Taylor *et al.* 1999). The debate into the safety of the MMR vaccine is ongoing. Parents seeking the latest developments should contact the National Autistic Society.

## Genetic factors

Bernard Rimland (1964) was among the first to suggest that the cause of autism was not psychological. Rimland speculated that genetics had an important role to play in explaining autism and suspected that bio-medical treatments could benefit these children.

Interest in genetics really took off at the end of the 1970s, follow-ing Susan Folstein and Michael Rutter's research (1977) into twins, where one or both children had autism. They found far more identical (monozygotic) twins who both had autism, than non-identical (dizygotic) twins. This was a clear indication that genetics was a factor in autism.

Folstein and Rutter's findings stimulated further research into this area. Interest focused on the search for specific genetic markers for autism. It quickly became apparent that a number of genes were impli-cated. Definite links have been established between certain genetic dis-orders and autism (e.g. fragile-X and tuberous sclerosis). The discovery of non-autistic people who possess many of the suspected genetic markers led to the conclusion that genetics was not the only answer to the cause of autism.

Subsequent research has led to more questions than answers. It is estimated that about 3 per cent of siblings of a child with autism will also have autism (Piven and Folstein 1994). This figure may be dis-torted by the fact that some parents choose to stop having children after having a child with autism. Studies with a wider focus have looked at extended family members and concluded that a range of difficulties (not specifically autism) can be present. Difficulties suggested include eating disorders, obsessive compulsive behaviours (Gillberg and Rastam 1992) and language disorders (Bolton *et al.* 1994). Siblings of a child with autism have an increased risk for what is known as the broader phenotype (LeCouteur *et al.*1996). This means that although some siblings are less affected than their brother or sister, they still have problems in similar areas (e.g. social communication and/or social interaction). This has muddied the waters for parents seeking simple reassurance that subsequent children will not be affected by autism. The majority of families with a child with autism will also have other children without the condition. Parents concerned about this issue should seek genetic counselling from a specialist centre (referral is through your local doctor).

## Organic features

The large number of people with autism who also have learning difficulties and/or epilepsy indicates some degree of brain damage or dysfunction. Steffenburg (1991) found almost 90 per cent of the children studied (on the autistic spectrum) showed signs of brain damage/dysfunction. Studies of individuals with autism have found particular organic features. Areas of interest include the size of the cerebellum, abnormal functioning of the basal ganglia, blood flow through the temporal lobes and increased brain volume. However, no one feature has appeared consistently in all the people with autism studied. More recently, American researchers (Nelson et al. 2001) have found abnormally high levels of four specific brain chemicals in the blood of babies who later develop autism or learning disabilities. This has exciting potential for the future of diagnosis. Currently, organic features are not a reliable marker for autism.

## Cognitive deficits

Various theories have focused on cognitive deficits when trying to explain autism.

### Mindblindness

Baron-Cohen (1995) coined this term to describe the inability to make guesses about other people's emotional states (also referred to as a lack of theory of mind). The majority of us appear to 'mindread' because our empathic skills enable us to predict how others will feel and think. Research suggests that the vast majority of individuals with autism have some abnormality in the mindreading system. Due to mindblindness they are unable to 'put themselves in someone else's shoes', and as a result come across as uncaring to other people's feelings, and thoughtless in some actions. More able children can be helped to make simple associations between what they do and say, and the reactions of other people. For children who succeed in learning how to show concern and a degree of empathy, the process may always be a learned rather than natural response for them. Whether children with autism can be taught to mindread is addressed in Chapter 10, 'Social ability'.

## Weak central coherence

Frith (1989) proposed that a single cause at the cognitive level could account for the skills and deficits of autism. Through the theory of weak central coherence Frith suggests that the style of information processing found in people with autism is detail-focused. This means that there is excellent attention to the parts of something, rather than overall focus on the whole. This would explain why children with autism perform well on tests requiring piecemeal processing (e.g. embedded figures) and why some are so adept at activities like jigsaw puzzles (even picture-side down). However, their ability to use context to make sense of the ambiguous is impaired (e.g. if asked to complete 'The sea is full of salt and…' the child may reply 'vinegar', as she is attending to the prompt 'salt' rather than the meaning of the whole sentence). Tasks that require the recognition of global meaning pose problems.

Most of us have strong central coherence, a tendency to see the whole at the expense of details. This is the ability to view a film and gain the gist of the story, without necessarily absorbing all the details. The beauty of weak central coherence as a theory for autism is that it accounts for the skills displayed, as well as the deficits. The theory does not judge the right or wrong way to process information. In certain situations weak central coherence will be an advantage, in other situations strong central coherence will be a benefit. Tony Attwood, describing thought patterns in high functioning individuals, writes, 'the thinking is different, potentially highly original, often misunderstood, but is not defective'(1998, p.126).

### Executive functioning

Executive functioning allows an individual to plan and organise. Problem solving, impulse control, flexible thought and action are all part of this ability. Some researchers (e.g. Ozonoff *et al.* 1991) have attributed the impairments in autism to a disorder of executive control functions.

The frontal lobes of the brain are associated with executive function, and adults with acquired frontal lobe lesions show similar deficits in this area to people with autism. This has led to the suggestion that the frontal lobes are implicated in autism. However, Happé (1994) warns that it would be premature to conclude that these two groups fail executive functioning tasks for the same reason, given the large area occupied by the frontal lobes and the many regions within it.

## In conclusion

Although many questions still need answers, researchers have come to the agreement that autism is biological in nature. However, despite the importance of genetics and a predisposition towards autism, a whole range of environmental factors are also implicated. This means that a genetic predisposition to autism alone may not ensure the development of the condition. Certain environmental factors, encountered at critical stages in brain development, may provide the final essential components. Therefore the build-up of factors, and the end combination that results in autism, could vary from one child to the next. Interplay between biology and environment seems to offer the best explanation. Autism appears to be the culmination of a chain of events – the straw that breaks the camel's back.

# Suggested reading

Happé F. (1994) *Autism: An Introduction to Psychological Theory.* London: UCL Press.
   *An introduction to psychological theories in autism.*

## Chapter 3

# A concise history of autism

To fully explain the development of ideas and understanding about autism, it is necessary to go back to the early twentieth century. Around this time a Swiss psychiatrist, Eugen Bleuler, first used the term 'autistic' to describe the withdrawn behaviour found in schizophrenia. The word autism is derived from the Greek word for self, *autos* and refers to the tendency to retreat into a private world. Autism was not suddenly created with Bleuler's first use of the term. Autism as a condition undoubtedly existed in earlier centuries. Uta Frith (1989) in *Autism: Explaining the Enigma* provides a fascinating history and believes that accounts ranging from the blessed fools of Russia to abandoned children such as the wild boy of Aveyron are evidence of autism in earlier eras.

Leo Kanner, an Austrian psychiatrist, is credited as the first person to use the term 'autistic' to describe a group of children displaying signs of a unique syndrome, never formally recognised before. In a preliminary report, Kanner remarks that since 1938 a number of children has come to his attention, all under 12 years of age, and showing common characteristics. The paper, 'Autistic disturbances of affective contact', published in 1943, provides case studies of the children, and over fifty years later it still serves as a fascinating and informative account of the disorder. Kanner's conclusion shows a depth of understanding and an enlightened position, still supported today:

> We must, then, assume that these children have come into the world with innate inability to form the usual, biologically provided affective contact with people, just as other children come into the world with innate physical or intellectual handicaps… For here we seem to have pure-cultural examples of *inborn autistic disturbances of affective contact.* (1943, p.50)

Unbeknown to Kanner, working in Baltimore USA, similar conclusions were being drawn in Vienna. Hans Asperger had also discovered a group of children displaying particular features, indicative of a new syndrome. Asperger's first paper on the subject was published in 1944, just a year after Kanner. Within this work, Asperger described children who seemed unable to enjoy normal affective relationships with people. Like Kanner, Asperger believed the disturbance was present from the beginning of life. The children described in both papers all displayed problems of affective contact. However, the individuals in Asperger's paper spanned a wider range of abilities than Kanner's sample, and provided the earliest account of an autistic spectrum. Asperger syndrome is now a useful diagnostic label to describe individuals functioning at a higher level on the autistic spectrum.

Despite the overlap in Kanner's and Asperger's work and the coincidental use of the label autism, their ideas were formed independently of each other, and the two never met. Asperger's paper, written in German towards the end of World War II, has received belated recognition only recently, whereas, Kanner's work in the USA was immediately acknowledged, and major clinics of the time responded with their own cases of autism.

## Important dates in the history of autism

**1943** – Kanner publishes first paper 'Autistic disturbances of affective contact' to describe a unique disorder.

**1944** – Asperger publishes first paper '"Autistic psychopathy" in childhood' and the notion of an autistic spectrum is suggested.

**1956** – An article by Bruno Bettelheim is published, which suggests autism is caused by parents' failure to bond with their children.

**1962** – Parents in the UK form 'the Society for Autistic Children' the world's first voluntary organisation for the condition (later renamed the National Autistic Society).

**1964** – Sybil Elgar opens the first NAS school.

– Bernard Rimland's text *Infantile Autism* argues that autism is organic in nature.

**1966** – Victor Lotter's study into incidence rates is published. Lotter estimates that 4.5 children in every 10,000 will have autism.

– Division TEACCH (Treatment and Education of Autistic and Related Communication handicapped CHildren) is founded in North Carolina, USA.

**1972** – Division TEACCH becomes the first comprehensive, state-wide, community-based programme of services.

**1977** – Folstein and Rutter's study implicates a genetic basis for the cause of autism.

**1979** – The *Journal of Autism and Childhood Schizophrenia* is renamed the *Journal of Autism and Developmental Disorders*. This signals an important shift in the classification of the condition.

– The results from Wing and Gould's Camberwell study lead to the use of the term 'the triad of impairments'.

**1980** – Autistic spectrum disorders are first recognised by the third edition of the Diagnostic and Statistical Manual (DSM III), an international system to classify disorders. Previously autism had been regarded as a psychosis and a form of schizophrenia.

**1987** – Lovaas publishes results indicating that behavioural strategies can help the majority of children with autism. (See ABA entry in Chapter 13 'Therapies and approaches').

**1991** – Elliot House opens, the first centre in the UK to offer diagnosis, assessment and professional training in the field of ASDs.

**1995** – An international consortium is established for research into genetics.

**1996** – Autism-Europe's charter of rights is adopted as a written declaration by the European parliament.

**1998** – MIND Institute, an American centre for research into neurological disorders, is established.

**2000** – Following the Internet conference Autism99, **autism**connect is launched (www.autismconnect.org) providing a first port of call for anyone interested in autism.

*Chapter 4*

# Diagnosis

Autism is diagnosed on the basis of behaviour. Blood tests and brain scans cannot reveal if your child has autism. As autism is a developmental disorder, taking a developmental history from parents is an essential part of the assessment process. To get a diagnosis, the child (or adult) must show the core features found in autism. In addition, there may be other behavioural characteristics present that are not essential for diagnosis. Autism is the combination of the key core features, occurring in one individual. When taken singularly these features may occur in other disorders and sometimes in the 'normal' population. The behavioural characteristics in themselves are not 'autistic features' (Jordan 1999). Therefore, a lack of eye contact does not necessarily mean a child is autistic, as children with other disabilities can also display this feature. Turning this around, a family doctor who refuses an assessment request because the child has eye contact is misunderstanding the diagnostic criteria for autism. Standard diagnostic criteria for autism and Asperger syndrome, taken from DSM-IV (*Diagnostic and Statistical Manual of Mental Disorders*, fourth edition 1994), are reproduced in Figures 4.1 and 4.2. Another widely used text is ICD–10 (*International Statistical Classification of Diseases and Related Health Problems*, tenth edition 1992). Certain authors (e.g. Elhers and Gillberg 1993) have put forward alternative diagnostic systems for Asperger syndrome.

Table 4.1  Diagnostic criteria for Autistic Disorder
from DSM IV (1994)

A.  A total of six (or more) items from (1), (2), and (3), with at least
two from (1), and one each from (2) and (3):

(1) qualitative impairment in social interaction, as manifested by
at least two of the following:

(a) marked impairment in the use of multiple nonverbal
behaviors such as eye-to-eye gaze, facial expression, body
postures, and gestures to regulate social interaction

(b) failure to develop peer relationships appropriate to developmental level

(c) a lack of spontaneous seeking to share enjoyment,
interests, or achievements with other people (e.g., by a lack of
showing, bringing, or pointing out objects of interest)

(d) lack of social or emotional reciprocity

(2) qualitative impairments in communication as manifested by at
least one of the following:

(a) delay in, or total lack of, the development of spoken
language (not accompanied by an attempt to compensate
through alternative modes of communication such as gesture
or mime)

(b) in individuals with adequate speech, marked impairment
in the ability to initiate or sustain a conversation with others

(c) stereotyped and repetitive use of language or idiosyncratic
language

(d) lack of varied, spontaneous make-believe play or social
imitative play appropriate to developmental level

(3) restricted repetitive and stereotyped patterns of behavior,
interests, and activities, as manifested by at least one of the
following:

(a) encompassing preoccupation with one or more stereo-typed and restricted patterns of interest that is abnormal either in intensity or focus

(b) apparently inflexible adherence to specific, nonfunctional routines or rituals

(c) stereotyped and repetitive motor mannerisms (e.g., hand or finger flapping or twisting, or complex whole-body movements)

(d) persistent preoccupation with parts of objects

B. Delays or abnormal functioning in at least one of the following areas, with onset prior to age 3 years: (1) social interaction, (2) language as used in social communication, or (3) symbolic or imaginative play.

C. The disturbance is not better accounted for by Rett's Disorder or Childhood Disintegrative Disorder.

**Table 4.2 Diagnostic criteria for Asperger's Disorder from DSM IV (1994)**

A. Qualitative impairment in social interaction, as manifested by at least two of the following:

(1) marked impairment in the use of multiple nonverbal behaviors such as eye-to-eye gaze, facial expression, body postures, and gestures to regulate social interaction

(2) failure to develop peer relationships appropriate to developmental level

(3) a lack of spontaneous seeking to share enjoyment, interests, or achievements with other people (e.g., by a lack of showing, bringing, or pointing out objects of interest to other people)

(4) lack of social or emotional reciprocity

B. Restricted repetitive and stereotyped patterns of behavior, interests, and activities, as manifested by at least one of the following:

(1) encompassing preoccupation with one or more stereotyped and restricted patterns of interest that is abnormal either in intensity or focus

(2) apparently inflexible adherence to specific, nonfunctional routines or rituals

(3) stereotyped and repetitive motor mannerisms (e.g., hand or finger flapping or twisting, or complex whole-body movements)

(4) persistent preoccupation with parts of objects

C. The disturbance causes clinically significant impairment in social, occupational, or    other important areas of functioning.

D. There is no clinically significant general delay in language (e.g., single words used by age 2 years, communicative phrases used by age 3 years).

E. There is no clinically significant delay in cognitive development or in the development of age-appropriate self-help skills, adaptive behavior (other than in social interaction), and curiosity about the environment in childhood.

F. Criteria are not met for another specific Pervasive Developmental Disorder or Schizophrenia.

Reprinted with permission from the Diagnostic and Statistical Manual of Mental Disorders, Fourth edition. Copyright 1994 American Psychiatric Association.

## The role of the parent

Parents are extremely good judges of their children. Mums and dads worried by their child's development usually have good cause for concern. This is the finding regardless of the family's education, income or previous parenting experience (Glascoe 1997).

## Early concerns

Although autism is rarely diagnosed before a child is two or three years of age, many parents have suspicions in the first year of life. Howlin and Moore (1997) found that the average age of the child when parents first became concerned was 1.7 years. For certain families anxieties follow shortly after birth, while other parents are not alerted till later.

## What are the signs to look for?

Some say that if you look hard enough it is possible to diagnosis your child with anything and everything. Certainly, every child has 'off days', but this is very different to the child consistently behaving in a way that concerns parents. As each child is different, the behaviours that alert parents can vary widely. The age of the child is also a factor; therefore the following sections are divided into babyhood and childhood. Please note that this section is in no way a tick-list for deciding whether or not your child has autism, and the included features are not essential to diagnosis. It is unlikely that one baby will show all the behaviours noted. The aim is to illustrate a range of the behaviours that alert parents.

## Concerns in babyhood

The babies themselves can present very different pictures. Some mothers find their babies hard to pacify, and talk of days and nights filled with almost constant screaming and crying. Feeding, cuddling or changing nappies/diapers does little to calm or soothe. The other extreme is the placid baby. Initially, a parent may describe this child as 'angelic', or 'too good to be true', but later becomes worried by their baby's passivity.

Behaviours noted in babies include:

- no lifting of the arms in anticipation of being picked up
- indifference to/ dislike of being touched or cuddled (the baby may twist his body away to avoid contact)

- the baby holds its body rigidly, or becomes floppy when picked up
- lack of eye contact
- objects appear more interesting to the baby than human faces
- absence of imitation (the baby does not mirror the mother's facial gestures or movements)
- babbling is absent, delayed, or scarce in quantity and low in quality
- appears deaf at times, doesn't respond to sound and voices but shows good hearing in certain situations

## Concerns in childhood

Some parents report that their child was a normally developing baby. However, at a specific stage – usually occurring between 18 and 36 months – the child noticeably regressed. Parents are faced with a loss of previously mastered skills, and a range of behaviours never encountered before. Some of these children regress dramatically in a remarkably short space of time, whilst others change slowly over a longer period.

Past babyhood, by far the most frequent difficulty to alert parents is a delay, or some other abnormality, in language development (Howlin and Moore 1997). To a lesser extent, social difficulties and behaviour problems (tantrums, etc.) also serve as an early warning sign for parents.

## Average age of diagnosis

Average age of diagnosis has been found to be around six years of age (Howlin and Moore 1997). This leaves a considerable gap between a parent's first concerns at 1.7 years, and the eventual diagnosis. Many families find the diagnostic process a stressful, protracted and exhausting time. Clearly, the earlier a diagnosis, the earlier parents can fully understand their child's problems. Diagnosis is by no means an end to the journey, but it is an invaluable first step towards gaining insight and help. Early intervention prevents the child falling further behind developmental goals and reduces the time that parents need to struggle without professional help. The good news is that children are being diagnosed at a younger age than in previous decades. This is largely due to improvements in the recognition and understanding of autism, and the development of tools for early diagnosis.

## Tools for early diagnosis

The Checklist for Autism in Toddlers (CHAT) screens 18-month-old children. Checks are made for impaired behaviours such as: joint attention; pretend play; and proto-declarative pointing (i.e. pointing to indicate interest). There are two sections, the first to be answered by the parent, the second by the family doctor or health visitor. This entire procedure takes 5–10 minutes, and yet studies show CHAT successfully detects toddlers later diagnosed with autism (Baron-Cohen *et al.* 1996). The CHAT is not a diagnostic tool in itself, but toddlers who show difficulties in the target areas are highlighted as being in an increased risk group. Children who do not pass the CHAT for a second time (re-screening takes place one month later) should be referred on to a professional experienced in assessment and diagnosis.

The RED FLAGS for autism (Filipek *et al.* 1999) is another tool for professionals to use with the younger child. This system provides a range of characteristics that a parent may bring to a professional, including: 'appears deaf at times'; 'doesn't smile socially'; and 'is oversensitive to certain textures or sounds'. These concerns act as early warning signs for a possible autistic spectrum disorder. To complement the parental concerns, Filipek *et al.* outline several 'absolute indications' which, if found in a child, should lead to immediate investigation. The indications are as follows:

- no babbling by 12 months
- no gesturing (pointing, waving, bye-bye, etc.) by 12 months
- no single words by 16 months

- no 2-word spontaneous (not just echolalic) phrases by 24 months
- ANY loss of ANY language or social skills at ANY age

There is a wide range of screening tools and diagnostic instruments available. Bayley Scales II, the Wechsler (WPPSI-R), the Childhood Autism Rating Scale (CARS) and the Autism Behaviour Checklist (ABC) are but a few. The Diagnostic Interview for Social and Communication Disorders (DISCO) has been developed by staff at Elliot House. DISCO differs from other instruments as it is suitable for individuals of any age with any type of autistic spectrum disorder (Gould 1998). It encompasses internationally recognised diagnostic criteria (i.e. ICD 10 and DSM-IV) and can be used for conditions that overlap with the autistic spectrum (e.g. Obsessive Compulsive Disorder (OCD), AD/HD). DISCO can only be used by specially trained professionals. The NAS fact sheet 'Diagnostic options in autism: a guide for health professionals' offers more detailed information on this topic.

## Common questions

*'I think my child has autism, how do I get a diagnosis?'*

To get a clear diagnosis, you'll need a referral to an autism specialist. A specialist could be a paediatrician, a child psychologist or a child psychiatrist: someone with experience and knowledge of the autistic spectrum. Sometimes the diagnosis is made by a multidisciplinary team of professionals (this could also include speech and language therapists, social workers, educational psychologists, etc.). There are several routes to getting referred. Some parents initially share their concerns with a health visitor, who then arranges for them to see a community paediatrician. This professional may be in a position to make the diagnosis, or may refer the family on to a specialist who can. Families with a child already under a specialist (for other reasons) may be able to discuss their concerns with that professional. Some children are referred through the school doctor system. However, in most cases the first person to approach when you have concerns about your child will be your family doctor.

Ideally, you'll notice early on that your child behaves differently to other children of the same age. After speaking to your family doctor you will be referred on to a specialist who will assess your child and provide a firm diagnosis. Unfortunately, things don't always work out this smoothly. Here are some tips on how to tackle common problems.

*'We think our child has autism, but we don't really know how to bring up the subject with our doctor.'*

The chances are that if you're reading this you already know a fair bit about autism and how it affects your child. So the issue here is confidence rather than knowledge. Try to be sure of your facts before the appointment. Take your child with you if you can, but don't worry if you can't. Do take your partner or a friend if possible, especially if you are feeling nervous.

It is important to make your points clearly. Before the appointment make some notes about the aspects of your child's behaviour that worry you. If you do not structure what you want to say, the true picture of your child's difficulties may not come across in your appointment. A diagnosis of autism can only be given if your child displays difficulties in the three areas of social communication, interaction and imagination. Try to provide one main problem that your child has in each of these areas. Bear in mind that many doctors will have no more than a passing knowledge of autism. They may never heard of the triad of impairments, or its importance in diagnosis. To get a referral you may need to educate your doctor. You may wish to take some literature along with you which briefly describes the condition (ideally this should be left with your doctor so that they can be better prepared for their next autism query). The National Autistic Society's Information Centre can send out information packs to interested professionals.

*'Our doctor doesn't know who to refer us on to.'*

The National Autistic Society has a database of diagnosticians with experience of autism. You can always call their Autism Helpline for details of professionals working in your region (see 'Useful contacts' at the end of Chapter 1). Alternatively, parents involved with local support groups often have experience of local professionals and can offer advice on who you should try and see (details of support groups available from the NAS Helpline).

*'Our doctor says we have nothing to worry about, some children are just slower to develop than others.'*

This is true, but if you think your child has autism this reasoning will not allay your fears. Make an appointment to discuss your concerns with another doctor at the practice. You may be surprised at how doctors can differ in their manner and approach. Parents who feel that this is not an option should go back to the first doctor they saw, armed with more information. If this doesn't get you anywhere, you have two options: either register at a different practice or make a complaint. Anyone can ask at reception for a copy of their practice's complaints procedure. You should also get advice from your local Community Health Council before proceeding (please note that under current government plans Community Health Councils may cease to exist shortly and will be replaced with a different type of patient advocacy service). Complaints procedures can take a long time, but making a complaint may encourage your doctor to review their decision. Some parents find that before the complaints process is completed, their doctor has changed their mind and agreed to a referral.

*'We've got a referral but the waiting list is a mile long, we might not see anyone for a year.'*

This is a tricky one. You may have to accept that getting a clear diagnosis will take time. It is preferable to wait for the right professional than to choose a less qualified alternative. Do remember that it is possible to start helping your child, even without a firm diagnosis. Finding out about therapies and approaches, accessing speech and language therapy, finding a suitable nursery or school and starting the statementing process can all be done without a diagnosis. It's easy to get hooked into thinking that diagnosis is the key to getting the services your child will require, but the fact is that a diagnosis will only give you an official name for what your child has, it will not change your child's problems. If your child needs help, the earlier you ask for it, the better.

Faced with a lengthy wait, many parents consider funding a private referral. The problem with this route is that there are relatively few diagnosticians working privately, so most of them also have long waiting lists. If you do want to investigate this option, the Autism Helpline and parent support groups can provide contacts for professionals in your area.

### 'What will the diagnostic process be like?'

> A doctor had been to the house to assess him. Without looking at me he had rattled through a questionnaire as if he'd been conducting market research for double-glazing – and with about the same amount of feeling. I gave the replies in a trance as he rubber-stamped the situation. 'Do you have to do this often?' I enquired timidly as I felt myself being labelled from now on 'mother of mentally handicapped child'. 'All the time,' he replied airily. 'There's an awful lot of them about.' And without a word of sympathy, commiseration or advice, he picked up his briefcase and breezed out of the front door leaving me to reflect on my new status. (Rankin 2000, pp. 61–62)

> Dr R was the most charming and sympathetic person we could have wished to deal with and could not have been more helpful... I loved the way he referred to Gabriel as 'this interesting little boy' and 'this spectacular young man' in his reports and to us wrote how he had 'greatly enjoyed' seeing him. What a contrast this was to other professionals we had seen over the years who sometimes didn't even manage to spell his name correctly or in one case referred to him throughout as 'Gareth'. More than once we had been to consultations or received letters where Gabriel had been described as 'your daughter Gabrielle'. (*ibid.*, p.71)

The previous quotations are both written by the same mother describing two dramatically different encounters with professionals. Experiences will always vary, depending on who you see. Many professionals are sensitive to the ordeal that parents go through trying to find answers to their child's condition. It is hard to comment too much on personality differences between professionals, as some doctors have a rotten bedside manner but nevertheless are very good at what they do. However, as a parent there are features of the diagnostic process that you can expect.

A good assessment should include taking a detailed developmental history from parents and observing the child's current behaviour. Some diagnosticians will want to see the child at home or in school, others will be satisfied assessing them in the clinic setting. A range of diagnostic tools may be employed. Diagnostic schedules which are designed specifically to pick up on autism include the Diagnostic Interview for Social and Communication disOrders (DISCO) and the Childhood Autism Rating Scale (CARS). In addition, some professionals also use more general psychometric tests to establish the child's level of functioning in areas such as cognition and language. Occasionally brain scans and blood tests are obtained to rule out the possibility of other neurological or genetic conditions (e.g. epilepsy, Fragile X). These tests cannot confirm a diagnosis of autism.

Some assessments are completed within a day. Certain professionals prefer to see the child over a longer period of time before they issue a final report. It is unusual to receive the final diagnosis on the same day as the assessment, although this is not unheard of. Professionals who work as part of a multidisciplinary team may want to take time to discuss the case thoroughly before reaching a conclusion. There is no ideal model for the assessment process. The important thing is that you feel you have been listened to, and that all aspects of your child's case have been considered.

*'My child has seen a specialist and they've diagnosed "autistic tendencies."'*

Children either are, or are not, on the autistic spectrum. To give a diagnosis of 'autistic tendencies' or 'autistic traits' is both meaningless and unhelpful. Professionals who provide this 'diagnosis', should be asked to clarify exactly what they mean. It is important to have written confirmation that your child is indeed on the autistic spectrum.

If this isn't an option, try making another appointment to discuss this issue with the specialist. When you get to the stage where agreement looks unlikely, you should consider a second opinion. The protocol is to return to whoever made the first referral and request to see someone else. Unfortunately you do not have an absolute right to a second opinion, but it doesn't hurt to ask.

*'I've got more questions for the consultant.'*

> The doctor sat down to tell me his diagnosis after assessing my daughter for one hour. He said 'Have you heard of autism?'. After that I continued to give him eye contact and constantly nodded my head as he spoke but I heard nothing except the word 'AUTISM' constantly repeating in my head. (Mother of two-year-old, 2001, private correspondence to author)

Receiving a formal diagnosis for your child is a lot of information to take in. Many parents come away from the meeting feeling numbed by the news. It is natural that more questions will occur to you once you have had time to process what has happened. A good professional will recognise that parents may need to come back to them at a later date. Contact your consultant again if you feel you need more answers. The weeks following the meeting when your child is still fresh in their mind is a good time. Once you receive the formal report, make sure that you understand everything that has been written, and that you agree with the points made. The diagnostic report will be a useful document for you to refer to time and time again. It will help you explain your child's condition to others and will support your request for services. Therefore it is vital that the report accurately describes your child's skills and deficits. Any queries over the report should be directed back to the consultant.

### 'By pursuing a diagnosis will I be labelling my child?'

Some parents feel that a diagnosis could actually be detrimental to their child. An analogy may be useful here. If a professional told you that your child had diabetes, would you be reluctant to accept this 'label'? Knowledge and recognition of a particular disorder is incredibly important to the well-being and development of the child. It allows others to understand and to offer appropriate help. This should not change because we are talking about autism rather than diabetes. Ignoring or refusing to use a label will not change a child's problems, though it can make things worse. Unfortunately, labels can lead to pigeonholes. However, there will always be circumstances where this occurs, for all of us, and it is the practice of pigeonholing people together that is wrong, rather than the label itself.

Labels do not stigmatize, people do. Intolerance towards anyone different from the norm creates stigmas. Blaming the label is ignoring the underlying problem. Not having a label also leads to a child being singled out:

> Sadly, someone who is different will be stigmatized whether they have a label or not, and children with Asperger's who escape official labelling generally don't escape unofficial labelling. When I didn't have an official diagnostic label my teachers unofficially labelled me as 'emotionally disturbed', 'rude' and so on and my classmates unofficially labelled me 'weirdo', 'nerd' and 'freak'; frankly, I prefer the official label. It's the stigma that's attached to being different which is the problem, not the label. (Sainsbury 2000, p.31)

Many young people and adults with autism find their label a useful tool for explaining their condition to others, and for comprehending it themselves. In certain cases, when an individual is extremely high functioning, a diagnosis may not be necessary. However, before this decision is made, the pros and cons need to be considered. On balance, diagnosis is a positive, sometimes illuminating stage that benefits the vast majority.

### 'I need more help.'

Parents can encounter many other difficulties in trying to help their children. Where appropriate, helplines offering advice on specific problems are listed at the end of relevant chapters. If you are in doubt, the National Autistic Society Helpline can signpost parents on to the services they need.

## Useful contacts

If you experience difficulties gaining a diagnosis for your child or have queries over the diagnosis your child has received, call the **National Autistic Society (NAS) Helpline** for information and advice. Staff can provide details of professionals across the country who are interested in autistic spectrum disorders. Helpline workers are happy to be consulted on a range of topics and can signpost parents on to other relevant helplines. Contact details for the NAS Helpline, as well as for the Autism Society of America (ASA) Helpline are provided in 'Useful contacts' at the end of Chapter 1.

*First Signs* advises on diagnosis in the US. Their contact details are:

> **First Signs, Inc.**
> PO Box 358
> Merrimac
> MA 01560
> USA
> *Tel:* 978 346 4380
> *Email:* info@firstsigns.org
> *Website:* www.firstsigns.org

## Suggested reading

The National Autistic Society (2000) Information Sheet: *Diagnostic Options in Autism: A Guide for Health Professionals.*

*Although this information sheet is aimed at health professionals, it does provide a good overview of diagnostic systems and instruments. Available from the NAS Information Centre. Tel: 020 7903 3599.*

Wing L. (1995) *Autistic Spectrum Disorders: An Aid to Diagnosis.* London: The National Autistic Society.
*A clear, concise introduction to this area.*

*Chapter 5*

# Accepting the news

❦

Parents' reaction to finding out that their child has a disability can vary widely. Feelings of helplessness, anger, guilt and despair are possible. One mother recounts the day she was told her child had autism:

> I was suddenly in a 'world of my own' picturing my daughter in 30 years time clutching her favourite books, rocking on a chair and expecting the food she always had on that day. The doctor's strange stare suddenly made me realise that he knew I wasn't listening so I quickly returned to reality to face an uncertain future with the feelings of shock, hopelessness and a very deep sadness as I stared at my daughter's beautiful eyes for the first time in a new light. (Mother of two-year-old, 2001, private correspondence to author)

For parents who have long suspected autism, finally receiving the formal diagnosis may be an enormous relief:

> Well, I think it was a relief for both of us to know he had autism. Once the diagnosis was made it did help. We felt better, I know that this is a horrible thing to say but if there is a label on the child, you know where to go for help. You have a new start, it was like he was born again. (Midence and O'Neill 1999, p.280)

Families unaware that autism was a possible outcome may find the news shocking. This is particularly likely when early suggestions from professionals indicated less pervasive conditions that the child could grow through (e.g. developmental delays or the 'terrible twos'). Some parents previously told that their child's problems were due to their own mismanagement may cling to this idea. It can be easier to believe that a parenting approach needs to change (something parents have control over) than to accept that a child has a lifelong disability.

Gaining a formal diagnosis should not blur the fact that the child you bring home from the assessment is the same child you loved and lived with before. In light of the new information you may choose to change the way you communicate and respond to your child, but this is not something that should be rushed into. You still know your child as well as you ever did, only now you have a framework for understanding their difficulties. It is your perception of your child that has changed, and not your actual child.

Accepting a child's diagnosis is often likened to the mourning process. Parents may go through different stages of shock, numbness, anger, denial and despair. It is said that mourning their lost hopes for normality is an essential part of their recovery process. Only then can they build a realistic picture of their own child, and adjust their hopes for him or her accordingly. Although this popular analogy is useful to some parents, it cannot account for the full picture. The child with autism is ever present throughout this 'mourning process', and therefore a period of quiet reflection that often follows the loss of a loved one is not available to these families. Real life continues from the day of diagnosis, with the same trials and tribulations in place.

Jim Sinclair, an adult with autism, offers his own perspective to parents:

> You didn't lose a child to autism. You lost a child because the child you waited for never came into existence. This isn't the fault of the autistic child who does exist, and it shouldn't be our burden. We need and deserve families who can see us and value us for ourselves, not families whose vision of us is obscured by the ghosts of children who never lived. Grieve if you must, for your own lost

dreams. But don't mourn for *us*. We are alive. We are real. And we're here waiting for you. (Sinclair 1993)

## Different ways of responding

Family members need to move at their own pace, and deal with the news in their own way. Within one family, it is possible that different members will be at different stages of acceptance. Actual ways of responding to the news can differ according to gender. Fathers tend to concentrate on the need to work harder to fund resources, whereas mothers focus more on providing activities for the child and spending 'special time together' (Liwag 1989). The way parents consider the future also differs. Fathers are more likely to be optimistic and positive, whereas mothers are more concerned with the uncertainty of the future. Reactions to the stress of caring for a child with special needs have also been found to affect parents differently. Mothers report more feelings of inadequacy over parenting skills, guilt and physical symptoms. Stressed fathers seem more prone to depression, personality problems and difficulties in relationships (Meyer 1986).

On the positive side, there are numerous accounts of parents who have come to terms very successfully with their child's disability. The following quotations from Midence and O'Neill (1999) show that family life can still be a rewarding experience:

> Our son has made us closer, this bonds us together… He is part of the family. When he is not there, there is a big hole. (p.281)

> Over the years we might have got to love the autism too. It is part of her. We cannot imagine her without it, not any more. Autism is an integral part of her, it is not a problem any more. (p.282)

## Strategies and coping mechanisms

Everyone has their own ways of dealing with life's twists and turns. The way you respond to your child's autism will be personal to you. There are no right or wrong reactions. Families dealing with autism have been found to use a range of different strategies and coping mechanisms

(Gray 1993). The most common strategy is the use of services (respite centres, specialist schools, treatment centres, etc.). Other methods include: individualism, support from family members, religious faith, and withdrawal. Interestingly, no one method is found to be more effective than any other. Different families find different ways to cope.

## Maintaining a healthy balance in the family: individualism

Some parents cope by maintaining lives outside autism. In these families, caring for a child with autism is not the sole focus of the daily routine. Mothers may choose to resume their careers, using the workplace as a form of respite (an option dependent on family circumstances). Dedicating time to hobbies and/or a social life are alternative examples of individualism.

Other families report that, following diagnosis, family life becomes centred on the child with autism, with everything revolving around that one individual. This child-focused approach leads many parents to neglect their own need for an identity stretching beyond mum or dad. Randall and Parker (1999) found that many parents 'feel they have no individuality left, that they are merely sitters to their children with autism'(p.28). Inevitably, when this occurs, other relationships within the family suffer. Time needs to be built in for siblings and partners to be together alone. Individualism does not need to be too extreme, but maintaining interests in hobbies and other pursuits, and putting some time aside for a social life, are important parts of any family schedule. In order for this approach to work, parents need to share childcare responsibilities and accept help from other sources.

Temporary respite can be provided through professional agencies, local babysitters or family members/friends. Accepting that another can temporarily meet your child's needs is crucial for successful respite and the prevention of burnout. As an added bonus, your child widens their social interactions, and will not be as distressed when emergencies necessitate alternative care. One mother who has come to this realisation writes:

For her, the issue is clear. She needs a care-giver, but that care-giver need not be me. For me, the issue is far more ambivalent. My need is, simply put, to care for my child, and to see that she is cared for constantly and always. At the same time, I recognize my limitations, my chronic exhaustion, and, at a deeper level, the danger my dependency holds in keeping her back. (Namak 1990, p.13)

## Dealing with social isolation

Around this time we stopped going out. We stayed away from church, we stayed at home…we hardly ever went to visit the family. Everywhere it was the same thing: 'If he were one of mine he would be spanked.' (From Peeters 1997, p.175)

For some families, the difficulties presented by autism lead them to socially withdraw. Family life can feel limited and unrewarding. In extreme cases, parents can feel imprisoned by their children. Using different services and choosing specialist schools can increase feelings of social isolation and reduce the opportunity of mixing with other families in the community. It can feel as though you are following a different path in life to everyone else that you know. Making use of the avenues of help available (see 'Useful contacts' at the end of Chapter 1) can stop families from feeling so alienated and alone.

## An invisible disorder (…sometimes!)

The invisible nature of autism is a feature that many parents find hard to deal with. A child with autism shows no physical signs of his condition and may appear completely normal in certain situations. If this child then goes on to display behaviour problems, he is more likely to be seen by the average passer-by as naughty or spoilt. Children who are more visibly disabled (e.g. using a wheelchair) provide clear clues to the public that they have special needs, and as a result are permitted to behave in more unexpected or unpredictable ways. As a result, parents of children with autism may feel their parenting skills are being called into question by complete strangers. Some parents report that passers-by approach them and offer unwanted advice on how to 'control' their child, while others insist that all that is needed is 'a good spank'. If you have experienced these sort of problems yourself, the later section 'Managing other people' offers advice on this issue.

## The stigma of autism

Mothers have reported feeling more stigmatised by their child's autism, compared to fathers (Gray 1993). This in part could be due to the fact that in most families the mother is still the primary caregiver and spends more time in public with the child. This exposes mothers to an audience on a more regular basis, where comments and stares from ignorant passers can be a regular occurrence. The public arena is where many parents feel their competence in managing their child is most open to question.

However, sooner or later most people reach a point where they feel less sensitive about what other people might think or say. It is this tougher skin combined with a liberal sense of humour that sees many parents through. Being able to see the funny side of something is a sure sign of recovery. Kate Rankin (2000) writes 'laughter was the best antidote to feelings of negativity and stress' (p.86) – and:

> On Friday his teacher wrote how pleased she was with him, then finished: 'Only one bad incident this week – he ate the classroom goldfish.' (p.79)

> There often was a funny side. You couldn't help laughing as, refusing all help, he would battle to get into a pair of trousers *via the ankles*, or would appear with his Y-fronts back to front on top of his trousers, blissfully unaware that anything was amiss. One evening he seemed quite unconscious of the fact that he had his own shoe on one foot and an oversized brogue of Neil's on the other, even when he had to drag it along as he tried to run. For some inscrutable reason for several weeks he wandered about with a tea-strainer carefully balanced on the back of his neck. (p.86)

## Informing family members

Decide what members of your family you want to tell about your child's special needs. To begin with, inform only those who really need to know – people you have regular contact with, who help you care for your child. Valued friends that are sympathetic listeners should also be top of your list. Everyone else can wait for the family grapevine, or until you feel ready to pass on the news. Your child's grandparents, uncles and aunts are usually the most important. Provide just the basic information to begin with; if you have found a leaflet or chapter particularly useful, pass copies on. Pointers on telling your other children about their sibling's autism can be found in Chapter 7 'Siblings.'

Sadly, reports from some parents reveal that not all family members can not be relied upon for support. Pre-diagnosis, 60 per cent of parents in one survey reported problems within their extended family (Randall and Parker 1999). Even once a diagnosis is obtained, some parents may find that their 'nearest and dearest' are reluctant to accept the facts. In one research, 33 per cent of the families studied had experienced the most trouble from grandparents (DeMyer 1979). Some grandparents were affronted by suggestions that their grandchild might have a difficulty. Others made an issue of whose side of the family the disability came from, leading to pointless, painful arguments. Some parents found that extended family blamed them for the child's condition, or were not comfortable being in public with the affected child:

> Well, my mum is embarrassed…she doesn't want to go shopping with us…but if she is for some reason with us and Sam and he is acting up she whispers to the shop assistant 'He's handicapped' and the minute she sees me sort of look at her she's really embarrassed but, that's it, that's her whole attitude, she's embarrassed by him being handicapped… She says to me 'Doesn't come from our side of the family…' (From Gray 1993, p.112)

## Managing other people

Fullwood and Cronin (1989) *Facing the Crowd: Managing Other People's Insensitivities to your Disabled Child* is full of useful advice. The authors suggest that you divide people up into the following groups: people you want on side (e.g. relatives, close friends), people you need on side (e.g. professionals, baby-sitters), people you are stuck with (e.g. in-laws, nosey neighbours) and strangers/people you don't care about. This allows you to conserve energy and preserve patience by tailoring your reaction depending on the group a person belongs to. One mother explained, 'I just got so sick of spending twenty minutes at the bus-stop explaining my child's condition to someone I was never going to see again.'

People who have a regular role in your life are worth spending more time on (your close friends, babysitters, staff at the nursery, etc.). Simple information on the disorder as well as guidelines for communicating and disciplining your child need to be passed on. For example, if you have decided to 'praise good behaviour and ignore bad', or you have removed certain foods from your child's diet, other care-givers need to be informed. Consistency of approach is vital to the success of many interventions.

For dealing with strangers, different tactics are needed. Making up your mind over a description of your child that you feel happy with (e.g. 'communication disorder'), and preparing a short answer to be used as needed can remove some of the worry of venturing out. Alternatively, keeping some information cards handy (stating the basic facts about autism) to give out when necessary, can be a short-cut to informing the public. These cards are available from the NAS.

### Useful contacts
Staff at the **NAS Helpline** can provide details of local societies and parent support groups in your area. The NAS Helpline details, as well as the **ASA Helpline** details are provided in 'Useful contacts' at the end of Chapter 1.

### Suggested reading
Fullwood D. and Cronin P. (1989) *Facing the Crowd: Managing Other People's Insensitivities to your Disabled Child.* Melbourne: Royal Victorian Institute for the Blind.
*An excellent book which enables parents to deal with other people assertively.*

*Chapter 6*

# Moving forward after diagnosis

For parents who have already informally diagnosed their child as being on the autistic spectrum long before professionals made it official, suitable changes to the home and interaction styles may already have been put in place. Other families, enlightened by the diagnosis, will want to do all they can to provide a suitable environment for their child.

## What could be changed at home?

If you are a parent learning about autism for the first time, do not rush into any changes, even if there are features in the household that you feel need to be adapted. These are features that your child has become accustomed to, and removing them without warning could cause more stress. Changes should be carefully planned and introduced gradually, one at a time, so that your child is not overwhelmed. This method allows you to evaluate any benefit following a particular change, by carefully observing your child's mood and behaviour.

A home is for the whole family. Making a home autism-friendly should not cause too much disruption for other members. Any advantages could be easily outweighed if a sibling blames the child with autism for removing or adding features that they feel impinge upon their lifestyle. So changes should be made with the whole family in mind, and wherever possible siblings and the affected child should be helped to feel involved in the process. This may be a simple case of allowing children to choose from a selection of colours for a new paint scheme or to replace wallpaper.

There are some universal features that have long been known to aid a child with autism. These are elements that specialist schools and residential units build into the environment, and they are just as effective when used in the home.

## Low arousal surroundings

Humans are incredibly good at tuning out sensory bombardment, be it in the street, the workplace or the home. The majority of children on the spectrum cannot do this, and so perform consistently better in a space that makes fewer demands on their senses. You may be able to watch the television while the washing-machine is on in the next room, and your nextdoor neighbour is mowing their lawn. Your child may find it impossible to filter out the multitude of noises, to concentrate on one thing. Keeping the noises you can control to a minimum will improve your child's attention and increase the likelihood of effective communication.

This applies to visual information too. Whereas other children delight in bright colours, pictures, photos, posters, etc., covering the walls of their bedroom, your child may need a place that is easy on the eye as well as the ear. Walls painted in calm neutral tones or in a hue that you know your child finds soothing are best. Wall adornments should be kept to a minimum and reserved for information-providing charts and calendars. Certain images relax some children and stencils or murals can then be useful. The aim of the bedroom is to calm the child (especially if they have trouble sleeping), so favourite pictures that excite and lead to stimulatory behaviours like hand-flapping are not the best choice.

Taking simple measures will help you create a low arousal environment. Sitting with your child in a quiet corner or facing a blank wall when you are trying to interact one-to-one increases your chances of success. Do not give yourself unfair competition from a television set or much loved washing-machine. Play in a setting and at a time that lets you be the major component in your child's world.

## A relaxing atmosphere

As well as excluding certain elements from the household, introducing particular features can prove beneficial. The spinning of a tumble-dryer fascinates some children; others will find the noise unbearable. Background music from the radio may have a calming effect on one child, but irritate the next. It has been found that fast, upbeat music (like the theme tune to *Rocky*) can encourage better moods in some children than more traditionally calming scores (like Mozart). A certain degree of trial and error is necessary to discover what works for your child. Some parents recommend lit fishtanks, which can have an almost hypnotic effect on children who otherwise find it hard to wind down. Similarly, lava lamps can encourage sleepiness in some, and are especially attractive in favourite colours (work wonders for stressed mums and dads too). Obviously these objects will need to be childproof, or placed out of reach. Coloured light-bulbs that infuse a room with gentle colour have been useful for some families. Burning scented oils that induce peacefulness may also soothe. A few drops of lavender oil on the edge of a pillowcase at night-time helps some children drop off to sleep. A little educated guesswork is needed here; if your child is hypersensitive to smells you may need to experiment to achieve the right levels. For children who cocoon (i.e. fit themselves into tight spaces for comfort) a few heavy cushions or a heavy feather duvet to crawl under provide a welcome haven.

Physical activities may also calm your child. Household chores (sweeping the floor, helping with the hoovering) and gardening (digging, gathering leaves) are great for expending excess energy. Relaxing in a rocking chair, jumping on a mini-trampoline, using the swing in the garden, pounding bread dough, taking a brisk walk or run may also help.

More able children may benefit from relaxation exercises. 'In the mood' by Penny Moon is a very useful article, which suggests different relaxation techniques for schoolchildren with autism. The following excerpt is an example of what could be used with more able children:

> Listen to the sounds around, e.g. traffic, children talking, birds singing, music and the sound of my voice. As you hear all of these sounds be aware, let yourself become so still that you can hear the sound of your breathing and as you feel these sounds you will feel yourself becoming quieter, calmer and happier (use other qualities, e.g. more confident, kinder, etc.)
>
> Repeat this three times. Then say:
>
> I am going to count from five to one and when I get to one you can take a deep breath, yawn and stretch as if waking and stand up, bringing back with you all those wonderful feelings. (Moon 1996, p.33)

It has been noted that some children with autism actually find relaxation techniques stressful. Obviously this is counterproductive to the goal. If this is the case for your child you will need to investigate other ways to relax and de-stress them (e.g. rough-and-tumble play).

### A safe place

> All of us need a private place. Autistic children need their secret places, too, in which they can hide and retreat to their own world. After all, autism is a 'withinness' disability, and autistic children need the security of their own hideaways. I had mine and it was a place for me to think and recharge myself. (Grandin and Scariano 1986, p.147)

Identify an area – a room, corner, even a spacious cupboard if your child prefers – to be their retreat (although ideally your child will decide for themselves). This is to be used as a sanctuary whenever your child needs to wind down or get away from the rest of the household. A place with obvious physical boundaries works well – e.g. a space partitioned off by a curtain or separated from the rest of the room by a big piece of furniture. Alternatively, when less room is available a big comfy chair with soft cushions/beanbags (the rocking variety are often popular) or a sheet draped over a table to create a tent can work well too. For children who seek out womb-like spaces a baby bath filled with cushions can be appealing.

This safe place is not a means of punishment through isolation (children should never be 'sent' there in a similar vein to 'go to your room'), but rather to provide essential time away from unnecessary stimulation. With more able and older children the safe place may eventually be somewhere they can take themselves when they recognise that they are over-aroused, as a self-management technique. Initially you may need to prompt your child to use it regularly when you see they are agitated. Once you recognise which times are most stressful for your child (e.g. returning home from a busy day at school, when the house is full of guests, etc.), you can encourage him to unwind in his special spot. Providing props (e.g. stress balls and other sensory toys, books, etc.) and snacks in that place, will encourage your child to spend time there when needed. Other family members (especially siblings) need to accept that this place is off bounds (although brothers and sisters could also have their own location).

## Practical adaptations

DÉCOR

Non-toxic, wipe-clean paint is preferable to wallpaper, especially if your child is adept at finding tiny corners and engaging in unexpected DIY. Dark carpet can hide a multitude of sins, and heavy-duty matting withstands frequent sponging. Removable sofa covers (machine washable) will increase the life expectancy of a lounge suite. Wherever possible surfaces regularly used by the child should be hardy and easy to wipe down.

In the rest of the house precious breakables should be placed out of reach, and above the child's natural sight line. Display cabinets and high shelves will usually suffice. Discourage mountaineering by checking that there are no handy sofas or other possible springboards beneath tempting ornaments.

GADGETS

Many parents report that their child engages in pursuits that would make Houdini proud. Childproof catches on cupboards and the fridge may deter some for a while. To help maintain the mystery, block your child's view whenever you are undoing the catches.

If your child is a 'runner', several latches near the top (away from clever fingers) of the front and back door may give you some valuable time to hear your potential escapee, and prevent a breakout. Introducing your child to your neighbours and local police officers will aid identification if your child does go AWOL. An identification band worn around the wrist (the same as most hospitals use) or an engraved bracelet is useful with nonverbal children, or those too young to know their home address. More technology-minded families have gone to the extent of fitting sensor pads by exits, which beep whenever someone stands by the door. These can also been used in the child's room, to alert parents to night-time wanderings. Personal alarms secured to the body or carried on the back in a rucksack may be one way of keeping tabs on a child while out. The Disabled Living Foundation is a useful source of information for specialised equipment (see 'Useful contacts' at the end of this chapter). Advice and contacts can be provided on a range of products including extra strong harnesses and reins, buggies for the older child and car seats.

In the case of a reduced (or absent) sense of danger, windows must be securely fastened to prevent accidents. Your child may see no difference between popping out of the ground-floor window, and running up to a higher storey to do the same. As many children with autism do not learn from experience, being burnt once from the cooker will not ensure that it does not happen again. This means that as your child grows older, you still have to order the environment as you would for a much younger child. Teaching basic behaviour guidelines is important here, but these need to be combined with safe surroundings. The simplest way to do this is to get down on your child's level and see what they can get up to from down there. Bear in mind what interests them and what objects could attract inquisitive fingers.

## Visual information

It has been found that information presented in a visual way is easier for most children with autism to process. Verbally delivered information is unavoidable and necessary, but you can back this up with visual cues to aid your child's understanding. Timetables, schedules, wall charts, diaries and calendars are all useful tools. The age of your child and their level of functioning will determine to a certain extent what you use, but even able children with good language can benefit from simple visuals.

Many children with autism show a marked preference for sameness and a strong need to follow structured routines. The family home can be a chaotic, vibrant place. It is not feasible for many families to adhere to a rigid timetable, as things change from day to day without warning. However, within this, it is possible for any family to lay down a basic structure to reassure the child with autism. For instance, although dinner times may vary, with different members being missing or present, your child can still be informed of this ahead of time. Telling your child 'It's just you and me for dinner tonight', and helping them lay the table with the right number of place settings will fix this in their mind.

Some children can retain information better than others. One child who is briefed about the day's activities in the morning will still remember this later on in the day. Another child may need to be warned about up and coming events at regular intervals. Simple picture timetables work well for most children. Recognised symbols or line drawings can represent the morning's activities. A child swimming, a shopping trolley and a picture of a sandwich can denote a visit to the swimming pool, then to the supermarket, followed by lunch (see Figure 6.1). This timetable can be clearly displayed for your child to refer to when needed. If the symbols are attached with Velcro to a felt-board, completed activities can be pulled off and placed in the 'done' box. This way your child is always aware of what is finished and what is happening next. Days without big events can still be chronicled, e.g. painting and play dough before lunch, reading and nap time afterwards.

*Figure 6.1 Visual symbols for daily activities*

For the older, more able child, visual information can be a valuable way of increasing independence. Self-care skills can be broken down into clear steps for the child to follow. Initially a parent could oversee these proceedings, and play a major role in modelling what needs to be done for the child (e.g. putting their hand over the child's to demonstrate turning on a tap). Gradually, parents can ease off their supervision until the child is performing tasks alone. Visual instructions may be necessary for some children to remember what needs to be done, and in what order. Eventually, for higher functioning children, the instructions could become quite detailed, as in the following example:

---

### Cleaning my teeth – morning and evening

1. Squirt tooth paste (a pea-sized amount) onto my green toothbrush.

2. Brush the top row of my teeth (for about 10 seconds).

3. Spit out foamy toothpaste into the sink.

4. Rinse toothbrush briefly under the tap.

5. Brush bottom row of my teeth (for about 10 seconds).

---

6. Rinse my mouth out again and spit into sink.

7. Wash my toothbrush under the tap.

8. Put toothbrush back into the cup.

9. Pour out a capful of mouthwash and rinse my mouth out with this.

10. REMEMBER an extra ten minutes on the computer if I rinse with mouthwash.

If you are interested in using visual information with your child, *Making Visual Supports Work in the Home and Community* by Savner and Smith Myles (2000) is a good resource (see 'Suggested reading' at the end of this chapter for full details).

## Good communication

Whereas behaviour programmes can take a while to research and begin, improving the way you communicate with your child can quickly lead to positive results:

- language should be concrete, concise and specific. Sentences should only convey key information (e.g. 'Please come over here and sit down' can be reduced to 'sit here').

- speech should be delivered in a calm voice. If you are angry and your tone reflects this, your child has more information to process. Speak slowly and pronounce words clearly. Some children are very sensitive to high volume levels, so speaking in a loud voice may increase their anxiety and fearfulness, but not their comprehension.

- emotional pleas may not be understood by a child with autism (this is related to mindblindness). Therefore crying and expressing anger may achieve very little.

- make your instructions positive. Your child will know what to do if you tell them 'Toys away in box' but may be confused as to what is expected of them if you simply say 'Don't leave a mess on the floor'.

- use your child's name to gain their attention, before you continue speaking. Try not to overuse their name as this could reduce their response to you.

- give your child time to process what you are saying. Deliver your sentence and then wait. Your child may need more time to process the words than you usually give. Some children benefit from hearing the sentence for a second time, after the waiting period.

- back up verbal communication with other methods. Simple body language can clarify an instruction (e.g. 'sit here' combined with patting the seat). Statements can also be combined with objects of reference and related actions (e.g. 'Let's go to the park' paired with fetching and putting on a coat). Using visual information aids understanding.

- if your child is verbal, the best way of checking that they have understood what you have said is by asking them to retell it to you. Simply asking, 'Do you understand?' will not reveal if you are both thinking along the same lines. Your child may think they understand you, but their interpretation may be quite different from your own.

- rephrase questions. 'Do you know which mammal is the fastest?' may result in a simple 'Yes'. 'Tell me…' questions help prevent exasperation.

- provide straightforward instructions. 'Go and ask Grandma if she wants cake' may result in your child asking Grandma the question but never returning to tell you the answer. Children with autism have a strong tendency towards literal interpretations, at the expense of the true implicit meaning. 'Then come and tell me the answer' are the magic words to add.

- think about the speech you use. Often words can be confusing. One teacher couldn't understand why a pupil was wetting himself, as he often asked to use the bathroom. When the teacher thought about her language she realised she was saying, 'Go to the bathroom but come straight back', and her pupil was doing just that. Similarly, a mother who asked her daughter to 'Change into your slippers' was met with a baffled look and the retort, 'I'm not a magician'.

- open-ended questions like 'How was school today?' are much harder for your child to answer than more specific statements like 'You had storytime today…what was the story about?' Arranging with your child's teacher to write in their home book the main activities of the day will make conversing with your child easier. Objects of reference that respond to the day can be sent home too (this is especially useful if your child has little language).

- phrasing requests as 'First…, then…' can be useful. This gives your child a sense of what is happening next, e.g. 'First wash hands, then cake'.

- sayings like 'I could eat a horse', 'It's raining cats and dogs', etc., could be taken literally by your child. More able children can be taught the actual meaning of these phrases, but will still be misled by new versions. Constructing a simple dictionary which explains what sayings really mean helps prevent misunderstandings.

- try to avoid using 'perhaps' and 'maybe' when your child asks you questions. Wherever possible be more specific, e.g. replace 'maybe later' with 'after lunch'. Children with autism find it hard to deal with uncertainties. Some parents do not tell their child about things until they are sure they are happening.

- keep your promises whenever possible! Your child will only be reassured by what you tell them if you stay true to your word. It is better to say no than to mislead and disappoint.

- try and provide warnings for your child so they know when activities will end and start, e.g. 'Five more minutes watching television, then bathtime.' Some parents have found this strategy can prevent tantrums. Egg-timers, watch alarms and buzzers can also be used, and have the advantage of being less personal (i.e. you are not telling your child to do something, the timer is).

- prepare your child for change by giving them information in advance. Surprising your child at the last minute is likely to cause stress and anxiety.

- when unexpected changes do occur, visual timetables can help. For example, if your child usually goes swimming on Saturday mornings but this is not possible, you can remove the swim symbol from the velcro board, so your child is shown very clearly that this will not happen today. In these situations, emphasising the elements of the usual routine that still stay the same help reassure your child, e.g. 'No swimming today, but we still go to Grandma's for lunch.'

- if your child has little or no language, consider alternative methods of communication. Teaching your child some basic signs or symbols can make everyday life much easier. The Picture Exchange Communication System (PECS) (Frost and Bondy 1994) and Makaton are two options. (See 'Useful contacts' at the end of this chapter.)

- organisations like the Hanen Programme and Portage offer models of early intervention to parents. They are not specific to autism but teach the fundamentals of communication and interaction between parent and child (see 'Useful contacts').

## Handling key events

When major changes occur, the right information helps remove the uncertainty of a new venture. Information needs to be tailored to the child's level of understanding; some of the following suggestions may be handy.

### Moving home

Moving home is comparable in stress levels to getting a divorce. Obviously, on the day of the move mayhem rules, but some careful preparation in the calmer weeks beforehand will help your child accept the change.

- let your child visit the new house as many times as possible.

- take Polaroid pictures or draw pictures of the new place and talk about them with the child – 'This is where you will sleep,' etc.

- if possible, take your child to visit local points of interest in the new area (the nearest playground, nursery school, etc.), explain to her that this is where she will be coming to the swings, to school, etc.

- provide a countdown calendar for the day of the move.

- if your child enjoys reading, get a relevant picture book which explains the process of moving house.

- make a point of saying goodbye to the old house – 'Goodbye kitchen, goodbye lounge, goodbye garden' etc.– and hello to the new.

### Family holidays

- start to talk about the trip a few weeks before the actual event so your child has time to get used to the idea. (Some children worry and ask endless questions if given too much time, so this is something that each family will need to judge.)

- count down the days on a special calendar.

- make a picture scrap book with your child from brochures – 'This is the hotel we will stay in.' Describe activities you'll do once you arrive –'We will visit this castle.' The scrapbook can be consulted whenever your child has questions or worries.

- remind your child that many things will stay the same as when at home (e.g. bedtime routines), as this helps build a reassuring structure.

- pack some familiar objects (toys, a favourite quilt, etc.) so not everything is strange.

*Starting nursery school*

- visit the school before the start day. Wander around so that your child gets used to the surroundings.

- meet staff ahead of time so that they are not complete strangers on the day.

- let your child take a comfort toy.

- if your child has real trouble accepting change, slowly build up the time she stays at school over a couple of weeks.

## Moving forward – this family is more than autism

Many suggestions have been made in this chapter. However a point made right at the start – a home is for the whole family – is perhaps the most important. Trying to regain normality once you have digested the news of diagnosis, is perhaps the most valuable thing you can do for your child. An everyday family doing everyday things is the richest learning environment you can provide for your child, for the outside world is not an uncluttered, low arousal place, and this is something that, to a certain extent, the child with autism has to learn to cope with. Setting targets such as planning to take a proper family holiday each year are essential to everyone's well being. Within these plans you can build 'autism-friendly' measures in (e.g. maybe the first holiday will be close to home, self-catering and free from huge crowds). Targets can gradually become more ambitious as your child learns to adapt to the new experiences you introduce.

## Useful contacts

### 1. The Disabled Living Foundation (DLF)
*Works to empower disabled people by providing information on technology and equipment to enhance independence. DLF has a demonstration centre in London (to book an appointment with a trained adviser tel: 020 7289 6111 ext. 247), a helpline, and a website with factsheets, extensive link pages and on-line shopping.*

> **The Disabled Living Foundation**
> 380–384 Harrow Road
> London W9 2HU
> *Helpline:* 0845 1309177 (10am – 4pm, Monday – Friday)
> *Minicom:* 020 7432 8009
> *Fax:* 020 7266 2922
> *Email:* info@dlf.org.uk
> *Website:* www.dlf.org.uk

### 2. Childproofers.com
*Childproofers.com provide advice on childproofing and can put parents in touch with suppliers in North America.*

> *Tel:* 314 962 BABY (314 962 2229)
> *Email:* inf@childproofers.com
> *Website:* www.childproofers.com

### 3. The National Portage Association
> 127 Monk Dale
> Yeovil
> Somerset BA21 3JE
> *Tel/Fax:* 01935 471641

### 4. Hanen UK/Ireland
> 9 Dungoyne Street
> Maryhill
> Glasgow G20 0BA

Scotland
*Tel/Fax*: 0141 9465433

*In North America contact:*

**The Hanen Centre Canada**
The Hanen Centre
Suite 403
1075 Bay Street
Toronto ON
M5S 2B1
Canada
*Tel*: 416 921 1073
*Fax*: 416 921 1225
*Website*: www.hanen.org
*Email*: info@hanen.org

*The Hanen Programme has produced two parent guides for use with children of all abilities. 'It Takes Two to Talk' (£17.50) is excellent for early intervention ideas. The autism-specific programme 'More than Words' (£31.50) helps parents promote communication and social skills in their children. Both available from:*

**Winslow**
Goytside Road
Chesterfield
Derbyshire S40 2PH
*Tel*: 0845 9211777
*Fax*: 01246 551195
*Email*: sales@winslow-cat.com

## 5. The Picture Exchange Communication System (PECS)

*For more information contact:*

**Pyramid Educational Consultants UK Ltd.**
17 Prince Albert Street
Brighton
East Sussex BN1 1HF
*Tel*: 01273 728888
*Website*: www.pecs-uk.com

*In the US contact:*

**Pyramid Education Consultants**
226 West Park Place, Suite 1
Newark
DE 19711

USA
*Tel:* 302 368 2515
*Fax:* 302 368 2516
*Helpline:* 1 888 PECS INC (1 888 7327 462)
*Website:* www.pecs.com

### 6. Makaton

*For more information contact:*

**The Makaton Vocabulary Development Project**
31 Firwood Drive
Camberley
Surrey GU15 3QD
*Tel:* 01276 61390
*Fax:* 01276 681368
*Email:* mvdp@makaton.org
*Website:* www.makaton.org

## For contact details in all other countries go to:

*www.makaton.org/international/international.htm*

## Suggested reading

Savner JL. and Smith Myles B. (2000) *Making Visual Supports Work in the Home and Community: Strategies for Individuals with Autism and Asperger Syndrome.* Kansas: Autism Asperger Publishing Co.
*Practical ideas for using visual information.*

The Hanen Programme: *It Takes Two to Talk* and *More than Words.* See 'Useful contacts'.

*Chapter 7*

# Siblings

At times, all brothers and sisters wish they were an only child. Arguments and jealousies have long been accepted as an inevitable part of sibling relationships. However, when a child has a disability, the balance of family life is shifted, and interaction between family members has to accommodate this shift. A child with special needs requires more time and energy, occupying a larger slice of the parental pie compared with other unaffected children.

> When I was a kid it seemed to me my brother Rich, who has autism, got the lion share of attention in our house. Now that I am an adult I can understand the jam my parents were in, but it was tough for me when I was younger. (from Harris 1994, p.25)

The arguments and jealousies that arise from this situation need to be recognised and responded to appropriately. In families where there is a child with autism, parents need to distinguish between problems found in any home, and problems arising specifically from living with a child with special needs.

## Common questions

### 'When do I tell my other children about autism?'

As a parent, you need time to come to terms with your own emotions concerning your child with autism. Until you have reached a level of acceptance and knowledge yourself, you cannot properly help your other children. Sandra Harris, in *Siblings of Children with Autism*, describes family life as a balancing act. Many parents can identify with the feeling of trying to juggle different tasks and responsibilities, 24 hours a day, 7 days a week. It can seem an endless and sometimes thankless job, without the wage, holidays or health benefits. Unsurprisingly then, finding time to tell your other children may not be a first priority, but it is a task that needs to be addressed when you feel ready.

Some children pick up vibes that something is 'not quite right' with their brother or sister remarkably early on. For very young siblings who are not ready for explanations, comfort and reassurance is the best response. Perhaps the child cannot understand the temper tantrum they have witnessed, but they can be removed from danger and helped to feel safe.

### 'What information do my other children need to know?'

Later on, when the quizzical looks and questions begin, your other children are ready for information. As a rule, answer questions as they arise, and try and keep responses as simple and specific as possible. Do not be tempted to provide too many facts too early on. One mother's rule of thumb is 'When her eyes start to glaze over I know I have said enough.' Answer your child's questions from your own understanding. Age-appropriate analogies can clarify certain problems for some children, e.g. 'Sam is like Data from *Star Trek*, he sometimes finds it hard to recognise your feelings.' When the term 'autism' is introduced make sure that it is meaningful to your child in relation to their sibling, and not just an empty phrase they have heard others use. There can be a big difference between telling siblings about autism and their fully understanding the condition.

It is important to provide the basic facts early on. Initial concerns may surround how you 'get' autism. Young children may worry about catching autism from their sibling in the way you may catch a cold, and as a result may avoid them. Assuring the child that babies are born with autism helps to dispel myths and ensure that your child does not blame himself for his brother or sister's condition. Howlin (1998) reports the sad case of a twin who had believed for some time that she had caused her sister's autism by hitting her on the head with a book when they were much younger (p.279). If a child is not given age-appropriate answers as soon as she is curious, it is natural that she will create her own logic and ideas about autism. There is the danger that the myths siblings invent may worry them more than the truth would.

Telling your other children about autism is not a one-off task. Their need for information changes as they grow older. Basic information needs to be retold with greater complexity and more detail. Harris elegantly explains that there 'should be a continuing open dialogue for the passage of information and emotions'. Young siblings need clear instructions on how to play with their brother and sister, as modelled by parents. Teenagers may be concerned about the risk of having a child with autism themselves, or about who will look after their brother or sister when you are no longer around. Issues over the long-term care of a child with autism should be discussed once the sibling is old enough to understand. Siblings should be told very clearly that they will not be expected to take responsibility, and that arrangements for the future will be made in advance.

### 'What is the best way to give information?'

Some parents have found it helpful to make a scrapbook with their children, where questions and answers are listed. Photographs and drawings could illustrate certain points, and the book could grow as you and your child cover more ground together. This is an aid that playmates coming into the home can also learn from. Younger children can benefit from acting out feelings with hand-puppets and learning through specialised storybooks. Novels and leaflets are appropriate for adolescents. (Resource list available from the NAS.)

### 'Am I asking too much of my other children?'

Whereas normally siblings argue amongst themselves, and in general 'give as good as they get', the siblings of a child with autism may feel guilty about this sort of behaviour. They may try and model themselves as the perfect son or daughter in an effort to compensate for a sibling they do not regard as normal.

> Justin is such a terrific kid. Sometimes I think he is almost too good. He spends so much time with his sister, Allie, who has autism. He acts like it is his job to do everything for her. I don't want him to resent that someday. To feel like she stole his child-hood… I'm not sure how much help is too much. (From Harris 1994, p.26)

With the juggling act already mentioned, parents may welcome this behaviour in their other children. Parents need to guard against their expectations being too high, and make sure that their other children are not burdened with too much responsibility. Parents often remark that other children in the family show compassion and understanding remarkable for their tender age. However, these children need to enjoy the carefree nature of childhood too. Although they may appear to enjoy the role of mini-caretakers, any contribution they make to the care of their sibling should be in relation to their age, and not at the expense of their own natural development. Parents should clearly lay down rules, e.g. 'When Sam has a tantrum, come and tell me straight away', so the children know they are not expected to intervene them-selves. Debriefing after the event may be necessary, and offers a chance to praise a child's swift action, and to acknowledge how scary the scene may have been for them.

*'How will having a sibling with autism affect my other children?'*

An important factor, often overlooked, is that genetically siblings have an increased risk for disorders of general intelligence, reading and language (Folstein and Rutter 1987). Fortunately many siblings do not experience these difficulties, and those who do are not as impaired as their brother of sister with autism. As the child with autism displays more obvious deficits, the less prominent problems of a sibling can sometimes pass unnoticed. It is essential that parents look out for difficulties in all of their children.

One concern from these children was the teasing and sometimes bullying they endured from other peers, due to their sibling being different. If this is happening to your child, tell class teachers and make sure your child feels supported and informed. It stands to reason that a child well versed about autism is much more likely to handle comments, questions and insults with confidence. In extreme cases, siblings at the same school as their brother or sister have asked to move to a new school when things have got too bad. This should only be considered as a last resort. Siblings can sometimes get labelled as bullies because they step in to defend their brother or sister from other kids at school. In this kind of scenario the whole class needs to be educated in a sensitive manner. (Perhaps a school assembly is needed on this topic.)

Various studies have investigated the impact on siblings when a brother or sister has autism. It is accepted that being sibling to a child with autism can be more demanding than with any other disability. When compared to siblings of children with Down's syndrome, both similarities and differences are found (Rodrique, Geffken and Morgan 1993). Parents reported more concerns over internalised problems (e.g. depression, anxiety, etc.) and externalised problems (e.g. aggression, defiance, running away, etc.) when their child had a sibling with autism. Although these problems were found to be more frequent in this group, overall behaviour still fell within the normal range.

The good news is that no difference was found in levels of self-esteem or academic competence between siblings of a child with autism and siblings of a child with Down's syndrome. Levels of self-concept are found to be higher than average and no adverse effects have been found on friendships or general quality of life (Mates 1990). Another reassuring point is that many parents feel that having a child with autism in the family teaches their other children patience, tolerance and compassion. These children also appear more certain about their own future and the goals they want to achieve. It has been noted that a number of siblings choose to work in caring professions, and make use of the interpersonal skills they developed through childhood.

> I guess it isn't an accident that I ended up as a pediatrician. All the time I was growing up I kept praying there would be a way to cure Rich. (From Harris 1994, p.25)

Other siblings respond very differently and choose vocations where 'people skills' are not essential to the job.

## Encouraging good relations between siblings

- For younger siblings, or when a bedroom is shared, provide a safe place that cannot be invaded for favourite toys and belongings. (A locker or chest will suffice.)

- For older siblings with their own room, provide a lock on the door for when they want some privacy.

- If belongings are destroyed, do your best to replace them.

- Dedicate some time for spending just with your other child. Arrange for your partner or someone else to babysit your child with autism. This time is precious, do not allow it to be taken over by your child with autism.

- Introduce games that depend on at least two players.

- If your child with autism has a token system to encourage good behaviour, let your other children also have goals and rewards. (Programmes are covered in Chapter 11 'Understaning behaviour').

- Give all your children household tasks (including your child with autism).

- Do things as a family. An afternoon bowling or a morning at the swimming pool can re-establish the fun that can be had when you are all together.

- Allow a grumbling time for the siblings, when they can moan and whinge and list all the complaints they have every right to have. This doesn't need to be every day, but a special allotted time will ensure it happens. Some children may be happier talking to someone who is independent and not part of the immediate family. Wherever possible, pragmatic solutions should be found to the problems expressed by the siblings. Things which cannot be changed can also be dealt with. Exercises where complaints and grudges are tied to the string of a balloon that is then popped is one way of helping the sibling let go of issues. Slipping the complaint into an empty glass bottle and then visiting the bottle bank can also be therapeutic. Screaming into a pillow or dancing furiously to a song can also release pent-up feelings. Encouraging the sibling to draw a picture or write a story opens up a channel for discussion.

- When schoolmates come round to play with your unaffected child, allow them some space and time without their sibling. This can be hard if you feel that the majority of your autistic child's social contact is through friends of their sibling. This play does not need to be completely ruled out, but it does need to be measured. It may be necessary to talk with friends of your children, explaining a little about autism. Talking directly to the parents of the friend may be helpful, so that they feel able to answer questions too.

- Contacts are available for children who have siblings with special needs. Being in touch with other children in a similar position can be helpful to some. The added bonus of a new pen-pal in a different country is also a draw (see 'Useful contacts' at the end of this chapter). Local parents' groups may also have provisions for siblings – social outings, discussion groups, or just a way of meeting others in the local area who also have a brother or sister with autism.

## Useful contacts

Various websites have been set up for children with a sibling with autism. As these addresses are often subject to change, just two are included here. The NAS website provides current details on various sites and mailing lists.

### 1. SibNet:

www.seattlechildrens.org/sibsupp/

### 2. The National Autistic Society:

www.nas.org.uk/family/sibling.html

Families without internet access can contact the NAS Helpline for alternative details.

## Suggested reading

Harris SL. (1994) *Topics in Autism. Siblings of Children with Autism: A Guide for Families.* Bethesda, USA: Woodbine House.
*For information on siblings, dealt with in a practical and sensitive manner.*

The National Autistic Society (2001) Resource List: *Autism: Books for Children and Siblings.*

Powell TP. and Gallagher PA. (1996) *Brothers and Sisters: A Special Part of Exceptional Families.* 2nd edition. Baltimore: Paul H. Brookes.
*An extensive guide with lots of helpful tips.*

# Chapter 8

# Sources of help

As the parent of a child with autism you may be entitled to receive help from your local authority and the Benefits Agency. Chapter 9 looks at how to ensure that your child receives the educational help he needs. This section focuses on where, when and how to seek other help.

This information applies to families living in Britain. The support services and financial aid available in the rest of the world may be very different. Readers in North America should contact the Autism Society of America (ASA) for information and contacts. Contact details for the ASA are given at the end of Chapter 1.

Following diagnosis, parents often ask what their family is entitled to. There is no definitive legislation or government guidance stating possible entitlements for a child with autism. This means that parents are provided with varying amounts of information, depending on the knowledge of the person they approach.

Decisions made about the services offered should be governed by the child's individual needs. Although there is a great raft of legislation which tells local authorities and health authorities what it is within their powers to do, this should be of less concern to you than what your child actually needs. If you are looking for a specific legal remedy, advice is given later in this chapter.

The primary source of help for most families will be their local community and extended family. Sensitive grandparents, neighbours and friends can reduce the burden of stress enormously. However, family and friends are not always as helpful as they could be.

Extended family may feel echoes of the loss felt by parents, as well as not knowing how to handle the situation. As with a bereavement, they may feel that they are powerless to help. If you do need help, make specific requests. Let your family and friends know how they can help, as they may feel awkward about offering assistance without being asked first. Ask for someone to babysit, or to spend time with your other children. If it is still too soon for you to talk about how you are feeling, say so, but keep the channels of communication open.

Beyond the family, local support networks can be helpful. Across the UK there are regional branches of the National Autistic Society, run by parents for parents. In addition to this, there are independent charities providing support either specifically to families affected by autism, or more broadly to those with special needs. Aside from these networks, churches and temples, toddler groups and playgroups all provide valuable opportunities to meet with other families and find support.

Support groups aren't for everyone. Some parents stay on the mailing list for their local groups but rarely attend meetings because they don't benefit from them. Others find the opportunity to sit and talk about having a child with autism really helpful. Local groups are a good resource centre for finding out about local services. Collectively, parents are in a far better position to campaign for improvements to the services in their area. Many schools, respite care units and holiday projects owe their existence to the dedication and perseverance of parents.

## Professional support

In most cases children with autism will fall under the definition of a disabled child used in the Children Act 1989. This means that they are entitled to receive services from their local authority to enable them to develop as fully as any other child. Local authorities have a duty to keep children with their families wherever possible. Consequently much of the help that is provided by local authorities to disabled children is given in the form of support to the family. Respite care is the best example of this. Respite care is short-term care designed to give parents a break from the stresses of caring for their child.

Respite can be offered in many different forms. Some children are matched with a link family with whom the child spends a weekend every so often. Others spend an occasional night or weekend in a children's home. Some local authorities offer home-based short-term care, where a carer comes to the home for a few hours each week to spend time with the child (or take them out). What your family is offered will depend partly on the needs of your child and partly on what is available in your area.

## Accessing respite care

First, you'll need your child to be assessed by your local social services department. Contact them and explain that you have a disabled child. Typically a social worker will then visit you at home to get an idea of your child's needs. A care plan will then be drawn up, outlining the amount and type of care your child needs and who will provide this. Recommendations about care will be offered to your family. Ideally, any service provision will begin at this point.

In practice, things do not always run so smoothly. Problems may arise for two reasons. First, families may be seen as not needing respite care. From the perspective of the social worker this may well be the case. However, autism can be a subtle disability, and the stresses it places upon families may be hard to gauge during a brief assessment. Second, many families have to wait a long time before they begin to receive any services.

What should parents in this position do? First, get hold of a copy of your local authority's complaints procedure. If you feel that the assessment your family received was unfair, or that the length of time you have had to wait for a service is unreasonable, then you may have grounds to complain. Making a complaint is the best first step you can take. Authorities have to respond to complaints within strict time limits. Within this time they should investigate whether your complaint is justified.

If you are unhappy with the response to your complaint you can decide to take it further. There two ways in which you can do this. The first is to make a further complaint to the Local Government Ombudsman. You can only do this if you have already used your local complaints procedure. The alternative is to take your local authority to judicial review. Judicial review is a legal process in which the High Court looks at an action, decision or omission of a public body, to see whether it is lawful. A useful explanation of judicial review can be found in *Taking Action* by John Wright and David Ruebain (2000) (see 'Suggested reading' at the end of Chapter 9).

Knowing your rights is not always enough. To convince local authorities that you are entitled to services and that you need them will probably take a lot of stamina and hard work. That doesn't mean that services are not worth fighting for. It is probably best to begin asking for help before your child or your family badly needs it. This way, if a crisis does arise, the social services department will already have some knowledge of your needs. Although it may be small consolation at the time, every time you teach your local authority something about the reality of living with autism you are making life a lot easier for the families that will come after you.

## Financial help

Raising children is expensive. Bringing up a child with a disability has been estimated to be approximately three times more expensive (although this depends on the severity of the child's condition) (Dobson and Middleton 1998). Many families find that in addition to benefits to meet day-to-day living costs, they also need one-off payments to cover major expenses such as house adaptations and holidays. This section looks at the benefits you could be entitled to and where to go for further financial help. The information contained in this section applies to Britain only.

Families of children with autism may well be entitled to receive one or more of the following benefits:

- disability living allowance
- invalid care allowance
- disabled facilities grants

Disability living allowance (DLA) is the benefit that you are most likely to be entitled to. DLA is a non–means-tested benefit. This means that you can claim regardless of what your family's income is. If you are already claiming other benefits they should not be affected. The award will be made in your child's name. DLA is made up of two components, mobility and care. The care component of DLA is paid at three rates, lower, middle and higher. The mobility component is only paid at lower and higher rates. To find out more about how to apply for DLA, contact the Autism Helpline or follow one of the internet links given at the end of this chapter.

If your child receives the middle or higher rates of DLA care component, you may also be entitled to receive invalid care allowance. This is paid to people caring for someone for more than 35 hours a week. You cannot be in full-time education or earn more than £72 a week to claim this benefit. Because of the effect that claiming ICA can have on other benefits you are receiving, it is not always to your advantage to claim this. It is advisable to seek specialist advice before putting in a claim for ICA (see 'Useful contacts').

If your home needs adaptations to make it safe for your child, you may be entitled to a disabled facilities grant. These can be paid up to a maximum of £20,000 in England and £24,000 in Wales. These grants are administered by local housing authorities rather than the Benefits Agency. You'll need to get an application form from your housing authority. You application will need to be backed up by a certificate stating that your child will live in the property for at least five years after the works are completed.

## Other sources of funding

If you are looking for one-off funding for something like a washing-machine or a family holiday, and you can demonstrate that this is something you need as a result of your child's disability, you may be entitled to a grant from the Family Fund Trust. The Family Fund Trust is an independent charity, but it is funded by the government. In addition to providing grants the Trust also provides information on a range of related issues. If you are applying for the first time someone from the Family Fund Trust may visit you to assess your claim. (See 'Useful Contacts' at the end of this chapter for contact details.)

If the Family Fund Trust is unable to help, you may wish to apply to other bodies that make grants to individuals. There are so many of these in the UK that it is impossible to list them all here. Interested parents should consult a copy of *A Guide to Grants for Individuals in Need* (Harland and Griffiths 2000), which provides a directory of trusts but also provides invaluable information on making an application.. This book should be available through your local library.

## Useful contacts

*1. For an application form for the **Family Fund Trust** write to:*

**The Family Fund Trust**
PO Box 50
York YO1 2ZX

*2. To get copies of the claim forms for DLA and ICA call the **Benefit Enquiry Line** on 0800 88 22 00. This service runs from 8:30am to 6:30pm Monday to Friday and 9am to 1pm on Saturdays.*

*3. Details of your local **Citizens Advice Bureau**, which can help with filling in benefit claim forms, can be found in your local phone book. **The National Association of Citizens Advice Bureaux** has a website at www.nacab.org.uk which also has details of all local Bureaux. Many local authorities also have **welfare rights departments**: to find out if your authority does, call the Town Hall.*

*4. For independent advice over the phone about disability benefits, call* **Disability Alliance Rights Advice Line** *on 020 7247 8763. This service is only available on Mondays and Wednesdays from 2pm to 4pm.*

*5. If you have concerns about your child's legal rights, the* **Children's Legal Centre** *may be able to help. Their contact details are:*

> **Children's Legal Centre**
> University of Essex
> Wivenhoe Park
> Colchester CO4 3SQ
> *Tel:* 01206 873820 (Monday to Friday, 10am to 12:30pm and 2pm to 4:30pm)
> *Fax:* 01206 874026
> *Email:* clc@essex.ac.uk

## Suggested reading

Harland S. and Griffiths D. (2001) *A Guide to Grants for Individuals in Need.* London: Directory of Social Change

Paterson J. (2001) *Disability Rights Handbook.* London: Disability Alliance

In the UK, you will probably find both of these books in your local library.

*Chapter 9*

# Education

When we got the diagnosis, we weren't even sure if our son would be allowed to go to school. (Parent of a twelve-year-old with autism, diagnosed at age two)

After diagnosis, the next problem many parents face is establishing what type of education their child needs. In this chapter, we examine the range of educational provision available to children with autism and how to access it. We also look at how to get extra help if your child is having problems, and how to tackle some common difficulties like bullying.

There are big differences between educational provision in Britain and the rest of the world. Most of the information in the following chapter applies only to Britain. Contacts for further information outside Britain are provided in 'Useful contacts' at the end of this chapter.

## Common questions

*'Will my child need to go to a special school?'*

Not necessarily. Children with autism vary enormously. Many thrive in mainstream schools, with some extra help. Others are better able to learn outside the mainstream environment. But the choice is not restricted to mainstream or specialist schools. There has been a shift in recent years towards including children with special educational needs in mainstream schools. This means that an increasing number of schools are equipped and able to support children with autism. Equally, more and more special schools are encouraging an inclusive ethos and supporting their students to attend mainstream schools for some lessons. And some are encouraging students from mainstream schools to join the school for certain lessons. As the boundaries between provisions become blurred, it has become increasingly important for parents to visit individual schools and decide for themselves what might suit their child.

*'I know my child is going to need extra help, how do I make sure he'll get it?'*

The Department for Education and Skills (DfES) estimate that as many as 20 per cent of children will need extra help with learning at some point during their school careers. In order to target extra help (and funding) at those who need it most, a complicated system of identification and assessment has developed. For those children with the most complex needs, a statement of special educational needs may be drawn up. The statement will outline the nature of their needs and the provision that is required in order to meet them. Extra funding will then be earmarked for that child to pay for this. Most children with special educational needs will not need a statement. They will be provided with extra help through the school's own funds. It isn't clear what proportion of children with autism have statements and how many are just helped within their schools. Due to the subtle nature of autism in some pupils, a child who appears to function on the surface may actually be experiencing real difficulties. Once supported, such a child can make dramatic gains in performance. Adequate support could be the difference between the pupil who just about keeps up, and the one that excels.

### 'Should my child go to an autism specific school?'

Again, this depends on your child. Some children will thrive in this environment and others will fare better elsewhere. Not every family will have autism specific provision near to them and whilst more provision is being developed and more Local Education Authorities (LEAs) now recognise how important it can be, we are a long way from universal coverage. Whatever you feel is right for your child it's worth remembering that autism specific schools can be invaluable resources when you are looking for ideas on how best to support your child.

## Pre-school provision

> It wasn't until Annie started nursery that we realised how different from the other children she was. (Parent of a four-year-old with high functioning autism.)

The term 'pre-school provision' covers a vast range of different services. Any services offered to children below statutory school age fall into this category. They can include childminders, playgroups and nursery schools. Even within these categories a diverse range of services is offered. For example, nursery schools could follow a specific teaching approach such as the Montessori method; they could be specialist nurseries for children with special needs; they could even be autism specific. Some may be state funded, others are privately operated. Some are attached to schools, others stand alone. However, what may seem like a bewildering array of choice may boil down to a very few settings suitable for a child with autism.

> Annie would just wander around the room by herself. The helpers tried to get her to play but she'd sit down for a minute or two and then she'd be off again.

Most settings for this age group don't offer a particularly formal education. Instead, they often promote learning through play. For children with autism this can pose problems, as they may not intuitively develop play skills and will need much support from an adult in order to gain from this type of environment. They may also find a noisy and unstructured nursery very stressful to be in. Making a child's first experience of school positive is very important in order to motivate them through the rest of their education. So it is definitely worth looking around for a placement where the staff understand your child's needs, where there is some structure and routine to reassure your child and space for her to have time out if it all gets a bit much. If you feel that none of your local nurseries will meet your child's needs without extra funding, it is worth requesting that the LEA conduct a statutory assessment.

## Alternative models of early intervention

Sending a child with autism to nursery when they are very small may not be the right choice for them. In many cases, young children with autism will not have developed the skills they need to cope with a teaching environment and, equally, may need a great deal of support in order to learn through play. Many parents choose home-based programmes for this age group. In Britain, the most popular approach for early years home-based intervention is Applied Behaviour Analysis. Other parents opt for the Options programme (for more information about both of these approaches turn to Chapter 13 'Therapies and approaches'). And many more set up their own programme based on a combination of approaches, with input from speech and language therapy services and specialists in the field, such as Portage teachers. Portage teachers visit children with special needs at home on a regular basis to observe and give advice to their parents on activities and exercises that could help the child. Not all areas run a Portage scheme and those that do will not necessarily have expertise in autism.

If you received your diagnosis from a recognised health professional such as a child psychiatrist or psychologist, then they should notify the LEA of your child's needs. Sometimes this does not happen or parents are not informed that it has happened. Make sure you ask the professionals involved with your child if they have made a referral. It is also worth requesting an assessment in your own right.

## Choosing a school

Many parents of children with autism have problems finding the right school. They are frequently presented with a bewildering choice of placements and little guidance on what would be best for their child. The following are just a few tips on what to look for and what to ask.

### 1. Make sure you know what's available

If your child is pre-school and in the process of being statemented, then your LEA should provide you with a list of suitable schools which are close to you. They may provide you with a complete list of mainstream and specialist provision, with guidance on which are the right places to look, or they may give you a selected list of schools which they feel are right for your child. You can always ask for a more comprehensive list if you feel you don't have enough information.

In addition to this you can obtain a list of schools accredited by the National Autistic Society for free by calling the Autism Helpline. You can also buy a booklet called 'Schools, Units and Classes' which lists every autism specific provision in Britain that the NAS is aware of. This is priced £5.99 and is available from NAS Publications. If you are considering an independent school you can find information on independent schools which take children with autism or Asperger syndrome in *The Gabbitas Guide to Schools for Special Needs*, which will probably be in your local library, or from an information service such as Gabbitas or the Independent Schools Information Service (ISIS). Further details are provided at the end of this chapter.

## 2. Visit as many types of provision as you can

You don't need to visit every school you hear about (and it would not be possible anyway) but it's a good idea to visit as many different types of school as you can. This will give you a much broader picture of what is available and what features you think are important. You may also find that something you would not normally have considered is just right for your child.

> I wouldn't have considered a mainstream school for Ryan but then I visited our local infant school just in case and thought it was great. It was quite small (only three classes) and the head teacher and reception class teacher were really enthusiastic about the fact that Ryan had autism. They really seemed to want him to come to the school and this made me feel much more confident about his prospects. (Parent of a six-year-old with autism.)

You may find that whilst some schools are not suitable, they still have elements which appeal to you. For example, a speech and language therapy unit in a mainstream school might not be appropriate, but the fact that children there spend a lot of time in mainstream classes would be appropriate. As a result you might want to look at the arrangements for integration or inclusion at other schools you visit.

## 3. Decide which features are crucial to you

This will vary among families, but there are a few features which are going to be important for all children with autism.

- Parents should feel that they are able to feed-back any concerns they have to the school and vice versa, so it's important that the staff seem approachable and open.

- Schools should be in a position to respond to the varying needs of children with autism. They should be aware that the approaches which work for one child may not work for another and that flexibility is crucial to effective provision.

- Children with special educational needs (SEN) are statistically more likely to be involved in bullying than children without SEN. They may be either perpetrators or victims, and so it is crucial that the school has a clear policy on bullying. This applies to special schools every bit as much as it does to mainstream schools.

- Careful and consistent planning is vital for children with autism, as mixed messages can cause them acute anxiety. So communication inside the school is as important for them as their communication with parents. Ask about arrangements for staff meetings, and how often teachers and learning support staff are able to meet.

There are many more features of a school which will be equally important but specific to your child. If you can ask family and friends to contribute to drawing up this list of features, this may prove very helpful. People outside the immediate family may see your child's needs very differently to you.

> My favourite thing about Ryan's school is that his teachers are always happy to talk to me. And they don't just let me know if he's had a bad day or flipped out at something. His class teacher will come out to the playground and say 'He did some really good work today. I was really impressed.'

### 4. Make a shortlist

Try and narrow your choice down to just two or three schools which you feel are acceptable. They don't all have to be perfect, so long as you can see your child being happy or settled there. Very few parents feel totally happy about their child's school, and most placements are the result of a compromise between the school and the family. This is true for children without SEN as well. However, if you feel that you can communicate effectively with the school should problems arise, then this is probably the best basis for a long-term working relationship.

It is probably better to focus on two or three schools rather than just one in case you are unable to get a place at your preferred school. And it is probably better to be open-minded about the future. If the placement doesn't suit your child you do have the option of moving them at a later date. Although change is difficult for children with autism this does not necessarily mean that it should always be avoided. Learning to handle change is an inevitable part of growing up.

## Tips on visiting schools

It is not possible to ask too many questions at this stage. You have made no commitment to the school; don't worry about being labelled as an overanxious parent – if the staff think that, that is their problem. If you were buying a house you wouldn't be embarrassed about asking questions, and the same should apply to choosing a school.

Decide what exactly you need to know in advance, and try to get exact answers. Take a list of questions if this helps.

- Where possible try to speak to the class teachers and classroom assistants as well as whoever is showing you around (usually the headteacher).

- If you can watch the children in the playground as well as during lessons, this could be helpful. This way you can find out how involved the staff are in the children's play, what activities are available and whether there are any bullying blackspots (places in the playground which are isolated and hard for teachers to observe).

- Try and see some paperwork as well. The school will probably tell you about how they plan each child's education and what kind of assessments they do, but looking at some actual paperwork will help you to see both how relevant it is to your child and how seriously it is taken.

- If you can, take your child with you to visit at least one school. Pre-schoolers won't have been to a school before and it may be the first opportunity you get to see how they cope in a school environment. However, for some parents it may be that taking their young child with them will add immeasurably to the stress involved and make evaluating the visit very difficult. Most schools will, however, want to meet your child before offering him/her a place.

- If both parents can go that's desirable, but often this can be difficult. If you aren't able to go with your partner it might be helpful to ask a friend or relative who knows your child to come too.

- If you get the chance to talk to other parents of children at the school at the end of the day, then make use of it. Ask questions about their experience of talking with teachers and other staff and having their concerns addressed. Be aware that some parents will have had negative experiences, but these won't necessarily be relevant to you or your child.

## Assessments and statementing

The law regarding the educational rights of children with special educational needs is outlined in the Education Act 1996. Specific guidance has also been given to local education authorities about how they assess and fund this support in the Code of Practice on the Identification of Special Educational Needs (DfEE 1994).

A statement is a legal document which entitles a child to extra funding to cover the costs of the provision needed to meet their needs. Not all children with autism will need one, as many can be supported with funding from within the school's own SEN budget. These children may be on one of what are called the school-based stages of the Code of Practice. The three stages are not a series of hoops to jump through; if you feel that your child needs more support than this you can approach the LEA for a statutory assessment leading to a statement at any time. Briefly, the school-based stages work like this:

### Stage 1

Should be triggered by the child's class teacher noting that the child is having problems. In the case of children with autism or Asperger syndrome, these problems may not be to do with school work, as the child may well be of average or above average intelligence. Instead teachers may become aware that the child is not very sociable and has difficulty interacting with other children. There may be speech and language problems, particularly with regard to using expressive language. The child may also have difficulties being creative or exploring imaginative play. If teachers feel that any of these issues constitute a barrier to the child's learning, they should discuss these concerns with the parents.

At Stage 1 the teacher is not required to take any action beyond notifying the parents and the school Special Educational Needs Co-ordinator (SENCO), and considering ways of modifying the curriculum to include the child more effectively.

## Stage 2

At Stage 2 the SENCO takes over responsibility for assessing the child's SEN and planning appropriate provision. The decision to move onto Stage 2 should be taken by the class teacher in conjunction with the child's parents. At this stage, the SENCO may decide to contact other agencies such as health or social services, and then review all available information in order to decide whether to draw up an individual education plan or seek a further assessment. If the SENCO thinks a child has autism then he/she should consider asking for an educational psychology assessment and discuss the possibility of pursuing a formal diagnosis through the health service with the parents.

## Stage 3

At this stage the SENCO may decide to seek further advice. An educational psychologist or speech and language therapist may be called in to assess and comment on the child's support needs. Please note, schools can call in external professionals for advice at any of the preceding stages as well. The SENCO should still take a leading role at this stage. It may be appropriate for the child to start receiving additional learning support in the classroom. Once assessments have been completed the SENCO will meet with other involved people to make a decision. The decision regards whether they should move on to Stage 4 and request a statutory assessment and potential statement. In some cases, in light of reports received, the individual education plan is revised to include the recommendations of specialists with the possibility of increased support within school.

If the decision is made to move to what may be called Stage 4 – or statutory assessment – the LEA will take over responsibility at this point, as described in what now follows.

### 'Why is it better for me to request the assessment than my child's teacher or doctor?'

If you request the assessment as a parent, the LEA must respond to your request within six weeks. If they refuse your request you have a right to appeal to the SEN Tribunal. If a professional, whether a medical professional or a teacher, requests the assessment, there is no time limit within which the LEA must respond and there is no right of appeal if they refuse to assess.

### 'How do I request an assessment?'

Write to the top person at your LEA (this will normally be the Chief Education Officer or the Director of Education). Keep a copy of the letter for yourself and enclose copies of any consultants' reports which you have received. Once the LEA has received your letter they should respond, outlining what action they will be taking, within six weeks. If they agree to your request for an assessment then they will arrange for this to be carried out. Reports will be needed from an educational psychologist, a teacher or nursery teacher (if your child is already attending a school setting), a parent, a representative of the health authority (who will add any details from the child's medical record) and a representative of the social services department. (If you have never been in touch with your local social services then all they will say is that they have not heard of your family.) The findings of these assessors will be used by the LEA to draw up a statement, which will then be sent to you for approval. LEAs are expected to work to a target of completing the statement within two weeks of receiving the reports of the assessments. The entire assessment process should be completed within 26 weeks.

Once the LEA has finished writing up the statement you'll be sent a document known as the proposed statement, which you will have 15 days to read and respond to. This is probably the most challenging period in the whole process. It is at this stage that you may wish to consult voluntary organisations and your local parent partnership service for information and moral support. Some addresses are provided at the end of the book.

If the LEA does not agree to any proposed amendments, they are obliged to issue a final statement anyway. The next section outlines what action you can take if you are unhappy with this.

### 'What if I disagree with the statement?'

If you are unhappy with the proposed statement you should express your concerns in writing to the LEA within 15 days of receiving it. Problems with proposed statements tend to fall into two categories. The first is that of concerns about the nature of needs specified in Part 2 and the provision specified in Part 3, and the second is problems with the placement named in Part 4.

If your LEA still refuses to respond, and you feel that your case is backed up by the law, then you can take them to an independent special educational needs tribunal. To do this you may wish to consult a solicitor with experience of education law. A free booklet entitled *Special Educational Needs Tribunal: How to Appeal* is available from DfES publications on 0845 6022260.

Appealing against a statement is likely to be very complicated and we cannot do the subject justice here. If you are considering taking this step we would recommend you seek further advice from one of the organisations listed at the end of this book.

### 'What if I want to change the statement?'

Even once you have accepted a statement and your child is receiving the specified provision, it may be that you want to change elements of it. For example, you may feel that your child will need more support from a learning support assistant when he moves from primary to secondary school; or you may wish to change the amount of speech and language therapy your child receives as she gets older.

If these needs arise and are recognised by teachers straight away, it is possible that you will be able to negotiate changes to the statement quite easily. However, if you feel that there is a need for re-assessment, which is not addressed by the school, then you may have to write to your LEA with your request. As with other concerns relating to statementing, they have a responsibility to respond. If they are not prepared to consider re-assessment they will need to provide you with adequate reasons for this. You may also take your LEA to the SEN tribunal if they will not re-assess your child.

### 'Where can I get more help?'

The field of special education is very complicated and affected by a broad range of legislation. If you are grappling with your LEA or your child's school you can contact any of the organisations in 'Useful contacts' for further specific advice. Different organisations work in different ways, and you may find that your needs are met better by your local parent partnership service than by a national charity, or vice versa. However, all of these organisations provide their basic services free of charge.

There are a number of organisations which may be able to provide you with help and support with the statementing procedure. Broadly speaking these fall into three categories:

- parent partnerships, which are statutory advice services funded by LEAs to support parents of children with SEN

- local support groups, such as your local autism parents group

- national voluntary organisations such as the NAS or special education specific charities like Network 81 or IPSEA (details are given later).

*'OK, I've got the statement, my child's got their placement, what else should happen?'*

Provided you are happy with the placement or the level of support your child is receiving, and your child's needs continue to be met, there should be no attempts made to change the statement. However, you should still meet regularly with your child's class teacher to discuss his progress, and the school SENCO should also convene an annual review to which all relevant parties are invited to discuss progress made during the year and any changes which should take place. Parents have a right to attend these meetings and to voice any concerns they are having at the time. You also have the right to contact your child's school at any time if you wish to discuss any aspect of your child's education.

## Planning for the future

Once your child reaches Year 9 the head teacher of their school should include transition planning on the agenda of the Annual Review. This gives parents and professionals the opportunity to look ahead and think about what services your child may need in the future. As a parent, it is important that you ensure that this planning takes place and that you are fully involved in it.

In adulthood your child may continue to need help with independent living and finding employment. The earlier you start looking into what is available, the easier it will be to help your child transfer smoothly from child to adult services. Sadly, many young people still reach 19 and leave school with little or no provision being made for them. But it is possible to avoid this.

## General tips

For some people, it can be extremely difficult to get a statement which accurately reflects their child's needs. For others it is remarkably straightforward. There is no magic formula and provision can vary considerably across the country. The following are some useful tips that should be helpful to most people:

- Keep notes of everything. Obviously keeping all paperwork in a safe place is common sense, but it is often helpful to keep a note of every face-to-face and telephone conversation you have. Although these cannot be used as evidence it may be helpful for you to have a record of what has been said to you and when.

- Always get the name of whoever you are speaking to and if possible their position as well. For some reason professionals frequently assume that parents will automatically know who they are and that therefore introductions are pointless!

- Get in touch with your local parent partnership service. Although the NAS and other helplines try very hard to provide accurate and useful information, they are often not in a position to provide a specialist regional service. This is where Parent Partnership is invaluable, because it will have a far greater specific knowledge of services in your area.

- Be clear about what you are prepared to compromise on and what you are not. It can be very easy to be bullied into making concessions which you do not want to at meetings. If you know in advance which points you wish to stand firm on and which points you can be flexible about, you can argue much more clearly.

- Ask questions, as often and as many as possible. This serves two purposes: first, it may make things clearer to you, and second, people are less likely to waffle at you if they know you will ask for clarification.

## Glossary of useful terms

*DfES*    Department for Education and Skills, the government department responsible for all legislation and guidance relating to SEN; formerly known as the Department for Education and Employment (DfEE).

*EBD*    stands for 'emotional and behavioural difficulties'. Again, this is the term used in legislation to describe children with disruptive behaviour. The DfES considers all children with EBD to have special educational needs and expects schools to recognise that much disruptive behaviour is the result of unmet learning needs. This is particularly relevant to autism.

*EPS*     Educational Psychology Service. All LEAs will run an EPS employing psychologists who all come from an educational background and can offer specialist advice on meeting a child's SEN in the mainstream or potentially transferring to special school.

*FE*       further or post-16 education.

*IEP*      Individual Education Plan. This should be drawn up by your child's class teacher in conjunction with you and other involved professionals. The IEP should be reviewed annually and include target achievements which will enable you to monitor your child's progress.

*LEA*     Local Education Authority

*SALT*    speech and language therapy or therapist. This is the same service as speech therapy. The name change reflects the way in which the services offered by SALTs have changed over the last few years.

*SEN*     special educational needs. This is the term used in education law to describe all children who, for whatever reason, need additional support to attend school. They may not have learning disabilities such as dyslexia or Down syndrome – a child who uses a wheelchair and therefore needs assistance to get around at school will also count as having special educational needs.

## Bullying

I was livid when I found out Alex was being bullied. I knew I couldn't deal with it because I was too angry. In the end one of my friends spoke to his school for me. (Mother of a ten-year-old with semantic pragmatic disorder)

Bullying is common. Almost all children are affected by it at some point during their education. Sadly, children with autism seem to be particularly vulnerable to bullying for a number of reasons:

- They are different, and besides being different they are often not motivated to fit in. This makes them prime targets for bullying.

- They sometimes aren't aware that they are being bullied. Although children with autism still feel hurt by name calling, teasing and being ignored, they often don't realise that these behaviours are bullying. As a result they don't tell anyone how upset they are.

- They lack the communication skills to let people know that they are being bullied. In particular they find it hard to talk about their feelings, so may seem not to care about the emotional pain they are experiencing.

- They retaliate and are then seen to be equally to blame.

- They are seen as 'provocative victims'. This is a phrase used by the DfEE (1999) to describe those children who are seen to provoke bullying by behaving oddly. Their guidance states clearly that no child deserves to be bullied, no matter how oddly they might behave. Children with autism often have no awareness that their behaviour might be seen as strange.

Alex just didn't have a clue what he was doing wrong. It was like the more he tried to get the other kids to like him the more horrible they were. His teacher was fed up with him being class clown but Alex had no idea that his mad behaviour in class was what was making everyone so annoyed with him.

### Strategies to tackle bullying

Bullying can begin at any age, but is most common once children begin secondary school. It is never too early to start teaching your child about bullying and ways to tackle it. The first problem that many children with autism face is that they often aren't sure what bullying is. A very simple definition of bullying is any action that someone undertakes deliberately to make another person feel hurt or sad or upset. Explaining this by itself might not be effective, as a child with autism will not necessarily understand why bullies do what they do and when something is done just to hurt them. You and the school can work with your child to define bullying and who bullies might be.

> I like it now I'm at secondary school. I joined the computer club and chess club and sometimes I help out in the library at lunchtimes. Now bullies can't get me and it's a lot more fun than standing in the rain. (twelve-year-old with Asperger syndrome)

All schools should have an anti-bullying policy which parents are entitled to see. Many will also have appointed a teacher with specific responsibility for co-ordinating and monitoring the anti-bullying policy. If your child is starting school it might be helpful to meet with this teacher to discuss your concerns.

It is important to emphasise to the school that while your child may appear to understand this, she may still have difficulty in applying it to her own experiences. She may need to be reminded of it frequently (you can write this down on cue cards which could be stuck in a homework diary as a reminder) and teachers will still need to watch out for signs of bullying.

A number of other strategies are also being used by schools to address bullying. More information about these approaches is available from *The Anti Bullying Handbook* (Sullivan 2000). Some of them are briefly summarised here:

CIRCLE OF FRIENDS

A circle of friends is a group of students who volunteer to befriend the pupil with autism. They can provide positive input on developing social skills and also give the young person some protection from bullies particularly during lunch hours and break times.

THE NO-BLAME APPROACH

The idea behind the no-blame approach is that addressing the problem of bullying is more important than punishing the perpetrator. The victim is given the opportunity to show in private what effect the bullying has had on them. They might be asked to draw a picture or write a story to show how they feel.

All those involved in the bullying, including those who may just have watched what happened, are asked to come to a meeting with a teacher. Other students may be involved as well. They discuss how the victim is feeling and make suggestions about how to help the victim feel better. They are then expected to put their ideas into practice and all make an effort to make life better for the victim.

This approach has some merits. The complex nature of autism and the fact that children with it may not react emotionally when distressed means that bullies may not know how much distress they are causing. The opportunity to learn how much pain they have caused the victim gives the bullies the opportunities to mend their ways with dignity and may also pave the way to a better understand of the child's needs across the whole peer group. However, children with autism may need support to understand that the bullying is not their fault and that the bullies are in the wrong, and if the bully receives no punishment this may be hard to demonstrate.

## CIRCLE TIME

Circle time is an approach used in lots of schools to encourage discussion among children on a range of topics. These could include bullying. This approach enables teachers to address bullying indirectly. Circle time is difficult for many children with autism. It is often largely unstructured and they may find this situation stressful. They are unlikely to feel comfortable talking about their own experiences in this environment. Consequently circle time cannot really be more than a part of the solution when addressing the bullying of a child with autism.

## PEER GROUP PROGRAMMES

This approach aims to eradicate bullying by ensuring that the whole school culture recognises that bullying is unacceptable and should not go ignored. Older children are trained to act as bullying counsellors and are then identified by wearing a ribbon or badge. Younger children can then approach them if they are bullied to ask for support and advice. This approach acknowledges that many children will find it easier to talk to someone their own age than a teacher. Other measures are taken to ensure that children who are vulnerable to bullying have places other than the playground to go at lunchtime.

Ensuring that the school culture promotes tolerance and respect for differences can only be a good thing for children with autism. Many aspects of this approach seem very positive to us, but children with autism will find it easier to approach a teacher who already knows them than another pupil who may not.

## Useful contacts

*1. If you wish to order a copy of **Schools, Units and Classes** from **NAS Publications**, then call **01268 522872**. The line is open between 10am and 4pm. Or you can send a mail order in if you request a copy of the publications catalogue, either from the helpline or the publications department.*

> **NAS Publications**
> Barnardos Despatch Services
> Paycocke Road
> Basildon
> Essex SS14 3DR
> *Email:* beverley.bennett@barnardos.org.uk

*2. **Gabbitas Educational Consultants** provide a service to parents wanting to find an independent school suitable for their child. They will charge for this service. You can find out more from:*

> **Gabbitas Educational Consultants**
> Carrington House
> 126–130 Regent Street
> London W1R 6EE
> *Tel:* 020 7734 0161
> *Fax:* 020 7437 1764
> *Email:* market@gabbitas.co.uk
> *Website:* www.gabbitas.co.uk

*They also publish the* Gabbitas Guide to Schools for Special Needs *(ISBN 0749429984, published by Kogan Page, £14.99) which lists all special schools in Britain as well as independent schools prepared to take students with SEN. This can be ordered from your local library or found in major bookshops.*

*3. A similar service is offered by the* **Independent Schools Information Service (ISIS)**. *You can find out more by contacting:*

The Director
**National ISIS**
Grosvenor Gardens House
35–37 Grosvenor Gardens
London SW1W 0BS
*Tel :* 020 7798 1500
*Fax :* 020 7798 1501
*Email:* national@isis.org.uk
*Website:* www.isis.org.uk

**4. Parent Partnership Services (PPS)** *are independent advice services for parents of children with SEN. They are funded by central government and offer support around all aspects of finding the appropriate placement and support for your child. If you have not been put in touch with your local service you can ask the LEA or your child's current school for their contact details.*

*5. Details of the* **National Portage Association** *are provided in 'Useful contacts' at the end of Chapter 6.*

*6. The* **National Association of Protection and Advocacy Systems** *can put parents in touch with advocacy services which can help with special education, disability rights and social security issues.*

**National Association of Protection and Advocacy Systems**
900 2nd Street, NE, Suite 211
Washington
DC 20002
USA
*Tel:* 202 408 9514

*7. A complete list of legal and advocacy services can also be found on the internet at*
*www.patientcenters.com/autism*

## Suggested reading

Elliott M. (1997) *101 Ways to Deal with Bullying: A Guide for Parents*. London: Hodder and Stoughton.

Sullivan K. (2000) *The Anti Bullying Handbook*. Melbourne: Oxford University Press.

Wright J. and Ruebain D. (2000) *Taking Action! Your Child's Right to Special Education*. Birmingham: Questors Publishing Company.

The following titles are all available for free from the DfES:

*Special Educational Needs: A Guide for Parents*. ISBN 0855224452

*Special Educational Needs Tribunal: How to Appeal*. ISBN 085522553

*Code of Practice on the Identification and Assessment of Special Educational Needs*.

The 1994 edition of the Code of Practice is now out of print. The 2001 edition should be available from September 2000.

*Chapter 10*

# Social ability

Humans are social creatures. From babyhood onwards, many show strong preference for the company of others. Even a young child can show clear understanding of social rules. The ability to behave in socially appropriate ways is fundamental to being human (though admittedly we do not always exercise this skill). Socialisation of the young child is mainly a natural process. Although there is valid input from parents and peers, children largely modify and adapt themselves to fit into their social world. Many implicit rules of social behaviour are never explicitly taught. Despite this, the majority of children show a firm grasp of these hidden codes of conduct.

The child with autism provides a frustrating contrast for parents. Here is a child who may need direct teachings to learn even the very basics of social behaviour. The ease of social learning with sponge-like absorbency is not apparent (although it may be present in other spheres such as special interests). Parents of a child with autism act as social teacher, guide and interpreter. Adults writing about their autism often use the analogy of aliens from another planet, arriving on earth without an instruction manual. One woman describes her autism as 'Ooops wrong planet syndrome'(see 'Useful contacts' at the end of this chapter). We can only try to imagine how bewildering, terrifying and exhausting this daily experience must be. Getting lost in a foreign country where you don't speak the language would be mildly comparable, although even in that situation the majority of us could still rely on universal body language.

Parents of a child with autism play a major role in their son or daughter's social development. Children with autism who are involved in social activities become more socially responsive and stereotyped and ritualistic behaviours decrease (Volkmar and Cohen 1982). Social interaction can be encouraged through activities that the child finds pleasurable. Focusing on special interests and favoured pursuits forms a starting point for initiating contact. There are different techniques that parents can use to become important partners in their child's world. A child's communication skills and thought-processing abilities will determine what parents try and what proves successful; as always, different things work for different children. Displaying desired objects out of reach, placing tempting objects in childproof transparent containers and rough-and-tumble play all require social contact and help teach your child that being with someone else is useful and fun.

Children with autism need a basic instruction manual which tells them everything they need to know about social life. They are not privy to the same information that other people instinctively know, realise or assume. Now clearly there are limitations between what can and can't be taught. If you take even a relatively simple social interaction you find there are infinite possibilities and conclusions. For every rule there is the exception, and for every likely outcome there could be several unexpected possibilities. To begin with, parents need to be aware of the particular difficulties that affect their child's social ability.

## The main problem areas

### Mindblindness, or a lack of 'theory of mind'

Mindblindness describes the inability to make guesses about the mental and emotional states of another person. When humans empathise, we use a highly developed ability to imagine what someone else is feeling and thinking. This in turn can influence our own thoughts and actions. By the age of three or four, most children have developed this skill, known as the 'theory of mind'. The majority of children with autism display mindblindness, and as a result, their social interactions are limited.

A child who does not have a theory of mind is more vulnerable as she cannot consider other people's motives and personal agendas. In some cases children can be exploited by so called 'friends' because of this naïvety:

> I am unable to perceive whether people wish me well or ill. Instead, I try to calculate with my intellect, and the result is not always that good. I've realised that people can sense if someone wishes them well or ill. They seem to accumulate some kind of experience of others, which they use in order to read them. I have no such sense, no special place in which to accumulate those experiences. (Gerland 1997, p.244)

(See last section in this chapter: 'Can children be taught to mind-read?')

### Recognising trouble, understanding and talking about feelings and emotions

Many children with autism do not match emotions with corresponding facial expressions in other people. They are unable to discern someone's feelings from their body language, unless it is made explicit. Some children may be able to recognise and describe very simple and extreme emotions (e.g. when someone is very happy or very sad) but they miss the more subtle range of feelings in between (e.g. jealousy, irritation, etc.). These difficulties are related to mindblindness, as we use a person's outward signs (e.g. smiles, raised eyebrows, depressed tone of voice, etc.) to form a hypothesis about their inward thoughts and feelings.

Your child's own emotions may be limited or extreme in range. Intense anger may be expressed at small setbacks. When happy, the child may get extremely overexcited. Other children feel the full range of emotions but have trouble expressing those feelings. Despite the emotions felt inside by the child, facial expression and tone of voice may betray little.

Sad family events, like the death of a loved one, may not be handled well by the child with autism. There may be little sign of sadness or depth of feeling. This is illustrated well by one child who asked her mother, 'Should I be sad when someone dies?' Your child may show grief in less obvious ways (usually through his behaviour). For example, the child may ask inappropriate questions about what has happened, which can be very upsetting for others to hear. Although it is easy to be hurt by your child's apparent thoughtlessness at these painful times, certainly no malice is intended. Your child is having difficulty judging what is expected of him and behaving accordingly.

### Difficulty reading and following social rules

As already mentioned, children with autism do not recognise and correctly interpret social rules. They may be able to learn basic principles, but then may apply these rules very rigidly in a black and white fashion. Some children with autism earn the title 'class policeman' as they tell tales on classmates who are not following the rules strictly. Judging when it is necessary to adapt or break the rules is a decision that the majority of children with autism have difficulty with.

### Inability to mix normally with peer group

Due to their social impairment, children with autism rarely blend in with their peers. Playing with, rather than just alongside, schoolmates demands numerous skills. Initiating successful play, taking turns, making and maintaining friendships, can pose problems. It is not uncommon for the child with autism to prefer the company of adults or younger children, where fewer demands are made and communication is clearer. Understanding what qualities make up a friendship, who is a friend and, just as importantly, who is not, are hard concepts to teach and learn.

## Overcoming social problems

Now the difficulties have been made explicit, responding to these areas will be addressed. You may find the following suggestions useful when approaching social behaviour issues. They may seem straightforward and in themselves unremarkable; however, once applied they could make a big difference to your child's social behaviour.

- Teach your young child the 'adult rules' of behaviour (e.g. only undress in a private place). This allows your child to learn appropriate conduct that will see her through into adulthood. Behaviours that are tolerated because of a child's age can quickly become part of a routine. The usual reasoning that 'he'll grow out of it' does not apply. Growing out of age-inappropriate things depends on the child recognising outside social forces, which may not happen with your child.

- Try to predict the future. If your child has habits that you are not sure whether to address, project ahead 15 years. Will you still be happy if your teenager has the same behaviours then? Some habits which appear odd are harmless and perhaps serve an important function for your child (e.g. they could be a way for your child to de-stress). Other behaviours are highly irritating or have the potential of becoming seriously anti-social. The age of your child makes a tremendous difference to how they are perceived by others. A tendency to remove clothing in public has very different consequences, depending on whether you are five or fifteen years old.

- Start strict. Do not kid yourself that you will toughen up once your child is older. You will make much more work for yourself and limit your chances of success. A wilful toddler is easier to deal with than an adolescent who has become stuck in their ways. Your child's love of rules can be used to your advantage. Provide clear, concise rules initially (e.g. 'never speak to strangers'). Rules can always be relaxed and modified at a later stage once your child has learnt them satisfactorily. As real life experiences widen and your child's expertise grows, clauses and exceptions can be added (e.g. '...unless they are a policeman/woman').

- Keep any explanations short and use concrete language. Don't spend too much time explaining the why and wherefore of each rule. Lengthy explanations rarely aid understanding and instead may lead to confusion and endless discussions. Sometimes your child just needs to know that that's simply the rule. If you feel a certain way of behaving is important, make it a rule and enforce it.

- Set boundaries. Make sure your child knows exactly what is expected of him in a given situation. Be direct and provide instructions. Do not assume that your child knows anything about new situations.

- Be consistent. Once decided, enforce the boundaries laid down. Your child may push against the boundaries just to be reassured as to where they are. Once they realise that your response is always the same, they will accept this as the status quo. Try to make sure that everyone who cares for your child knows the rules of social behaviour and sticks by them.

### Tools to aid social behaviour

Siblings can be involved in many of the following ideas. The aim is to make learning about social behaviour more like a game to be enjoyed rather than a lesson to be endured. Special interests of the child are the best starting point, and wherever possible should be incorporated into teaching. This is a sure-fire way of gaining your child's attention and making the experience enjoyable for him. Initially, reinforcers may be needed to encourage your child to participate. (See Chapter 11 'Understanding behaviour' for ideas on reinforcers.)

Able children with Asperger syndrome who are strongly motivated to make friends (and hence improve their social skills) will be very different to work with compared to children who are happiest alone. The time spent on social skills should reflect this. Although all children need encouragement to interact and exposure to social situations, time allowed alone is also very important. If your child has been at school all day surrounded by people, solitude may be essential to allow her to de-stress and relax. A balance needs to be struck between private and social time.

Some of the ideas presented here are for more able children on the spectrum, others can be used with children with a lower level of functioning. In some cases, the basic idea can be simplified so it is suitable for less able children.

## FACES

If your child has difficulty describing the way he is feeling, visual representations of faces could help. Draw some circles on a piece of paper and fill in and label different emotions e.g. a happy face, sad face, angry face, etc. Keep the representation very simple and use colour to further differentiate between the faces (e.g. an angry face could be placed on a bright red background). To begin with you will need to model for your child how to use the faces, e.g. with a big smile on your face point to the happy face and say, ' I am happy'. Next time your child is displaying a particular emotion, use the face chart to show them the appropriate symbol to describe their mood. With encouragement, your child will learn to explain how she is feeling, though initially she may need prompts. Over time you can add a wider range of faces; an 'I am in pain' face may be especially useful. If you are not feeling artistically inspired, 'How do you feel today?' and 'Face Games' are available commercially. (See 'Useful contacts': tools for parents.)

Mirror games can also be used to help your child learn facial expressions. Games where your child has to guess the emotion, or pair statements with the right face, can be educational and fun. Masks displaying different emotions are also useful.

You can also aid learning by consistently labelling your child's emotional states as they occur. Stating 'You look bored' before directing your child to an activity will help them to connect feelings with appropriate behaviours.

### EMOTION SCRAPBOOKS

> Thomas can't read facial expressions at all. He didn't use to be able to understand when an adult was cross with him, he often started to laugh when someone's face changed expression suddenly. Since then I've taught him the difference between 'happy' and 'frightened' and 'angry'. We practised with dozens of pictures and little Thomas can now name them all perfectly. But unfortunately for him we don't all have the same face and it is still difficult for him. When his sister Elisabeth looked at him crossly the other day, he asked quite seriously, 'Elisabeth, what are all those lines on your face for?'
>
> (Hilde De Clercq in Peeters 1997, p.122)

If you want to work on your child's recognition of moods in other people, and enhance their understanding of emotions, consider a scrapbook. To begin a happy scrapbook, look through different magazines with your child, tearing out as many happy people as you can find. This helps demonstrate to your child all the different ways that people can express their happiness physically. Next add some photos of your family, taken at happy moments (birthdays, holidays, etc.). Add captions explaining the happiness shown ('Sarah is happy because she has a new bike', 'Mum is happy because the sun is shining'). Lists of things that make you happy can also be added and illustrated.

As the quotation by Hilde De Clercq demonstrates, your child may have problems generalising mastered skills to new faces. Pointing out universal features – e.g. when most people are surprised their eyebrows are raised – can be useful to an extent. However, it is likely that you child will recognise moods most effectively in people best known to her who have been used as models for teaching.

EMOTION THERMOMETERS

Children with autism are limited in their ways of expressing emotions. This seems to be a problem of expression rather than a deficit of feeling, as personal accounts by able adults demonstrate a varied range of internal emotions. You may find that there are only subtle differences between your child's showing annoyance and showing serious distress. Therefore, when something goes wrong, she responds in the same over-blown way, regardless of whether it is a major or minor problem.

Tony Attwood (1998) suggests that emotion thermometers can help children to learn to express emotions more appropriately. Begin by drawing a thermometer on a big sheet of paper. The bulb of the thermometer should be white and labelled 0. The tip at the other end should be vivid red and labelled 5. The space in between should be coloured from light to stronger red (1–4).

Decide what emotion you want to work on with your child first. Next time your child displays that emotion (e.g. anger) use his real life experience as an example, i.e. show him the thermometer and say 'You are very angry, you are here at number 5'.) Once he has cooled down, talk to him about how he expressed his feelings in the given example. If he accidentally tipped a drink over and went into a wild rage, this is too strong a reaction. This incident should be the lowest rating on the thermometer. Write the example down alongside some suggestions for expressing mild irritation (e.g. stamping your foot, saying 'sugar', or whatever else you condone in your family). Talk about different ways to calm down when angry, e.g. 'We can go and splash our face with cold water,' and write them onto the paper for next time. You can carry on in this way, helping your child to rate his emotions from everyday events.

THE ALERT PROGRAMME FOR SELF-REGULATION

This programme has some parallels with the previous technique. As with the emotional thermometer, the child is directed to recognise and respond to the way she is feeling. Using the analogy of the body as a car engine, Williams and Shellenberger's (1994) programme teaches the child to monitor her own levels of alertness. The child is taught that sometimes her 'engine' runs too high, sometimes too low, and sometimes just right. Once a child can recognise her sensory needs, she can respond with appropriate strategies for self-relaxation or stimulation.

ROLE-PLAY AND VIDEO REPLAY

Repeatedly watching videos of simple, appropriate conversations and reproducing them with adults has been found to benefit some children with autism. Children involved in one study rapidly improved their conversational skills; an accomplishment they could generalise to different topics with other people.

Certain principles are best demonstrated. For instance, teaching the art of proxemics (i.e. judging personal distances) can be clearly displayed through role-play. By video-taping the proceedings the child can comment on his own performance and understand how he appears to other people. General body language, facial expressions, volume and tone of voice can also be monitored. This can be particularly effective for children who grimace, rock or have other socially 'odd' behaviours. Video feedback helps some to become aware of how they appear, and can lead to changes desired by the child herself. Care should be taken when using video feedback. This technique works best for socially motivated children who actively want to learn, e.g. the child who asks questions about where he is going wrong. Video feedback should never be used in a punitive fashion.

Role-play games revolving around what not to do (*Mr Bean* videos can be useful for this exercise) keep learning enjoyable. Role-play sessions can also be used to expose your child to new scenarios. Once they are well practised, the new behaviours can be moved to real-life situations. This should happen gradually, starting with lots of parental support that fades away as your child becomes more skilled. For instance, if you are teaching your child how to buy a comic at the local shop, initially you will prompt him through all the necessary actions. Over time, he may be able to perform independently, or without such a high degree of intervention. You may start standing right next to him, and slowly increase your distance away from them until you are at the other end of the shop. For more able children independence goals can be more ambitious, but still need to be approached in a simple, support- ive manner.

Teaching your child how to begin a conversation, and how to respond when someone else talks to her, are foundation social skills. Any starters you teach should be kept non-specific (e.g. 'How are you?', 'What did you do today?'), so that they can be used with anyone, anywhere.

Encouraging your child to pause until her conversation partner has replied also needs to be worked on. This is only part of the art of con- versation. Teaching her to listen to a response is also necessary. Games where only the person holding the ball can talk, can help promote turn-taking and listening skills. Once the basics have been mastered, games can become more sophisticated, e.g. someone asks a question and throws the ball to the person they want to answer, who then asks the next question.

Unfortunately, unless your child is socially motivated, her conversa- tion skills are likely to remain at a basic level. You cannot teach a child how to be interested in other people and in what they are saying, which is a vital ingredient in the recipe. Despite these limits, a child who is polite and makes an attempt at interaction is likely to be viewed more positively by other people.

SOCIAL SKILLS GROUPS

Social skills groups designed specifically for children or adolescents with autism have been found to improve certain aspects of social func- tioning (Williams 1989). Most of the children involved in Williams's group (aged nine to sixteen years) enjoyed themselves, although one child jokingly nicknamed the class 'social kills'. Videotaped material suggests improvements in social behaviour; by the end some children appeared more adept at introductions and starting conversations. An added bonus was that children made friends within the group, and remained in contact even after the meetings stopped. Many of the topics covered in this group were taken from Spence (1995). (See 'Useful contacts' at the end of this chapter.)

Non-specialist groups that do not focus on the impairments found in autism are unlikely to produce the same results. Putting reported successes aside, a common concern is that skills taught within social skills groups are often not generalised to real-life situations. It is widely agreed that social skills are best taught 'on the job', using everyday examples as and when they occur. Skills taught within a group need to be practised outside in the real world.

## CARTOONING

Cartoons have long been used by speech and language therapists to increase comprehension of social interactions. More recently, Carol Gray has revamped this technique with her *Comic Strip Conversations* (1994). Through the use of simple figure drawings, symbols and thought bubbles, the child is made aware of the hidden messages lurking within communication. This is an excellent way of demonstrating that people can say one thing but actually think something very different. Cartooning specific conversations freezes the moment, allowing the child time to analyse (with help) what is going on.

## SOCIAL SCRIPTS

Scripting particular scenarios can help to develop communication skills. Scripts are tailored to the areas your child needs help with, e.g. starting conversations, expanding vocabulary or knowing when to change the subject. Writing a simple script for your child and taking him through it step by step helps prepare him for the real-life situation. If your child consistently encounters a problem that she does not have the resources to deal with (bullying is a clear example) a script with clear instructions could make all the difference. Providing different options for likely eventualities increases the value of the social script, e.g. 'If the boys shout at you again, find a teacher. If you can't find a teacher, tell a friend/sibling what has happened.'

## SOCIAL AUTOPSIES

If your child asks you for guidance when there has been a misunder-standing with peers, you could consider performing a social skills autopsy. The child, with the help of an adult, dissects a recent incident to understand why the error occurred. The child provides his interpreta-tion of events and the adult pieces together what may have happened. The child is given direct help to understand why the misunderstanding occurred, and a plan is developed to prevent the same scenario happen-ing again in the future. Importantly, no blame is laid on the child and the autopsy is not used as a form of punishment.

## PICTURES OF ME

*Pictures of Me* (Gray 1997) is a scrapbook the child makes about herself, with help from other adults. Gray describes this exercise as a way of introducing a student to their talents, personality and diagnosis. This is a handy tool for encouraging your child to develop a balanced view of herself and hence increase self-esteem. It can be too easy to focus on what is going wrong, unless there are reminders of all the positive things in life. The child is helped to list all the things she is good at, all the important people in her life and all the things she enjoys. Problems and areas that need to be worked on are also covered. The author suggests that the exercise could be used to explain the diagnosis to the child in a meaningful way (i.e. through the skills and deficits they have).

Parents may find it useful to keep adding pages to the book as the child reaches new stages and discovers new skills, concerns, etc. This way the young person has a self-reference book that he can consult whenever it is needed (e.g. it could be a suggestion from the parent as a way of cheering up the child, preventing him from focusing on isolated failures, or to discourage him from lingering on what he doesn't like about himself).

*I am Special* by Peter Vermeulen expands upon Gray's basic idea, and is filled with different exercises for child and adult to work through. Other books designed especially for the more able young person to read (e.g. Gerland 2000; Ives 1999), help provide facts about autism in a balanced way. (See details provided in 'Suggested reading' at the end of this chapter).

### SOCIAL STORIES

Another innovation from Carol Gray (1994, 1995) for more able children. Social stories is a formula for writing short stories to explain a specific situation, a concept or a social skill. Each story is written specifically for the child it is to be used with. Consideration and respect of the child's perspective is paramount to this process. Through reading the story, the child is helped to understand what is happening and how she should *try* to behave.

### USING HUMOUR AND GAMES

One way to work on flexibility and social empathy in children with autism is through the use of humour. Newson (2000) believes it important to deliberately cultivate a sense of humour in verbal children. Teaching your child to see the amusing side of something can help to defuse anxiety. One able child moved on from learning to understand puns and metaphors to creating his own: '"Too big for your boots" doesn't mean you're too big to get into Boots (the chemist) in Nottingham!'. Jokes and riddles such as the 'Knock knock' and 'Waiter, waiter' variety, require flexibility of thought and considering someone else's perspective. Older children can venture on to comic books and humorous stories. (Raymond Briggs' revoltingly funny *Fungus the Bogeyman* and the works of Roald Dahl are particularly popular).

Certain games require players to guess what their competitors are thinking, and therefore provide a lesson in empathy for high functioning children. 'Guess Who?' (M and B Games) and the card game 'Cheat!' are good examples suitable for younger players. Newson particularly recommends the game 'Scruples' (Milton Bradley) for use with older, more able children. Opponents have to guess what other players would do in certain social dilemmas. Players can answer 'yes', 'no' or 'it depends', the last option being especially effective in teaching greater flexibility and consideration of other people's opinions...

> On this first occasion James was aghast when I answered 'It depends' to the dilemma of whether I would appear naked on the centrefold of a magazine, and firmly argued that my answer *must* be 'No' because I was 'too old and too fat'. However, he was prepared to consider my argument that it depended on the amount of money offered and (crucially) whether my face would be shown. (Newson 2000, p.104)

Many games can be adapted and modified to suit your child's age and needs, and there are also some specially designed games for teaching aspects of social skills (e.g. 'The Social Skills Game' – see 'Useful contacts' at the end of this chapter for full details). Games and humour can be an informal way of opening up discussions and assessing what your child need help with. Many children with autism show a distinct lack of competitive spirit, so parents may need to employ other means to motivate and reinforce them. (See Chapter 11 'Understanding behaviour').

SULP, THE HANEN PROGRAMME AND OTHER RESOURCES

Various videos, games and commercially available aids are listed in 'Useful contacts' at the end of this chapter. Details of packages for professionals, including SULP – the Social Use of Language Programme – (Rinaldi 1992) are also provided.

BUDDIES

If you are worried that your child is not getting enough social interaction you may want to consider finding a buddy. Some parents may shrink away from the idea of providing friends for their child, but if they are unable to initiate and maintain friendships for themselves your intervention may be necessary.

With the increasing drive towards integration, more children with disabilities are mixing with non-disabled peer groups. However, being physically in the same space as peers does not ensure interaction. Some studies have suggested that children with autism can benefit from regular opportunities to play with normally developing peers. Essential to the success of these endeavours is an appropriate social context: peers making the first move (Roeyers 1996) with adults on hand to prompt (Laushey and Heflin 2000). Certain studies have found that some children with autism can sustain interaction once approached, but do not initiate contact themselves. This is not true for all children with autism, as some do initiate contact with peers, but not always appropriately.

Providing buddies for children who need extra help is becoming a common strategy for the classroom. Although the teacher needs to be involved and can arrange pairings, buddies are most successful when they volunteer themselves. The buddy needs to be compassionate and sensitive towards the target child. A little help and direction from a buddy could make a big difference to a child who finds it hard to fit in. Buddy tasks could include: making sure the child knows what class is next/what books are needed; approaching the child in the playground if they look lost and inviting them to play; and sitting next to them at lunch.

As already mentioned, younger children with less complicated interaction styles, or older children who enjoy mothering others, may make ideal buddies. Same-aged peers tend to be more complicated and harder for your child to understand. Some parents have reported very positive results from inviting a local college student to play with their child. Students who are studying psychology or childcare may be particularly suitable, though it is vital that you warm to them and that their references are thoroughly checked. The nice thing about college-aged buddies is that they can provide an independent social contact for your child. Some families, once they have got to know the buddy and are happy for them to be alone with their child, allow outings to the cinema, swimming, etc. (although this is dependent on the commitment the buddy is able or willing to make). A more formalised version of this is available through the National Autistic Society's befriending service (see 'Useful contacts' at the end of this chapter.)

Some parents who did not know any willing children have offered a small 'fee' as encouragement to suitable candidates:

> I thought my friend's child would make an ideal buddy for my son Luke. However, Katie had been put off by Luke's early refusals to play. I decided to offer a little encouragement, and knowing Katie loved stickers I brought a whole selection and allowed her to choose one at the end of each play session with Luke. I was worried about 'buying' friends for Luke, so I also allowed him to choose a sticker too, so it didn't appear too much like payment. I needn't have worried, over time Luke and Katie developed a friendship and no incentives are needed for her to come over now. I think being on hand to make sure the play sessions were fun was essential at the beginning. This also enabled me to give Katie a few tips for playing with Luke. (Mother of six-year-old, 2001, private correspondence to author).

It is natural that some parents may feel uncomfortable about such an arrangement. However, some kind of incentive helps ensure the play-mate is motivated and enthusiastic. Providing a favourite dessert and making sure play sessions are enjoyable and full of activities are less contrived ways of keeping playmates happy. An important point to make before considering this option is that your child (especially if more able) may be very sensitive if he finds out that you have arranged a buddy for him. Also, as your child gets older, it may become increasingly hard to find suitable buddies.

Finally, if your child has had social contact all day at school it may be very important for him to have some time to himself when he does not have to interact with other children. If you do engineer play partners for your child, make sure that sessions are short and well spaced. It is better that your child enjoys playing for an hour, rather than have a whole afternoon which may prove too tiring. Forcing a child into social situations is often counterproductive.

## Setting realistic goals with your child in mind

It is natural for parents to want their child to live a normal life as possible, and a social life plays an important role within that. However, some parents have found that it is their own expectations for their child that lead to subsequent disappointments. This mother reached an important stage when she realised that what made her child happy was different to what she personally wanted for him:

> That disparity between what we want for our children and what they want for themselves is at the root of our grief. Once we recognize this, it is easier to set sensible goals and to be of real help to our children. When Ed was very young, he was invited to a neighbourhood birthday party. Of course, I declined for him; neither he nor the party would have benefited from his presence. But I was not so cool and rational when the day itself arrived. The party, complete with balloons in the trees and a pony ride, was only two houses away – clearly visible and audible from our patio, where Ed was autistically driving his matchbox cars in circles. I looked at him, I looked at the party, and I wept. He seemed to me to be so hopelessly outside life. But then I realized the real reason for my tears. Ed wasn't unhappy about missing a party; he was having a perfectly fine afternoon. I was unhappy because he wasn't! In other words, his expectations for himself differed from mine for him…I think I smartened up a lot that afternoon. I realized I would have to adopt as goals for him what would make him happy and fulfilled as he was, not as I wished him to be. (Akerley 1984, p.94)

For success is often dependent on having realistic goals. These goals should take into consideration the needs, abilities and desires of the young person they are set for. This last extract shows that sometimes it is the pressure to conform to social norms that leads to feelings of inadequacy, rather than a true desire to fit in. Being alone and being lonely are two very different things:

> I was very lonely, and was increasingly suffering from it – not from my actual solitude, but more from comparing myself with others and wanting to be as normal, right and ordinary as they were. My actual solitude – being on my own – was easy. I found it much easier to be on my own than to be with other people. I never missed other people when I was drawing, reading or writing poems, or when I was examining and investigating things. I never felt I ought to have wanted to share them with anyone; in fact, the thought never even entered my head. (Gerland 1997, p.139)

### Can children with autism be taught to mind-read?

It has already been established that children with autism have difficulty understanding that other people have thoughts, beliefs, intentions and desires. The majority of children with autism do not grasp the concept of belief normally shown by three- to four-year-olds. A minority (20–35 per cent) can function at this level, but are unable to match the abilities of normal six- to seven-year-old children, even when in their teens (Baron-Cohen, Leslie and Frith, 1985).

So this inability to mind-read (also referred to as mindblindness and lack of theory of mind) is very real and appears intrinsic to autism. In this area, children with autism are found to fall behind children with learning disabilities of a younger mental age. In everyday life, it is difficult to connect with someone that you do not understand. Mind-reading provides a key to another person, a way through to meaningful communication. If it is possible to teach children with autism to mind-read, their social and communicative skills could benefit significantly. So can a skill, naturally learnt by most children, be explicitly taught?

The answer seems to be yes, although it is early days. Recent studies utilising a variety of techniques indicate that children with autism can be taught to interpret other people's mind states. Following repetitive instruction, the majority of children were able to pass tasks involving some level of mind-reading, with a number retaining their performance at least two months later. Success in other respects was more limited. When the children were required to complete mind-reading tasks that they had not been taught previously, they were unable to generalise the skills they had demonstrated earlier. Any learning appeared to be dependent on the context in which it was taught.

Patricia Howlin and her colleagues (1999) address these issues in *Teaching Children with Autism to Mind-read: A Practical Guide.* The guide is aimed at anyone working with or caring for a child with autism. The authors suggest that specifically teaching underlying principles of mind-reading, rather than just simple instruction, may be one way of overcoming problems of generalisation. Other teaching principles described in the book include: breaking information down into small steps; using naturalistic teaching that takes account of the child's environment, interests and skills; and systematically reinforcing the child when they are successful. After using these methods with children with autism (four- to thirteen-year-olds, but with a language age of at least five years), Howlin *et al.* found significant improvements. After only a brief period of training the children displayed progress in selected areas, changes that remained long after teaching finished. The authors suspect that the added involvement of families over a longer training period could lead to even better results. If you are interested in trying these methods with your child, see 'Suggested reading' at the end of this chapter for full details.

## Useful contacts

**1.** *For information on the **NAS Befriending Scheme** contact:*

**action for AUTISM UK**
The National Autistic Society Volunteering Network
4$^{th}$ Floor, Castle Heights
Maid Marian Way
Nottingham NG1 6BJ
*Email*: volunteers@nas.org.uk
*Website*: www.oneworld.org/autism_uk/

**2.** *More information on **Ooops wrong planet syndrome** can be found at www.isn.net/~jypsy*

**3. Pen-pal clubs for children with special needs**
*Write Away provides a penfriend club for children and adults with disabilities and special needs. Has a children's club (8–18 years) and adults club (over 18's).*

**Write Away**
1 Thorpe Close
London W10 5XL
*Tel*: 020 8964 4225
*Fax*: 020 8964 3532
*Email*: penfriends@writeaway.demon.co.uk

*For a pen-pal registration form to join the Morning News in the USA contact:*

**Karen Lind**
The Morning News
Jenison Public Schools
2140 Bauer Road, Jenison
MI 49428
USA
*Fax*: 616 4578442

## Tools for parents

*1. How do you feel today? (drawn illustrations which represent different feelings)*
*is reproduced in Attwood 1998, p.194. Taken from: Kroehnert G. (1991)* 100
training games. *Sydney: McGraw-Hill Book Company.*

*2. Face Games (a range of photographs to aid understanding of facial expression) is*
*available from:*

**Nottingham Rehab Supplies (Novara Group Ltd.)**
Novara House, Excelsior Road
Ashby Park, Ashby De La Zouch
Leicestershire LE65 1NG
*Tel*: 0870 6000197
*Fax*: 01530 419150
*Website*: www.nrs-uk.co.uk

*3. See what I mean? is a video produced by ICAN (a national charity for children*
*with special needs) which displays 31 emotions/attitudes (ranging from the very*
*simple to the more subtle). This is a basic yet useful resource – actors display various*
*facial expressions and perform simple role plays to demonstrate different feelings. The*
*video has no sound and would need to be paired with a voice over from a parent. It is*
*a good starting point for teaching your child how to recognise moods and emotions in*
*other people. Priced at £20, the video is available from:*

**ICAN**
The Information Officer
4 Dyers Buildings
Holborn
London EC1N 2QP
*Tel*: 0870 0104066

**4. What would you do?** *is a set of cards covering a range of issues including bullying, vandalism and friendships. Helps children to connect their actions with the effect they can have on other people. Good for parents wanting to develop reasoning skills and decision making in their children. Priced at £10.95 + VAT, available from:*

> **LDA (Learning Development Aids)**
> Duke Street
> Wishbech
> Cambridgeshire PE13 2AE
> *Tel*: 01945 463441

*(The LDA Primary and Special Needs Catalogue is full of useful resources, including a whole section on motivation and self-esteem.)*

**5. Can you make it through the day?** *by Debbie Standaloft is a board game about social behaviour and personal routines. For two or more players, it is suitable for three- to seven-year-olds with adult supervision, or older children unaided. The simple rules make it accessible to children with learning difficulties. Priced at £9.95 + VAT, it is available from:*

> **Taskmaster Ltd**
> Morris Road
> Leicester
> LE2 6BR
> *Tel*: 0116 2704286

*The UK distributor of the Morning News (a newsletter edited by Carol Gray) is:*

> **Rosalyn Lord**
> Pleasant View Farm
> Goodshawfold, Rossendale
> Lancashire BB4 8UF
> *Tel*: 01706 222657
> *Email*: actionasd@talk21.com

## Tools for teachers and other professionals

### 1. SULP (the Social Use of Language Programme)
*Developed by Dr Wendy Rinaldi, this assessment and teaching procedure is suitable for children with a wide range of special needs. There are two versions of SULP, one for*

*infant/primary school-aged children (four to eleven years) and one for secondary school/adult students. Different sections of the programme cover different issues (e.g. eye contact, listening, self/other awareness). The primary/infant school package comprises manuals, stories and picture books and story packs, which can be used separately or in conjunction with the rest of the programme. This package can be used as part of the National Curriculum (for English or Personal/Social Education). For more details on publications and training contact:*

**Dr Wendy Rinaldi**
Child Communication and Learning
18 Dorking Road
Chilworth
Surrey GU4 8NR
*Tel*: 01483 458411

*The Programme for secondary school and adult students (priced at £82.85) can be ordered directly from:*

**NFER Nelson Education**
Darville House
2 Oxford Road
Windsor
Berks SL4 1DF
*Tel*: 01753 827249

*Story packs suitable for this age group are available directly from Dr Wendy Rinaldi (see previous address).*

### 2. Social skills training: enhancing social competence with children and adolescents *(Spence).*

*This comprehensive package includes questionnaires, charts and checklists for assessing social skills. Practical guidelines and lesson plans help teachers improve social competence in the children they are working with. Adaptable to suit a range of clients, but most appropriate for more able children with fair language skills. Teachers may find they need to work through this material at a slower pace than suggested. Available from NFER-Nelson, priced at £106.55 + VAT.(Contact details as for NFER Nelson Education on previous page)*

**The Social Skills Game** *is a therapeutic board game for use within a group by skilled therapists/teachers. A good resource for children and adolescents who have difficulty with relationships, the game focuses on different areas including self-awareness, assertiveness, verbal and nonverbal communication and interpersonal* *relationships. A fun starting point for encouraging discussions of relevant topics. Adaptable for older and younger children. Priced £35.00 + VAT, available from:*

**Jessica Kingsley Publishers**
116 Pentonville Road
London N1 9JB
*Tel:* 020 7833 2307
*Fax:* 020 7837 2917

**How does your engine run?** *(Williams and Shellenberger)*
*Information on the Alert Programme can be found at:*

www.AlertProgram.com

*Products can be ordered from:*

**Therapy Works Inc.**
4901 Butte Place N.W.
Alburqurque
NM 87120
USA
*Website:* www.AlertProgram.com/products.html

**Talkabout** *by Alex Kelly, is a social communication skills package designed for use with children/adolescents with social and communication difficulties. It is a practical manual for therapists and teachers. There are six levels, each covering a particular aspect of communication. Priced at £32.50 and available from:*

**Speechmark**
Telford Road
Bicester
Oxon OX26 4LQ
*Tel:* 01869 244644
*Fax:* 01869 320040
*Website:* www.speechmark.net

## Suggested reading

Aarons M. and Gittens T. (1998) *Autism: A Social Skills Approach for Children and Adolescents.* Oxon: Winslow Press Ltd.
*Practical ideas to help parents and professionals work on social skills, or start a social skills group.*

Attwood T. (1998) *Asperger Syndrome: A Guide for Parents and Professionals.* London: Jessica Kingsley Publishers.
*Includes an excellent chapter on social behaviour for the more able child.*

Barratt P., Joy H., Potter M., Thomas G. and Whitaker P. (1988) 'Children with autism and peer group support: using circles of friends'. *British Journal of Special Education,* 25(2).
*For parents and teachers interested in setting up a circle of friends.*

Gerland G. (2000) *Finding Out about Asperger Syndrome, High Functioning Autism and PDD.* London: Jessica Kingsley Publishers.

Howlin P., Baron-Cohen S. and Hadwin J. (1999) *Teaching Children with Autism to Mind-read: A Practical Guide.* Chichester: John Wiley & Sons.
*Suitable for anyone working with or caring for a child with autism. An easy-to-follow book containing pictorial exercises for structuring teaching sessions and forms to record progress.*

Ives M. (1999) *What is Asperger Syndrome, and How Will it Affect Me?* London: The National Autistic Society (Suitable for nine- to thirteen-year-olds)
*For young readers with autistic spectrum disorders.*

Vermeulen P. (2000) *I am Special: Introducing Children and Young People to their Autistic Spectrum Disorder.* London: Jessica Kingsley Publishers.
*A workbook for parents, teachers or other professionals to work through with the child. Suitable for ten-year-olds with average IQ or young people from twelve years upwards with below average IQ.*

*Chapter 11*

# Understanding behaviour

It is important to appreciate that, for much of their lives, they are expected to cope with a world in which they are able to understand almost nothing of what is happening around them; in which they are thrown daily into an ever-changing and unpredictable environment; where they lack even the rudimentary verbal skills necessary to make their needs known; and where they have no access to the internalised, imaginative facilities that are so crucial for dealing effectively with anxiety, uncertainty and distress. It is hardly surprising, therefore, that from time to time they resort to behaviours that can be difficult for other people to deal with. (Howlin 1998, p.55)

## Behaviour as communication

Children with autism are living in a world they do not understand. Not only do they have trouble understanding what *we* want, but also in communicating *their* needs and desires to us. Even the most able children with good speech will misunderstand and be misunderstood, frustrate and be frustrated. Many parents will be caring for children with minimal or no functional speech. Is it any wonder, then, that behaviour becomes the major channel of communication in many families? Commonly it is the behaviours that challenge parents – aggression, destruction, self-injury, etc. – that receive the most attention. Yet, who has never slammed a door in anger, indulged in comfort eating/ drinking or bitten their fingernails with anxiety? Take a look around. Everywhere people are providing information about themselves through their actions. Sometimes the messages are mixed, some behaviours contradict others, but the clues are all there. Children with autism do not control and self-manage their actions in the same way as other people, hence their behaviour sends an undiluted, powerful message. In order to understand autism, it is essential to see your child's behaviour as their way of communicating with you.

## Behaviour serves a function

The second point, when trying to understand behaviour, is that actions are useful. All behaviour serves a function. Even actions that in themselves appear useless or counterproductive have a purpose, e.g. the child who rocks backwards and forwards endlessly is stimulating herself through physical movement; the child who hits his playmate gains some time alone. Looking at behaviour in this way is referred to as functional analysis (fa). Sometimes the purpose of a behaviour may be quite obvious, at other times actions may not be so easy to explain. The most readily available explanation is not always correct. Over time, parents can work up a vocabulary of behavioural expressions that help them to better understand their child.

> When Rashid first started banging his head I thought it was to get my attention. Over the next couple of weeks I made sure that I was more available for him, but to my dismay his head banging increased. It was only through a chance conversation with another mother that I considered that the cause might be

physical. A trip to the doctor's revealed that Rashid had a major ear infection. Once this was treated, his head banging disappeared. (Mother of a three-year-old child, private correspondence to the author)

## Behaviour does not occur in a vacuum

When trying to comprehend behaviour, it does not make sense to focus just on the action itself. The environment in which the behaviour occurs is very important. The traditional 'ABC' approach requires carers to consider the **A**ntecedant (what happened before the action), the **B**ehaviour (the action itself) and the **C**onsequences (what happened after the action). For example:

**A –**    Mum and Jo walk past the sweet aisle in the supermarket.

**B –**    Jo throws himself on the floor, screaming and kicking his legs against the floor.

**C –**    Mum picks up Jo's favourite sweets from the shelf to help calm him down. Jo sees the sweets and stops screaming.

This simple scenario demonstrates the need to consider the three steps of ABC. If Mum and Jo had been walking down the frozen foods aisle, the tantrum would probably not have occurred. If Jo's behaviour had been to ask for some sweets the situation would also have changed. If Mum had reacted differently (e.g. if she had ignored Jo's tantrum) Jo's behaviour may also have altered. Each behaviour has its own antecedents and consequences which must be taken into account.

When enlarging on the ABC format, the following questions are useful:

- When does the behaviour take place?
- Where does the behaviour take place?
- With whom does it occur?
- How frequently does it occur?

## 'Autism problems are like the tip of an iceberg' (Peeters 1997, p.153)

The analogy of behaviour as an iceberg is an incredibly useful one. In this metaphor, the behaviour of your child is seen as only the tip of the iceberg. Below the water-line are the deficits found in autism, as well as trigger mechanisms that could set off the behaviour. Figure 11.1 demonstrates how to apply the iceberg metaphor using aggressive behaviour as an example.

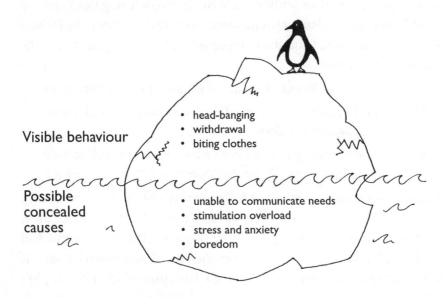

*Figure 11.1 Using the iceberg metaphor*

*The Parent Survival Manual* (Schopler 1995) is a valuable tool for parents interested in the iceberg metaphor. (See 'Suggested reading'.)

## Behaviour programmes

The most effective way to tackle behaviour issues is by devising and following a programme. Some parents may be able to access professional services that implement and maintain behavioural programmes. The advice in this chapter is certainly not intended to replace professional help, especially when dealing with behaviour that is dangerous to the child or other people. However, if you are currently waiting to see your clinical psychologist or if these services are not available to you, you may want to consider your own programme.

### 'What is a programme?'

You may automatically connect 'programme' with the American packages on the market (such as Lovaas, The Son Rise Institute). However, 'programme' in this case should be taken to mean parents devising and carrying out a practical plan of action for dealing with a target behaviour. Programmes can be tailored to meet different aims: to eliminate unwanted behaviours, to encourage desirable behaviours, to reduce the frequency/duration/intensity of certain actions and to teach new skills. Programmes are not intended to be a permanent fixture. As your child progresses, her needs will change, and the time will come when the programme can be faded away. You may then decide to embark on a new programme which addresses fresh issues.

### 'Why do we need a programme?'

It may seem a bit formal to actually follow a programme when you are dealing with your own child in your own home. However, it is essential to approach behaviour modification in a systematic, objective way. Everyone has 'off' days and times when they do not feel able to give 100 per cent. Having a programme makes life just that little bit easier, as you will already have planned how to respond to behaviour, how to reinforce, etc. Another important point is that all the people who take care of your child will also need to be informed (babysitters, relatives, etc.). If everyone is consistent in the way they respond to your child's good and bad behaviour, behaviour modification is much more likely to succeed.

### 'Where do we start?'

Seeing your child's behaviour as communication is the first stage. You need to put aside previous views you may have held concerning behaviour. Believing that your child is 'deliberately trying to wind you up', or that they know 'exactly what buttons to push' is starting off on the wrong foot. Your child may have inadvertently learnt how to get their own way, perhaps with a great deal of success. However, the majority of children with autism are simply not capable of advanced mind games and manipulation (this relates directly to their lack of theory of mind).

Next, choose the behaviour that you want to focus on. It is advisable to concentrate on only one or two behaviours at a time. Put yourself in your child's position. When does the behaviour occur? What happens before the behaviour? What happens as a consequence of the behaviour? In asking these questions you are following the ABC technique. Consider when, where, with whom and how frequently the behaviour occurs.

Now, ask yourself 'What function does this behaviour serve for my child?' Do they receive anything as a result of their behaviour? You may need to think laterally here. It may not seem immediately obvious, but as a result of their behaviour your child may receive any one of a whole range of benefits, e.g.:

- your attention (even if you are angry, negative attention is still attention)
- affection (comfort, kisses, cuddles, verbal reassurances)
- removal to a quieter room
- separation from a sibling or peer
- food/drink
- play activities with you
- bath/clean up (for behaviours like smearing faeces, raiding the fridge, etc.)
- stimulation (escape from boredom)
- release from pain and other physical sensations (particularly relevant for self-stimulatory and self-injurious behaviour)
- a combination of any of the above.

This is not an exclusive list, so you may come up with other possible benefits.

By now you should be starting to develop a picture of the function and context of the behaviour. As this is a first attempt at devising a plan, do not be surprised if the reasons you believe your child is behaving in a certain way prove to be wrong. Establishing the ABC of behaviour is usually relatively straightforward. Trying to work out the function of the behaviour for your child can be much more complex. The real function may not be the first thing that springs to mind.

Bear in mind the iceberg that represents your child's behaviour. The specific behaviour is what you can see (above the water-line), but the underlying deficits not on show (below the water-line) are what you actually have to deal with. Therefore, a child's aggressive behaviour is more than just hitting and pushing a playmate. The child is also display-ing poor social judgement and a lack of empathy for other people. Focusing on just the aggression is treating the symptom rather than the cause. Successful intervention must take account of the underlying deficits found in autism.

### Seeing the programme through to the end

The following account describes how one mother implemented her child's programme. The behaviour tackled was her son screaming for cola whenever he returned from school.

> The intervention I used to stop Jack screaming was as follows: After telling Jack there was no cola (I had no cola in the house that day. It made it much easier for me to be consistent), I totally ignored him when he started to scream. In other words, I did not give him what he usually got. On the first day he screamed for 15 minutes; we then went up to his nannie's, and she gave him a bottle with about an inch of cola in it, so he was not totally deprived of his favourite drink. The next day his screaming lasted 30 minutes. Behaviour analysts have called this an 'extinction burst' and have found that it is part of the pattern to be expected when behaviour is successfully put on extinction. That is, it gets worse before it gets better. When Jack's screaming behaviour

followed this expected pattern I knew we were going in the right direction. The following day he came in from school, and the tantrum lasted only 5 minutes. Eventually his tantrums disappeared. During the programme, we also taught Jack how to ask appropriately if he wanted something, thereby replacing the inappropriate behaviour with appropriate behaviour. (From Keenan *et al.* 2000, p.30)

This account illustrates a common phenomenon found when modifying behaviour – the dreaded extinction burst. Simply put, when your child realises that his old behaviours are not working any more, he will try a little bit harder (i.e. scream louder, hit harder, etc.) before he learns that his usual way of behaving is now pointless. There are a number of important points to make related to the extinction burst.

Intermittent reinforcers (provided every now and then) are more powerful than constant reinforcers (provided each time). This means that programmes should never be embarked upon half-heartedly. If the mum from the last case study had successfully ignored her child's screaming on the first day, but then on the second day had given in and provided cola, she would have intermittently reinforced the negative behaviour. This could have lead to her child learning that 'Mum will eventually give in, as long as I scream enough'. The next time this mother attempted to carry out the programme she would have had a much harder task on her hands. Behaviour that is intermittently reinforced is often much more resistant to change. So before you go ahead and begin a programme, ask yourself the following questions:

- Is this the right time? (Do you have an extra busy few months ahead of you? Have you got any other big commitments?)

- Are other family members also available to help you? (Never underestimate the benefits of emotional and practical support from others.)

- Does everyone agree on the behaviour that is being targeted? (Be very specific in your goal. 'Improving Tom's relationship with his sister' is too vague. 'Stopping Tom hitting his sister' is much clearer.)

- Does everyone agree on alternative behaviours that you wish to encourage in your child? (Behaviours cannot just be removed. The chances are that something bigger and uglier will take its place. Once you are aware of the function of the behaviour you need to think of an alternative, acceptable action that you wish your child to use instead. This proposed behaviour must serve the same function as the old in order for it to successfully replace it. In the earlier example, not only was screaming for cola ignored, Jack was also taught to ask appropriately for things he wanted, and reinforced for doing so.)

- Will everyone reinforce your child in the same way? (This needs to be discussed thoroughly. Your child needs to receive consistent messages from all carers.)

## Using token systems/star charts for reinforcement

For some children, token systems and star charts can prove highly motivating. This removes the need to provide a tangible reinforcer every time your child behaves well (although verbal praise is still essential as a regular reinforcer). Instead, you can award points to your child, which add up to a bigger reward once the agreed amount has been achieved. This sort of system can be more manageable for parents on an everyday basis, as it removes the daily need to provide constant reinforcers. Sticking a star on a board or ticking a chart is less time-consuming. Certain children may be hard to motivate with the promise of toys and food, but would respond to more substantial rewards (e.g. a visit to the zoo).

In order for the system to enhance your child's behaviour, your child must be able to understand the concept of tokens building up to be exchanged for a prize. Therefore basic counting and memory skills are necessary. For some children, the actual mathematics involved with a token system are more reinforcing than the end reward:

It was Jessy who awarded the points or subtracted them for such behaviors as hitting and screaming, even though I was not present. Sometimes she graphed the points, decorative bar-graphs in lovely colors; the day she reached 134, when our goal was only 100, I realized that for mathematical Jessy, the points were their own reward. (Park 1986, p.86)

As in this example, more able children can become involved in regulating their own token system. This is an area where a child's love of rules can be used to a parent's advantage. In order for this to be successful, you have to be very clear with your child about the behaviours that will earn points.

Wherever possible, token systems should work on the positive, i.e. awarding points for good behaviour rather than taking away for bad. An alternative would be awarding your child a certain amount of points at the start of the day, and points are then subtracted for any bad behaviour that occurs. With this system, it is important to provide your child with opportunities to regain points that she has lost, so the emphasis is once again on the positive and good behaviour. At the end of the day, the child can then choose a prize, depending on how many points she has (e.g. 5 points: a fizzy drink at dinner time; 10 points: an ice-cream for dessert). This way, the child can start afresh each day with the same number of points.

Colourful bar-graphs and tables may appeal to children who enjoy using computers or children with artistic streaks. Star stickers are often popular, especially when the child can add them to the chart himself. This is a good visual way of showing your child the progress he is making. Alternatively, collecting coins in a tall glass jar (say 5p or 10p for every good behaviour) can be visually motivating, especially if your child loves counting and playing with money. Compiling a menu of possible gifts to swap for a certain amount of points encourages your child to choose for himself the rewards he wishes to work for. (See Figure 11.2.)

*Figure 11.2 Menu of rewards for token system of reinforcement*

## Monitoring progress

It is not only your child that needs reinforcing! Programmes take time and energy and it is important that parents can see the benefits of their hard work. For this reason, before beginning on a programme, establish a base line, i.e. the stage of development your child is at presently. This can be used as a basis for comparison in monitoring your child's progress once intervention has begun. Some parents ask friends who do not see the child every day to provide a behaviour report when they do visit, based on an afternoon's observation. (This should be evenly spaced, say monthly, to allow room for progress.) It can be difficult to recognise progress when you work with your child week in, week out. Someone else who knows your child but sees her less often is in a better position to notice improvements.

There are different ways to monitor progress yourself. What you choose should depend on what you can realistically see yourself sticking to. Some parents choose a diary-style format, and write down important events as they happen. Other families with the right equipment have opted for videotaping their child in hourly bursts each week. (NB if you do this it is advisable to keep the video camera in the child's play area at all times. This way you can discreetly switch it on when it is needed and your child will not be disturbed by the sudden presence of a camera.) It may feel as though any changes are minimal, but looking back at old diary entries and video tapes can help you appreciate how much you have moved on, even if the steps forward are small and gradual.

Taking the time to draw up a frequency chart (which can then be photocopied each week) reduces the minutes you need to spend monitoring. Obviously it is impossible to monitor every occurrence of every behaviour. Watching your child for a set period of time each day (say 30 minutes each afternoon) can solve this. By recording how frequently/ rarely the target behaviour occurs, you will be able to gain a weekly average. An example of a frequency tick chart is provided in Table 11.1.

## Reinforcement

*'How do I get my child to co-operate?'*

Many parents remark that their children are very hard to motivate, as the normal rewards and pleasures that people enjoy are not attractive to them. This can make behaviour management difficult, as the child is not affected by the traditional sanctions that parents usually employ. Whereas another child may work solely for praise and recognition, the child with autism may need more concrete encouragement. As children with autism are less able to learn from ordinary teaching methods, there is a real need for deliberate rewards (Carr 1998). It is vital that you have a way of reinforcing your child's good behaviour, to increase the likelihood of her behaving in that way again. Therefore, reinforcers are essential when working with your child. If you wish to modify elements

new vegetable from my cupboard to carry around with him. He has now learnt that when he has been good he can add another turnip (his current favourite) to his collection. (Private correspondence with author, 2001).

Other reinforcers known to the author include:

- tickling
- 'posting' things behind the radiator
- bubble blowing
- putting on nail varnish
- singing favourite songs
- quick bursts of a favourite video
- talking about a special interest
- whizzes (parent holds child round waist and spins him around their body so that his legs are off the ground)
- worm-hunting
- spinning tops
- wind-up toys
- chocolate buttons
- sucking ice-cubes
- popcorn
- time alone
- tearing up paper
- smashing glass and crockery
- playing computer games

*'But **nothing** seems to motivate my child.'*

Some parents find it very difficult to find a reinforcer for their child. Nothing seems to work. If you are in this position consider following the Premack principle. This principle states: 'A high-frequency behaviour may be used to reinforce a low-frequency behaviour' (Premack 1959).

So whatever your child does when left to her own devices could be used as a reinforcer. For example, if she often rocks, allowing her to do so after she has co-operated will be a way of reinforcing her positive behaviour. Naturally, some parents worry that this practice may lead to an increase in their child's stereotyped behaviour. But this has not been found to be the case. On the contrary, the Premack principle is often used to establish more appropriate behaviour, so the child actually spends less time engaged in stereotyped actions.

### 'I've found a reinforcer, how do I use it?'

Finding a suitable reinforcer is not the end of the story. You will need to deliver the reinforcer in the right way. Bear in mind the following points:

- Make sure the reinforcer is immediately at hand. This will allow you to reward the good behaviour the instant it occurs. A trip to the local swings is time-consuming and interrupts what you are trying to accomplish with your child. A spinning-top can be produced from a pocket at a moment's notice and can provide enjoyment in a short space of time.

- Provide reinforcement immediately after the desired behaviour. This allows your child to connect what he has just done with what he receives. If you delay reinforcement your child will not understand what he is being rewarded for. There is also the risk that other behaviours (perhaps unwanted, e.g. hand-biting) could occur in between the desired behaviour and the reinforcement, and due to the time lapse these unwanted actions could be reinforced instead.

- Check regularly that the reinforcer is still working with your child. Some reinforcers have a limited shelf-life and may only be briefly effective. Something that reinforces your child one day or even one session may lose its power the next time you try to use it. This means that you need to assess reinforcers regularly, and keep some fresh ones up your sleeve. Star charts and token systems help preserve the appeal of a reward.

- Only use the reinforcer for rewarding the desired behaviour. Making sure that the reinforcer is used only for rewarding a particular target behaviour helps to preserve its appeal. Therefore, if your child loves popcorn and you wish to use this as a reward, make sure that popcorn is not freely available to your child at other times. If using food, use as little as you can get away with. Positive behaviour can be rewarded with a half of a chocolate button, whereas a whole packet will satisfy your child's desire way too quickly, removing the power of the treat.

- Manage the reinforcer. Some reinforcers may be quite destructive if unmonitored and uncontrolled. Tearing up paper and smashing glass are good examples. However, if creatively managed these activities can still be of use. Tearing up paper is only a nuisance if your child chooses important paperwork, books, etc., and strews litter all over the house. If your child is clearly instructed – i.e. 'You can tear any papers in this box, when you are sitting at the kitchen table' – the behaviour can be managed and used as a motivation. Similarly, for a child who loves smashing glass, glass collected in a marked box can be taken to the bottle bank and safely reduced to smithereens. (This could be used as a weekly reward in conjunction with a star chart or token system.)

- Don't give up on praising your child. Although your child may not appear to respond to praise, still provide it alongside the primary reinforcer (e.g. something tangible like chocolate). Some children will eventually be able to associate praise with positive things and recognise that it indicates they have done well. In time, your child may respond to praise alone (praise will become a secondary reinforcer). When delivering praise make sure that it is specific – e.g. 'good sitting' rather than 'good boy'. This enables you to send a clear message to your child about exactly why he is being praised, which in turn makes it easier for him to please you again. Over time, as he becomes more competent and has successfully learnt the desired behaviour, praise can become a less contrived and more natural 'well done'.

### Direct teaching – 'I am using reinforcers but I think my child needs more help.'

Sometimes, however strong a reinforcer is, it is not enough. Reinforcement can only be used if your child displays the desired behaviour. There may be many skills that you would like your child to master (e.g. washing, dressing and feeding herself) but as they are not yet in place, you cannot reinforce them. If you feel your child needs to be taught as well as rewarded, consider some of the following techniques:

#### SHAPING

Start by focusing on a behaviour that you want your child to learn. Establish how much he can already do alone (e.g. if you want him to learn to put on his own trousers, maybe he already puts his feet through the trouser legs). Initially reinforce him for getting to that stage, but then keep reinforcement back until he goes a tiny bit further. Now the next step may well happen accidentally, which doesn't matter as long as it happens and you reinforce him for it. Once the new step becomes established, you hold back reinforcement again until you see a little more progress, and so on and so on. As you can probably tell, shaping is a slow and sometimes arduous business. This is because it relies on the child taking the next step. Because of this limitation other methods may be more attractive to you, being both quicker and more effective.

PROMPTING

There are three main types of prompt: physical, gestural and verbal.

When a child is physically prompted, her body is moved by an adult but she is reinforced for performing this action. This increases the chances of her repeating the action alone. Physical prompts are useful because they allow the child to learn what an action feels like, through the movement of the adult. Therefore the child who is phys-

ically prompted to turn on a tap (i.e. the adult's hand is over the top of the child's) gets to experience the necessary movements, the pressure needed to turn the tap, etc. Eventually the child will perform the action of her own accord – although the adult's hand is still in place, it is just 'shadowing' what the child is doing for herself. The final stage is known as 'fading'. The adult gradually reduces their role (they may loosen their pressure on the child's hand, and then start to rest just lightly on the child's wrist, then her arm etc.). Fading must not be rushed, as the child must be capable and confident in what she is doing before she is allowed to perform solo. If this stage moves too quickly and fading occurs before the child is ready, she may fail at the task, setting the whole process back.

Gestural and verbal prompts are more straightforward. Verbally telling your child what to do (e.g. 'sit here') is the most commonly used prompt. If he has limited understanding, pairing the words with a gestural prompt (e.g. patting the chair with your hand) helps him understand what you mean. After a time, if he can carry out actions independently the prompts can be faded.

As well as physical, verbal and gestural prompts, the environment can be tailored and better equipped to encourage your child's progress with new skills. A child who is learning to put on her shoes will find velcro much easier than laces. Jumpers with extra wide necks are far easier to learn to dress with than tight, polo-necked jumpers. Learning to use cutlery is made simple with chunky forks and spoons and non-slip placemats. Rearranging or altering the child's surroundings can prevent behaviours ever happening and possibly becoming a problem. Many suggestions are provided in Chapter 6 'Moving forward after diagnosis'. Once again, environmental prompts can be faded as the child becomes more proficient and able to use commonplace objects.

CHAINING

Other teaching methods focus on breaking down activities into manageable chunks. (This is known as task analysis.) This allows the child to learn a new activity through a series of steps, aimed at his skill level. When using this technique a child can learn activities that would be too complex if presented in their entirety. The steps are chained together so he can eventually move through the whole activity from start to finish. Forward chaining teaches the steps by following the normal sequence of the activity (i.e. a child learning to put on trousers begins by stepping into the trouser legs). In backward chaining this is turned around, with the final step of the activity being taught first (i.e. the child would learn to pull his trousers up from his thighs to his waist). The method parents decide to use will depend on the activity to be taught as well as the attention span of the child. Backward chaining is particularly useful as it provides the child with immediate success – he finishes the task. With forward chaining it takes longer for the child to reach the final goal. (This will depend to an extent on how long it takes them to master the different stages.)

## Other methods for tackling behaviour

When it is an old behaviour you want to stop rather than a new activity you want to teach, different methods are needed. Common sense dictates that a child who is busy playing pat-a-cake will not be able to bite her hands at the same time. This in itself is actually a behaviour management technique – differential reinforcement of other behaviours (DRO). New, positive behaviours are encouraged which are incompatible with the old behaviour.

## EXTINCTION

This involves removing the reinforcement that usually follows the child's undesirable behaviour. If this is a constant consequence, the child will eventually stop using the target behaviour. Extinction is only successful if the reinforcer is correctly identified, and is something that can be controlled (i.e. something that can be removed).

Establishing complementary programmes alongside extinction encourages the development of positive skills. Replacement skills should serve the same function as the old behaviour. For example, a child screams to gain attention and therefore screaming is ignored (extinction). At the same time, she is taught to indicate when she wants attention from an adult. When she carries out this appropriate behaviour she is reinforced with the adult's attention. This works well as long as the child is given time and attention when she behaves well. If for any reason the adult stops responding to the new behaviour, it is no longer serving the desired function for the child. In this scenario she may resort once more to negative behaviour patterns to get what she wants.

## TIME OUT

This is a concept which is often misunderstood. In its extreme form it can involve removing the child to a specific room following undesirable behaviour. However, in its purest form it is time out from a reinforcer. Therefore a child who hits her brother while watching the television would have the set turned off for a set amount of time (or until the undesirable behaviour stops). This child has experienced time out from something she found enjoyable/ reinforcing. Time out is only effective when the child is reinforced by what you are removing. If she stops hitting her brother, the television is turned on again. This consequence is repeated every time negative behaviour is observed, so the child learns to associate the loss of something pleasurable with the event of a certain behaviour. Once this connection has been made, the unwanted behaviour is likely to decrease.

Time out can be effective with a whole range of reinforcers. For instance, if negative behaviour occurs during rough-and-tumble play (assuming this is something the child loves), the activity is stopped until that particular behaviour finishes. Kisses, cuddles, even eye contact can be halted if a child begins unwanted behaviour. Time out can be a powerful tool for adapting your child's conduct. (NB if a child is removed to a certain room following unwanted behaviour, this may act as a reinforcer. If the child dislikes being with other people, an empty, quiet room may be very appealing to him. He may inadvertently learn that the quickest way to escape from busy situations is to behave in a certain way.)

STIMULUS CONTROL

This is another way to manage behaviour. The child learns to recognise when his behaviour is acceptable through the use of signals or cues. This technique is suitable for repetitive behaviours that are not dangerous. It is a way of reducing how often the behaviour takes place, rather than completely eradicating it. The following example involves a child who constantly asked repetitive questions.

> Robert was given a coloured sticker to wear on his jumper, and told that so long as he was wearing the sticker his questions would be answered. When the sticker was removed the questions would not be answered… The programme was at first set up to run only between 9 and 10 a.m., and the sticker was removed for four 15-second periods. On the first day, when the sticker was removed, Robert bombarded the staff with questions, but they told him, 'No, you haven't got your sticker, wait till you get it back.' After this first day his attempts at questioning reduced rapidly over the eight weeks of the programme, until there were none in the last four weeks. At the same time the teachers noticed that even when he was wearing the sticker he would, if staff were busy, wait until they were less busy to ask a question. (Carr 1980, p.93)

TIMELY REMINDERS

Timely reminders can aid children who have trouble retaining what they have been taught, especially in exciting and stimulating situations. Try and identify what these situations are for your child so that you are aware of when particular behaviours are most likely to happen. Then remind your child of how she is expected to behave, immediately before the situation that usually triggers unwanted behaviour occurs (This increases the likelihood that your child will employ newly learnt behaviours. The following example illustrates this technique (referred to as 'pre-teaching' in the USA):

> Alicia usually squeals and turns her head away when she sees a friend. She is learning to greet people by saying 'Hi' and waving. Before going into the hallway, Mr. Wilson reminds Alicia by saying 'Show me what you do when a friend walks by'. He waves his hand and pretends to say 'Hi'. Mr. Wilson is using a preteaching strategy before greeting behaviours occur. This increases the probability that Alicia will use an acceptable behaviour. (From Fouse and Wheeler 1997, p.146)

RESPONSE COST TECHNIQUES

These techniques involve teaching your child what happens as a result of his behaviour. Unwanted behaviour is paired with a logical consequence as in the following example:

> As soon as Billy had eaten his fill he pushed his plate onto the floor. Every time this happened I insisted that he cleaned up the mess he had made. Billy hated doing this. In a short space of time his behaviour altered and he learnt to leave his plate on the table when he had had enough. (Mother of five-year-old, 2001, in personal correspondence to the author)

This is an example of simple correction, where Billy's task directly redresses his behaviour. For more able children, more sophisticated response cost techniques can be used:

> Saskia has never liked wearing shoes. She has been taking them off ever since she has been able to remove them herself. Saskia would often try to leave her shoes at bus stops (I would not realise until we drove past a familiar pair of shoes abandoned on the pavement). When she was younger nothing seemed to matter to her, which made stopping this behaviour difficult. However, when Saskia was a little older she started really looking forward to birthday presents. In the run up to her ninth birthday I told her

'You realise that if you throw your shoes away you'll have to spend some of your birthday money on shoes.' This turned out to be a very meaningful reinforcer for her, and she hasn't 'lost' her shoes since. (Mother of nine-year-old with Asperger's syndrome, 2001, in private correspondence with the author)

OVER-CORRECTION

Over-correction takes simple correction one step further, and restores the environment to a better state than it was originally. For example, Billy would not only clean the mess he made but he would also complete other related tasks, e.g. mopping the whole kitchen floor. This sends a very clear message to the child – 'If you do x, you will also have to do y.' For this reason it is important that the task that follows is a logical consequence of the unwanted behaviour. Pairing an unrelated task with behaviour could result in the child not understanding the connection with his earlier actions.

## Remember mindblindness when considering your child's actions

When dealing with behaviour it is crucial to remember the principal deficits found in autism. The problems and different perceptions that stem from a lack of theory of mind have been referred to in previous chapters. A particularly important aspect of mindblindness is that your child may find it hard to differentiate between what she knows and what you know; she may believe that you know everything that she knows. This tendency can have important implications for her behaviour, as illustrated in the following hypothetical examples:

> Tina is thirsty. She believes that her mum knows that too. Tina finds it incredibly frustrating when she is not given a drink from the fridge. The way she sees it, mum is just carrying on as if she doesn't care. Because Tina believes that her mum's knowledge is the same as her own she sees no purpose in actually requesting a drink. Tina thinks – why should I ask for a drink? Why should saying the words 'I want a drink' make any difference at all?

Now clearly, in the above example, problems of communication are combining with a lack of theory of mind. These deficits should never be underestimated. One father reported how his son found communicating so hard that he preferred to drink from the toilet bowl rather than ask for a glass of water. The next example illustrates a different problem:

> Philip is upset and panics. His first priority is to leave the room as quickly as possible. His sister Jane is sitting in a chair en route to the exit. In Philip's mind everyone in the room knows how he is feeling and what his intention is. Therefore, everyone should know that he needs to escape and should get out of his way to allow this to happen. Philip barrels into his sister (who has not moved position), the chair and Jane go flying. Jane feels very angry and hurt by Philip's behaviour which she believes was intentional.

If your child engages in behaviour of this kind a few principles can prevent it reoccurring in the future:

- Make sure exit routes are clear. Do a dry run of the route yourself. Can your child get there easily and quickly without encountering objects and obstacles on the way?

- Encourage your child to go out to the garden, go to the punch-bag in the garage etc., whenever he feels himself/you recognise him getting angry or upset. This does not need to be done in a reproachful way. Asking him to take the dog to play in the garden, or giving him a task you know he enjoys/finds calming is a less obvious way of preventing explosions.

- Arrange a signal that you can deliver quickly to alert other family members when they need to give your child a wider berth. This can be especially helpful for siblings old enough to take part. A simple 'Come and help me in the kitchen' or two claps of your hands could be a pre-arranged code to quickly remove siblings from your other child's space.

# Suggested reading

Schopler E. (ed.) (1995) *Parent Survival Manual: A Guide to Crisis Resolution in Autism and Related Developmental Disorders.* New York: Plenum Press.
    *For parents interested in the iceberg metaphor, this book looks at a wide range of specific behaviours and underlying deficits.*

*Chapter 12*

# Responding to behaviour

A variety of behaviours can be tackled using the principles put forward in 'Understanding behaviour'. However, time and time again the same message comes back from parents – 'How do we make the theory work with our child, in our home?' Understanding how a principle works in theory is the easy bit, applying it to your own situation is considerably trickier. Suddenly the wonderful concept that you thought you understood fully when the professional (or book!) explained it, becomes vague and abstract when you try to make it your own.

In response, this section looks at five areas of behaviour – feeding, sleeping, playing, toilet training and self-injurious behaviour. For each behaviour, common problem areas are covered and tips are suggested. Wherever possible case studies are included to illustrate how other parents have found solutions to widespread issues. Some of the solutions described are theory driven, some are a product of common sense and a few are simply discovered by chance.

The aim of this section is not to answer every question parents have ever asked, but to present a range of problems and their possible solutions. It is hoped that as a parent, you can use this section as a starting point when focusing on target behaviours in your own child. Perhaps you have a similar problem to one covered in this section, or perhaps you can adapt or extend an idea to fit your own situation. Combining these ideas with the information already covered in 'Understanding behaviour', you can start to approach your child's unwanted behaviour in a creative, flexible and responsive manner.

## FEEDING

A child with eating problems can be a real emotive issue for parents. This section looks at some common feeding concerns.

*'My child seems to have physical problems eating.'*

Before you address eating difficulties through intervention, you need to rule out a physical cause to your child's problems. Some children have not developed the right muscle tone to enable them to chew and swallow food successfully. If you feel this is relevant to your child, speak to your family doctor. Request a referral to a speech and language therapist, as they will be able to assess your child's motor oral capacity. There are simple exercises, depending on the particular problem (e.g. drinking through straws, blowing bubbles, eating chewy foods), which can help your child's development. In some cases parents take a more active role and help their child learn by holding their jaw and going through the motions of eating. Eating problems could also be related to sore or swollen gums, sensitive or painful teeth, so regular check-ups at the dentist should not be overlooked.

*'My child eats inedible objects.'*

Pica (eating inedibles) is not unusual in children with autism.

> When Jim was just a toddler, he moved around very fast and paid no attention to language. He would pick up anything and everything from the floor and put it in his mouth. When we gave him a pacifier and hung it around his neck so that he could always find it, he started to use that instead. (From Schopler 1995, p.137)

This parent worked out that Jim needed something to mouth, and if nothing was provided he would find his own objects. With young children who do not comprehend instructions, altering the environment and/or providing replacement props can work best. Jim could not suck his pacifier and fit other objects in his mouth too. Some parents have reported that engaging the child in alternative oral activities (e.g. blowing bubbles, whistles, chewing gum, mouthing rings, etc.) distracts the child from eating inedibles. If your child mainly behaves this way in unstructured time alone, you may need to engage him in regular activities and provide alternative amusements to prevent pica.

The most appropriate intervention can depend on what inedibles your child is attempting to eat. Sucking clothes and chewing cuffs can usually be discouraged by applying an unpleasant liquid to the surface. (The revolting taste of the fluid to prevent nail biting is ideal.) Bitter lemon juice or detested flavours (strong ones like aniseed can work well) are more cost-effective. Time out from reinforcers when pica occurs proved effective in the following examples:

> Whenever we are in the garden and Sarah puts mud and stones into her mouth, I immediately stop playing with her and cease talking and eye contact. As soon as she stops, I smile and praise her strongly. Since I have stopped paying attention to her 'feasts' they have become less and less regular. It was very hard for me to ignore this behaviour in the beginning, but I now realise my horrified reaction was just encouraging Sarah.

> My son Matthew always used to chew the cushions in the lounge when he was watching television. I decided to tackle this and began watching his favourite cartoons with him. As soon as the chewing began, I turned off the television for the count of ten (I had the remote control ready in my hand) and said, 'No chewing'. He was very angry when I started this but quickly associated chewing with the disappearance of whatever he was enjoying. Over the next few weeks Matthew stopped chewing the furniture entirely.

These techniques both proved successful, even though the reinforcers involved were quite different. Sarah desired her mum's attention. If she was a child who wanted time alone, her mum's technique would only have encouraged her to continue eating mud and stones. Matthew was able to make the connection between sucking furniture and his cartoon being stopped. He understood the verbal message given ('No chewing'). A child unable to associate his behaviour with a consequence could not have benefited from this approach.

### 'My child always eats on the move.'

> Our youngest son Mark disrupted every mealtime by wandering around the kitchen in between mouthfuls. Mark enjoyed the food I cooked but never listened to my instructions to sit nicely at the table. One day my husband decided to take action. The first time Mark left the table his dad picked up his plate and said loudly, 'Mark's finished'. I think Mark was quite shocked to find his dinner gone once he returned, and even more surprised when he was not given it back. This carried on for a few days until Mark realised that if he left the table his dinner would not be there on his return. Very quickly Mark became a very well-behaved diner, who finished everything on his plate, remaining seated the whole time.

Some parents may feel uncomfortable about removing a nearly full plate when they know their child is hungry. However, this technique proved very effective in only a couple of days. Alternatively, reinforcers could have been provided every time Mark managed to stay seated for a set amount of time, e.g. if he remained seated until the sand ran through an egg-timer, Mark could be rewarded with a sip of his favourite fizzy drink. The goals could gradually be increased until Mark was able to sit for an entire mealtime.

### 'My child will only eat particular brands.'

If your child is a fussy eater it can be very tempting to indulge whatever eating preferences and obsessions they do have. As children with autism are resistant to change it is not uncommon for some to become very fixated on certain brands of food. For this reason, try to nip potential problems in the bud and swap around the brands of favourite foods you buy. This way your child will not expect always to receive a particular product. If your child has already become very set in what he will and will not eat, you may need to be a little more devious in your ways:

> Mel would only ever eat one brand of cornflakes. I didn't realise until his favourite type had sold out at the local mini-market, and I bought the store's own brand. As soon as he saw the box he started screaming, I tried to pour him a bowl hoping it would calm him down but it just made matters worse and soon breakfast was all over the wall. I was shocked to see how dependent he had become on that one brand, and when I experimented I realised that he was also choosy about brands of orange juice and biscuits. This was something that I knew I could ignore to make my life easier but I really didn't want him to be so fixed in his ways. I knew that if his favourite lines were ever discontinued or were not available for some reason there would be hell to pay. I started off with the cornflake issue. I bought his favourites but still kept the other box out of view. I couldn't taste any difference between the flakes, although the colour of one was slightly brighter than the other. I tipped a third of the new brand into Mel's preferred box. I gave it a good shake so the contents were all mixed up and looked constant. Mel seemed to accept the imposters so I carried on increasing the ratio of old brand to new until Mel was eating entire bowls of the new cereal. Finally I invested in a range of plastic containers and started pouring all cereals into those (this had the added bonus of keeping them fresher). To my surprise Mel was not at all bothered by this change. I have started to do the same with orange juice and biscuits and am confident that I will have the same success.

This mum decided to tackle her son's food obsessions head on, and in doing so prevented potential problems from escalating. Several points to mention. First, the mum in this example did some important research. She realised that it was mainly the box that the cornflakes came in that was important to her son. Mel did not appear to notice a difference in taste or slight variations in appearance. The technique of gradually introducing a new product through an old favourite can work very well, though it will depend on the similarity of the foods involved. Some children are expert in recognising their favourite brands through taste and smell alone, so for some, hiding the box or swapping containers will not be enough. This procedure may seem like a lot of work but it can also be a means of introducing new types of food to your child's diet.

### 'My child is a fussy eater.'

> Pretty much all Monica would eat when she was younger was strawberry-flavoured yoghurt. This worried me a lot, I felt there was no way she could remain healthy with such limited intake. I bought some raspberries and pureed them to a fine liquid. I added a tiny splash to Monica's yoghurt, which she ate with her usual relish. I kept the rest in a jar in the fridge so it really wasn't a lot of bother to prepare. Over the weeks I slowly upped the amount added. Monica never objected to this change, I think because it was so gradual. I also experimented with peaches and she also accepted these. It just made me happier to know she was eating some fresh fruit each day.

Adding a minute portion of a new food to an established preference is a time-consuming business. There is also the risk that if you move too quickly and add too much at one time, your child will reject your offering. This mother seemed to get the balance just right, so even though the end product was distinctly different to the original in appearance and taste, Monica still accepted the staggered change.

Sometimes it is exposure to different situations and role models that create positive changes, as the following example shows:

> When Ian was four we took him to the nursery school in the village just for an afternoon. Up until then Ian had never eaten a sandwich. He refused to eat bread so I didn't give him any sandwiches to take with him. After a few days the teacher asked me to give Ian sandwiches for playtime because he took the other children's sandwiches from them and ate them. That was good, it was something new he had learned there and afterwards he also wanted to eat bread at home. (From Peeters 1997, p.173)

This mother did not put any pressure on her child to eat bread, his change of heart naturally followed his encounter with different norms. In some families siblings can play an important role in expanding restricted diets:

> At the age of seven, John was firmly entrenched in a pattern of only eating chips, chocolate and biscuits. His increasing weight was posing medical and management difficulties. He had just entered a phase of imitating his older brother, and his parents decided to try and turn this to their advantage. The brothers were seated opposite each other and each was given a small helping of John's favourite food. John was encouraged to look at and copy his brother as they each ate several small portions of the favourite. Once John was clearly aware of, and enjoying, this game, tiny amounts of unfamiliar food were introduced between the helpings of the favourite. The quantities and the range were built up gradually until John was eating a better, more balanced diet. The range remained somewhat restricted, but his parents felt that this was a fair compromise. (From Whitaker 2001, p.66)

The parents here made good use of a natural advantage – John's willingness to copy his brother. If you do not have other children, you could use the technique of 'first…, then…' to similar effect. You need two bowls, one filled with treats, the other filled with an unfamiliar food. Pop the new food into your child's mouth, and follow it immediately with the treat. This is a simple way to reinforce your child's experimentation of different foods.

Sometimes children can become quite fixated on the different characteristics of food that they will or will not eat. The same principle can work in these problem areas.

### 'My child dislikes certain textures/colours.'

Hypersensitivity has already been mentioned as a common feature in many children with autism. Eating is an area frequently affected, as the following quotation from Sean Barron demonstrates:

> I was supersensitive to the texture of food, and I had to touch
> everything with my fingers to see how it felt before I could put it
> into my mouth. I really hated it when food had things mixed with
> it, like noodles with vegetables or bread with fillings to make
> sandwiches. I could never put any of it into my mouth. I knew if I
> did I would get violently sick. (Barron and Barron 1992, p.96)

So what should you do if your child will not eat food because of its
texture? First, compile a diet sheet of the foods that your child will eat,
and note the characteristics of food she refuses (e.g. colour, texture,
crunchiness, etc.). Once you have this information you should be able to
build up a picture of what it is about food your child likes, and what she
dislikes. You may find that she will eat a certain food when it is prepared
in one way, but not another, e.g. boiled carrots are a firm favourite but
raw carrots are hated. This will provide big clues about what offends her
(e.g. raw carrots are noisy when crunched and a very vivid colour,
whereas boiled carrots are soft and duller in hue). Some children will
only eat food of a smooth consistency. If this is the case for your child
you can introduce her to a wider diet by liquidising meals to the
required puree. Gradually you can reduce the time the food is liquidised
so that your child starts to cope with more texture.

Dislike of colours can be approached in the same way. Some
children will only eat food of a particular colour (e.g. bread, milk,
potatoes), which once again restricts intake. Adding a tiny drop of food
colouring to accepted foods (so it is barely noticeable) and slowly
increasing this over time helps to expand the child's limited preferences.
This procedure does take a little time but can prove successful for some
children. Another father turned the problem around:

> Sam was very fussy about the colour of her food. Anything that
> was too brightly coloured (e.g. oranges, sweetcorn, green beans)
> was rejected. Following a trip to the seaside I brought Sam some
> sunglasses with coloured lenses, which she loved wearing. I
> noticed that when she wore them whilst eating she ate everything
> on her plate, regardless of colour. Once she had tried something
> and enjoyed its flavour she seemed to ignore the hue. Those
> glasses were a blessing in disguise.

Not a solution that would work for every child, but it worked perfectly for Sam. It ensured Sam ate a healthy range of foods in the short term, although ultimately, long-term strategies would also be needed.

*'How can I encourage table manners in my child?'*

Your child's table manners and self-feeding skills may have a big effect on family mealtimes. It is hard to relax and enjoy your own meal when your child is unable to feed himself or leaves the table resembling a battlefield. Once again, your technique will depend on the particular problem in hand. If you feel that your child's difficulty is mainly one of co-ordination, physically shaping his actions may help him learn new patterns of behaviour:

> Max never seemed able to judge distances between his mouth and his spoon and often banged his teeth with the cutlery through bad timing. I started sitting him on my lap when at the table, putting my hand over his hand so we were holding the spoon together. By going through the necessary motions of eating, Max began to learn from me how to eat. After a week I noticed that I could ease my grip on his hand and he could still successfully complete the action. Eventually my hand was just hovering above his and he did everything alone. Simply seeing other people eat did not help Max and he did not respond to my verbal instructions. Hand over hand was the best solution.

Props and aids can also be useful, perhaps in tandem with a shaping and fading approach similar to the one just described. In Max's case, a plastic baby spoon would have prevented him from hurting his teeth while learning to eat. Cutlery with chunky handles, and anti-slip placemats also make mealtimes easier. Pelican bibs with an extended lip to catch food that misses the target cuts down on mess.

Simple rules such as no toys/television/books at the table help your child to concentrate on the task in hand. If dinner is a noisy affair it may be easier to feed your child earlier so that you can focus on teaching him good table manners. Some children eat better when positioned in a high chair set a little way away from the main table. One parent reported that her child eats more when his high chair is facing the wall, so that there are fewer distractions. (This is different to making a child face the wall as punishment.) Willing siblings can be used as role models for encouraging and teaching new skills. One family hit upon an ingenious solution for teaching their son how to eat nicely in public. The parents were reluctant to practise in their favourite restaurants, so began visiting cafés within service stations. Because the other diners were anonymous motorists, the family did not feel so embarrassed when mishaps occurred (Aarons and Gittens 1999, p.50).

*Feeding tips*

- If your child is a fussy eater, try not to let it appear that this is a big deal. This can be incredibly hard to pull off, but it is important to stay cool and collected, keeping the emotion out of your voice when in the kitchen or at the dinner table.

- If you are worried that your child does not eat enough to be healthy, keep a food diary. Note down everything she eats throughout the day, including snacks. After a week or so, most parents are surprised and reassured by how much their child actually does eat. The diary also makes it easier to work out which vitamins and supplements your child could benefit from (i.e. by observing what she doesn't eat).

- If completing a food diary confirms your fears, ask your doctor to refer you on to a dietician. Such a professional can help you plan a balanced diet for your child, and may suggest form-building drinks or vitamin milkshakes to supplement meals. In extreme cases, referral to a feeding clinic like the one at Great Ormond Street Hospital for Sick Children may be necessary.

- Plan ahead so that you do not need to discuss things with other family members in front of your child. This will make it easier for you not to give attention to unwanted eating patterns. If siblings remark on their brother or sister's feeding habits, you may need to take them aside and ask them to stop. This should stop your child from being reinforced by comments from other diners.

- Make use of visual information. Fridge magnets, blackboards, timetables can inform your child of what's for dinner and who else will be present. These systems work especially well if your child is very anxious or asks relentless questions. The child can be directed to the displayed information, rather than relying on their carer's patience.

- Using simple objects of reference also conveys information – helping your child lay the correct number of placemats for dinner highlights who will be present, e.g. 'We need two extra mats for Grandma and Grandpa.' Velcro-backed photos on a feltboard entitled 'Who is at Dinner?' reinforce this message further. More able children may enjoy making place names for everyone present, which also ensures that the child knows who sits where in advance.

- If your child is very resistant to change, avoid entrenching him in too many food routines, e.g. 'We always have fish on Fridays.' If your child benefits from a routine, a timetable allows you to introduce changes each week in a controlled, predictable way. This allows room for variety and minimises disappointment when the expected fare is unavailable.

- Try and be constant about the time dinner is served. Mood swings and tantrums could be related to late or unpredictable dinner times. Low energy levels can lead to irritability and may increase the likelihood of unwanted behaviour.

- Finger- and hand-puppets work effectively for young children with short attention spans. Colourful characters can capture interest at mealtimes, but as their involvement may be quite messy, washable puppets are a good idea.

For information about special diets see Chapter 13 'Therapies and approaches'.

## Suggested reading

Schopler E. (ed.) (1995) *Parent Survival Manual: A Guide to Crisis Resolution in Autism and Related Developmental Disorders.* New York: Plenum Press.

Whitaker P. (2001) *Challenging Behaviour and Autism: Making Sense – Making Progress.* London: The National Autistic Society.

## SLEEP

By the age of one year, most children should be regularly sleeping through the night. Illness, holidays and stressful periods can have a negative impact on sleep patterns, but your child should quickly adapt back to normal routine within a few days. If you find that your child is often unable to get to sleep, or if their sleep is frequently disrupted, she is showing signs of a sleeping disorder.

Many children with autism have difficulty establishing consistent sleep patterns that tie in with the rest of the family. All children need to learn to sleep through the night, as during babyhood they got used to waking every few hours to be fed. There are no definite guidelines on how long a child should sleep; how much sleep each person needs can vary considerably. On average the amount of sleep a child needs per night decreases by fifteen minutes per year, until the age of sixteen. Following this rule of thumb, a five-year-old needs an average of eleven hours per night, whereas a sixteen-year-old needs eight-and-a-half hours.

It has been suggested that sleep problems fall into two main categories – settling and waking (Quine 1997). A child with settling problems

Table 12.1 Example of a sleep diary

| Week beginning: 04/06/01 | Monday | | Tuesday | | Wednesday | | Thursday | | Friday | | Saturday | | Sunday | |
|---|---|---|---|---|---|---|---|---|---|---|---|---|---|---|
| | When Jo slept | When we slept | When Jo slept | When we slept | When Jo slept | When we slept | When Jo slept | When we slept | When Jo slept | When we slept | When Jo slept | When we slept | When Jo slept | When we slept |
| 00:00–02:00am | 0.15–1.30am | 0.30–1.45 | 0.15– | 0.30– | | | 00.15– | | | | | | 1.00 | 1.15 |
| 02:00–04:00am | 3am– | 3.15– | | | | | | | 3.45 | | | | | |
| 04:00–06:00am | | | 5am | 5.30 | 5.00 | 5.05 | | 6.00 | 5.15– | 6.00 | | | 5.30– | 5.45– |
| 06:00–08:00am | 6.30am– | 6.45 | | | | | 6.15 | | 6.30 | | | | 7.30 | 7.32! |
| 08:00–10:00am | | | | | | | | | | | | 9.00 | | |
| 10:00–12:00pm | 10.30–11.15 | | | | | | 10.15–11.00 | | | | | | | |
| 12:00–14:00pm | | | | 12.00–1.15 | | | | | | | | | | |
| 14:00–16:00pm | | | | | | | | | | | | | | |
| 16:00–18:00pm | 16.30– | | 16.15– | | 16.30– | | | | | | | | 15.30– | |
| 18:00–20:00pm | 18.45 | | 19.00 | | 19.00 | | | | Jo goes | | Jo comes home | | 16.15 | |
| 20:00–22:00pm | | 20.00–20.15 | | | | | 22.00– | 21.45– | to stay with | 21.30– | 20.15–21.30 | | | |
| 22:00–00:00am | | | 22.30– | 23.00– | | 23.30– | | | his Gran | | 23.15– | 23.30– | | 23.45 |
| Total: | 7.25hrs | 5hrs | 8hrs | 7.25hrs | 7.5hrs | 5.5hrs | 8.75hrs | 8.25hrs | 5hrs | 8.5hrs | 2hrs | 9.5hrs | 3.75hrs | |

has difficulty going to sleep at the appropriate time, whereas a child with waking problems wakes repeatedly during the night.

If you think your child may have a sleep disorder it is advisable to start keeping a diary. Sleep diaries can be useful for a number of reasons. First, recording when and how long your child sleeps allows you to identify any patterns. Table 12.1 is an example of a sleep diary.

In this example, Jo's nap after returning from school disturbs his sleep for the night. If this became a consistent pattern Jo's parents should consider ways to keep him awake and stimulated during the time he tries to nap. It is also clear that Jo's most disturbed night's sleep follows the time he spends with his grandmother. This suggests that consistency and routine are important to Jo.

A sleep diary can also be used as a base-line comparison to demonstrate whether new interventions or routines are having a positive effect on your child. When trying to seek help for your child's sleep disorder, a sleep diary provides professionals with a clear picture of the problem. People may assume you are exaggerating if you tell them that you only get an average of two hours' sleep a night. If you can provide a chart with precise times it is more likely that you will be taken seriously. Certain benefit applications (e.g. the disability living allowance) ask you to specify how much your child sleeps and how often you have to get up in the night to help them. You can send in a copy of the sleep diary to support your application.

Table 12.2 is a blank sleep diary form that you can modify to suit your purposes. If you haven't time to fill in every detail, shading the chart to indicate when your child is asleep can be a good way of showing how much sleep you and your child are getting.

## Common sleep concerns

*'My child refuses to sleep in her own bed.'*

At some time or other, most children have spent at least a couple of nights in their parents' bed. Troubles arise when this becomes an established habit, resistant to change.

## Table 12.2 Blank sleep diary

| Week beginning: | Monday | | Tuesday | | Wednesday | | Thursday | | Friday | | Saturday | | Sunday | |
|---|---|---|---|---|---|---|---|---|---|---|---|---|---|---|
| | When slept | When we slept | When slept | When we slept | When slept | When we slept | When slept | When we slept | When slept | When we slept | When slept | When we slept | When slept | When we slept |
| 00:00–02:00am | | | | | | | | | | | | | | |
| 02:00–04:00am | | | | | | | | | | | | | | |
| 04:00–06:00am | | | | | | | | | | | | | | |
| 06:00–08:00am | | | | | | | | | | | | | | |
| 08:00–10:00am | | | | | | | | | | | | | | |
| 10:00–12:00pm | | | | | | | | | | | | | | |
| 12:00–14:00pm | | | | | | | | | | | | | | |
| 14:00–16:00pm | | | | | | | | | | | | | | |
| 16:00–18:00pm | | | | | | | | | | | | | | |
| 18:00–20:00pm | | | | | | | | | | | | | | |
| 20:00–22:00pm | | | | | | | | | | | | | | |
| 22:00–00:00am | | | | | | | | | | | | | | |
| Total: | | | | | | | | | | | | | | |

Sasha had meningitis when she was younger, and so I put her in my bed to keep an eye on her. Two years later she still sleeps with me and resists any attempt I make to settle her in her own room. She seems genuinely scared to sleep without me.

For some children, switching from sleeping in their parents' bedroom to sleeping in their own room is a big jump. This is especially so if the reason your child first slept alongside you was for comfort and reassurance. Therefore this issue should be dealt with gradually, over a period of time. To begin with, Sasha's mum started sleeping in her daughter's bed with her. Sasha accepted these new circumstances, as mum was still present. Next mum slept on an air mattress right next to Sasha's bed. Over the next few weeks, the mattress was moved a few inches each night until mum was sleeping in the hallway, still within Sasha's sight. Eventually mum was able to return to her own bed. This approach worked well because it acknowledged that the child's fear of sleeping alone was very real. Rather than forcing a confrontation, Sasha was given the reassurance that her mum was never far away should she need her. Donna Williams, writing as an adult with autism, explains her own fears of sleeping:

> Sleep was not a secure place. Sleep was a place where darkness ate you alive. Sleep was a place without colour or light. In the darkness you could not see your reflection. You couldn't get 'lost' in sleep. Sleep just came and stole you beyond your control. Anything that robbed me of total control was no friend of mine. (Williams 1994, p.6)

> I was afraid to sleep, always had been. I would sleep with my eyes open and I did this for years. I guess I did not appear to be terribly normal. 'Haunting' or 'haunted' would have been better adjectives. I was afraid of the dark, though I loved the early dawn and dusk. (*ibid.*, p.8)

Many children are afraid of the dark. Nightlights help to disperse the gloom, while lava lamps and lit fishtanks can have a soothing, almost hypnotic effect on some children. If you feel that fearfulness is a factor in your child's waking problems, fading could be suitable. Whenever you hear your child wake up, go into their bedroom briefly to check they are in bed and to reassure them that you are around. Slowly reduce the number of times you look in on your child so that she learns that her behaviour does not increase the attention you give.

### 'My child only sleeps for a few hours each night.'

In very young children waking problems are an indication that they still haven't developed mature sleep patterns. As babies they woke up to feed every couple of hours and this pattern hasn't yet been eradicated. In the older child with autism there may be an indication that they suffer from sleep disturbances. Anxieties or nightmares may be making it difficult for them to fall into a deep sleep. When your child's limited sleep pattern starts affecting other family members, direct action is needed. The following example describes the solution one family found:

> His parents made two 'Thomas' clocks for him. The 'morning' clock had its hands set at 7am and included a rising sun among the train illustrations. The 'bedtime' clock incorporated a moon. His parents knew that they could not make him sleep, but they did make sure that his bedroom contained plenty of toys that he could entertain himself with. Umar was shown how to tell when the times on his clocks tallied with the times on the real clock in his bedroom. He was taught to stay in his room until the 'morning' clock tallied with the real one, and to start getting ready for bed when his 'bedtime' clock and the real one said the same time. This seemed to work better than simply telling him what time he was allowed up and reminding him to look at the time. (Whitaker 2001, p.32)

This solution made use of Umar's interests as well as his ability to tell the time. Less able children could be told to wait for their alarm to go off, signalling that it's time to get up. As Umar's parents rightly recognise, they couldn't make him sleep. But the use of the clocks helped him to remain in his bedroom until a suitable hour.

*'My child is a night time wanderer.'*

Many children with autism go through periods when they need very little sleep. Unfortunately the same cannot be said for exhausted parents.

> I can never fully relax when I go to bed. My four-year-old son, David, had taken to waking in the middle of the night, leaving his room and wandering round the house. I constantly have to keep my ears peeled, and rarely get more than a few hours' sleep each night. I don't like the idea of closing him in his room. If he really needed me, I would want to hear him.

In this situation, David is getting by on very little sleep and waking in the early hours of the morning. Like most four-year-olds, he does not stay put once awake, and decides to explore the house. His dad finds this very worrying, he is worried about his son's safety when unsupervised and yet does not want to lock David inside his room. There are several options to be considered.

First, David may be wandering because he is bored. If this is the case, his father should make sure that there are things in the room for David to play with if he does wake up. Leaving a nightlight on will provide David with enough light to play by. Keeping a potty and a drink in the bedroom ensures thay there is no reason to wander to other parts of the house. Initially, David must be taught that when he is awake he must stay in his room. Quickly and calmly returning David whenever he wanders away from his bedroom means sleep deprivation for Dad in the short term, but it will help David understand where he is expected to stay.

Alternatively, David's father could consider minor adaptations to the house. A stable door arrangement, where the top half can be kept open when the bottom half is locked shut, allows David to be heard but not to physically leave. Safety gates serve a similar function and allow the child a clear view through to the rest of the house. A floor pad that buzzes whenever it is stepped on could alert parents to nighttime wanderings. Lastly, locking doors to other rooms in the house will keep valuables safe and minimise any mischief-making. Your child will be more likely to return to his bedroom if he finds nothing else to amuse him.

*'My child is easily disturbed from sleep by noises in the rest of the house.'*

> Michelle is very good at going to bed, I usually have no trouble getting her off to sleep. The problem is that she has supersensitive hearing and is woken up by even low-level noises. I have an older teenager who goes to bed several hours later and invariably this wakes up Michelle. Once woken she is really difficult to settle again.

It can be difficult juggling the needs of different children in the house. Once again, this problem could be approached in several ways. First, the positioning of Michelle's room should be considered. Is her bed in the best position, i.e. as far away as possible from the likeliest source of noise? If her older sister's room is next door, stereos and televisions should be positioned as far away as possible from a shared wall, and a volume level agreed on for after a certain time.

Shelving the shared wall and filling with books and games can muffle any noise getting through. In this instance, Michelle's dad stuck a layer of foam, followed by a layer of eggboxes, on both sides of the shared wall, which significantly cut down on noise. A soothing, sounds of nature tape (in this case gentle rain) was put on in Michelle's room at a level that didn't disturb her sleep but did disguise what was going on in other parts of the house.

*'My child insists on lengthy bedtime routines.'*

> Somehow we have got into the situation where Dylan comes downstairs three or four times after I have put him to bed. It is not a simple case of tucking him in each time, we have to go through the rigmarole of saying goodnight to each of his numerous toys, and singing the 'Goodbye, farewell' song from *The Sound of Music*. Anything less causes a tantrum. I find this whole process exhausting and irritating but don't know how to break out of this cycle.

The issue in this example seems to be the number of times the bedtime ritual has to take place, rather than the actual ritual itself. There are several issues to consider. Perhaps Dylan's mother needs to spend longer ensuring that her son is really asleep before she leaves him. Second, she needs to decide how much time she wants to spend putting her child to bed (it is always best to think about how much patience you have on a bad day and use this as your measure). If Dylan was intercepted before he made his way downstairs, there might be less fuss about getting back into bed and going to sleep. By the time Dylan has walked all the way downstairs into the bright light of the lounge he has completely woken up. It could be beneficial for mum to remain upstairs for a few nights so she can hear as soon as Dylan attempts to leave his room. It is important, when Dylan is returned to bed, that this is done as quickly and with as little fuss as possible. To begin with Dylan may resist strongly when mum refuses to repeat the bedtime routine a second time. As long as Dylan's mum can hold out, Dylan will reach the stage when he realises his tantrum does not get him what he wants.

A few weeks of tantrums is enough to frazzle anyone's nerves, so, if you can, share the load with your partner. It is important not to give into the tantrum once intervention begins. As mentioned previously, intermittent reinforcers are much more powerful and can make behaviour more resistant to change.

### 'My child sleeps very heavily and is difficult to wake in the mornings.'

If your child rarely sleeps, hypersomnia (excessive sleeping) may seem like a parent's dream come true. However, this sleep disorder can (sometimes severely) interfere with the child's daily activities. Waking a child from heavy sleep can lead to a grumpy, unhappy individual, as well as a bad start to the day. One parent found a novel solution:

> John had difficulty waking up on time to get ready for school. If awakened by us, he was usually in a very bad mood. I discovered that if I let his pet cat into the house, the cat would go jump on his bed, nuzzle up to his face, and pester him until he woke up – in a good mood. (Schopler 1995, p.152)

Petless households could try using finger-puppets or favourite cuddly toys to wake up their children amicably. Setting a clock radio on low volume to come on ten minutes before getting-up time works for some children. Stereos that can be set to play chosen CDs at a certain time also make waking up a more pleasant experience. For children who are motivated by food, breakfast can be used as an incentive for getting up.

In some cases, family doctors recommend the drug ritalin for hypersomnia. Ritalin is not effective for every child, and many parents are understandably reluctant about using regular medication. If you are in this position, ask your doctor to refer you on to a paediatrician with experience of autistic spectrum disorders. This will allow you to receive up-to-date information about treatments and expert advice about possible courses of action.

In older children and teenagers, motivational difficulties need to be tackled differently. Some may have very real fears about the day ahead, especially if school has become a challenging, stressful place. Depression can affect motivation, and people who are depressed tend to sleep more (and spend more time in bed) than other people. Excessive sleep problems which appear to be laziness could actually indicate psychological problems.

*'I have heard a supplement called melatonin can improve sleep patterns.'*

Some families report benefits from using melatonin with their child. The following quotation is from a grandfather who was impressed with the calming affect melatonin had on his granddaughter:

> ...turned my little Idaho tornado into a slight breeze. I kept Rachel over the weekend, her first time of being out of her own bed with the exception of when she was in the hospital three years ago. And with the melatonin she was not any different from any other kid.

Melatonin is a hormone secreted by the pineal gland which, among other things, has been shown to regulate sleep patterns in animals. Studies show that taking melatonin supplements can help ward off jet-lag following long flights. It has been suggested that children with autism have irregular patterns of melatonin secretion, which in turn affects their sleep cycle. That is, they do produce melatonin, just not at the right times of day.

Melatonin supplements are not licensed for sale in this country (being a hormone it is classified as a drug), but it can be prescribed by your doctor. In America melatonin is available over the counter because it is classified as a food supplement. Foods such as plums, bananas and brazil nuts are naturally rich in melatonin. It is not known whether a melatonin-rich diet could improve sleep patterns. Research is inconclusive, although anecdotally some parents report that melatonin supplements have improved their child's sleep.

## 'Should I consider medication to help my child sleep?'

Medical interventions are typically seen as a last resort in treating sleep disorders in children as they can be habit-forming and they don't treat the root cause of the problem. As a general rule it is better to minimise the medication your child is on but at certain times it may be desirable to have a mild sedative to hand – for example, if you are going on holiday and are concerned about the consequences of jet-lag, or if you feel that your child's health is suffering through lack of sleep. Most family doctors will be prepared to prescribe under these circumstances.

Some parents have also found that using medication in tandem with a behavioural approach can help to restore a good sleep pattern. The combination is crucial, as without the behavioural intervention, when the medical treatment ends the child is likely to return to his old sleep patterns.

## 'Are there more natural ways to induce sleep?'

Many of the natural remedies available from health food stores claim to treat insomnia and other sleep disorders. Homeopathic treatments do not carry the same risk of side-effects and addiction as found with conventional sedatives. Homeopathy is a holistic approach to healing that aims to work in harmony with the body. If you would like to try this method with your child, you need to get in touch with a reputable, qualified homeopath. The Society of Homeopaths can provide details of local professionals working in this field. (See 'Useful contacts' at the end of this chapter.)

*Sleeping tips*

- Keep a sleep diary.

- Use relaxation techniques to help your child wind down. A few drops of lavender oil added to bathwater has a soothing effect. Children who can tolerate and enjoy physical contact can be relaxed through massage (this can be on bare skin or over the top of clothes). Relaxation tapes (music and simple exercises) have been found useful by some families. However, some children with autism find formal relaxation techniques distressing, which makes them counterproductive to your goal. Physical exertion during the day can increase the chance of a peaceful night. As much as possible, the hour before bed should be quiet time, free from arousing distractions and demands.

- Get some sleep yourself. Sleep deprivation is a powerful form of torture. If your night's sleep is consistently interrupted you should consider getting some respite. Unfortunately, respite services are notoriously limited, despite the very real need for them. Parents with a named social worker should ask them about local provision. Otherwise, contact your local social services department and speak to the duty social worker.

- If possible, share night duties with other family members. Taking turns with your partner will allow you those vital extra hours of sleep.

- Routine and structure will help your child feel safe and in control. Stick to a firm bedtime routine that your child is aware of, e.g. bathtime > glass of warm milk > story > sleep.

- When you need to return your child to bed, do it as quickly and simply as possible. Give little attention, simply tuck him back into bed and leave. Reading stories, hot drinks, lullabies, should only be part of the first bed routine, otherwise your child may get up simply to enjoy the routine all over again.

- Make sleep more comfortable. Children with autism can have significant problems with hypersensitivity to touch, visual stimuli or sound. This can be both distracting and distressing and make the process of falling asleep very difficult. Assess your child's sleeping environment to see if there is any way to reduce unnecessary distractions. Simple measures like making sure the door can be shut quietly can make a big difference to some children.

- If your child enjoys deep pressure they may prefer heavier blankets to lightweight duvets. The weight of a blanket can prove reassuring to some children.

- Children with autism are perhaps more likely than their peers to be sensitive to foodstuffs like sugar, caffeine and additives, which can keep people awake. If your child frequently has sweet or caffeine-rich drinks and foodstuffs near bedtime then it is worth investigating whether this could be disturbing her sleep. Removing stimulants from some children's diets (especially colourings and flavourings) can have positive effects on behaviour. As well as the obvious stimulants (e.g. tea, cola, chocolate) investigate the less well-known stimulants like oranges, fresh orange juice and hard cheeses.

- If you decide to cut out certain foodstuffs it is best to phase them out gradually (particularly if your child consumes a lot). This prevents your child from missing these elements from their diet too much (some of these products can be addictive and therefore hard to give up; caffeine is the clearest example of this).

# Useful contacts

### 1. The Society of Homeopaths

*The Society of Homeopaths provides a register free of charge detailing professional practitioners working in different regions of the country. This register can be accessed by ringing the society, or visiting their website. The 'Friends of Homeopathy' Newsletter (four issues a year) is also available.*

> 4a Artizan Road
> Northampton
> NN1 4HU
> *Tel:* 01604 621400
> *Fax:* 01604 622622
> *Email:* info@homeopathy-soh.org
> *Website:* www.homeopathy-soh.org

### 2. Sleep Scotland

*A helpline for families in Scotland.*

> 8 Hope Park Square
> Edinburgh EH8 9NW
> *Tel:* 0131 6511392
> *Email:* sleepscotland@lycosmail.com

# Suggested reading

Durand VM. (1998) *Sleep Better! A Guide to Improving Sleep for Children with Special Needs.* Baltimore, MD: Paul H. Brookes Publishing.
*Available from NAS Publications Department (price £14.95). This comprehensive book is an excellent source of information and suggestions.*

Quine L. (1997) *Solving Children's Sleep Problems: A Step by Step Guide for Parents.* Huntingdon, Cambs: Beckett Karlson Publishing.
*This book does not deal specifically with children with special needs and is more of a practical manual for parents. However, many of the approaches featured could be adapted for children with autism.*

# PLAY

Every parent appreciates those parts of the day when they check on their child and find him happily engaged in play. Play provides a form of respite for the carer, removing the pressure to constantly entertain and direct the child. Normally, as the child grows older, he becomes more and more able to find his own diversions.

Play for most children is a natural, enjoyable activity. It is an invaluable way of helping the child explore new concepts, develop ideas and progress to higher levels of understanding. Through play, children learn skills of negotiation, turn-taking and socialising. Relationships with peers and siblings are strengthened through play opportunities.

Parents watching their child with autism may notice distinct differences. Children will vary in their play behaviours but common remarks from parents include:

> My son has loads of toys which he never even looks at. He is not curious like other children. He spends his free time playing over and over with his toy train.

> My son has two big sisters who were very excited to have a little brother to play with. He is the baby to be mothered, the patient to be healed and the puppy to be trained in most of their games. He passively tolerates his role with good humour, but never seeks to join in with the girls of his own accord.

> Ben gave up trying to play with Thomas years ago. Whatever Ben tries to initiate an activity, Thomas will ignore the approach and carry on with whatever he was doing. To start with, this made Ben try even harder to engage his brother, but then Thomas found out that hitting Ben made him go away. They have very little contact now, unless I am there to supervise play.

> Tina loves to play with other children but has very few social skills. To start play she may go and grab another child's toy, which usually leads to tears rather than a shared game. She plays best with very passive, younger kids who do not make demands on

her. She controls the game and will stop playing if her rules are not followed.

Charlie screams with delight when his daddy lets him jump up and down on his stomach (my husband is of generous proportions). He will happily continue for hours (or until my husband's stomach has had enough) giving good eye contact and his full attention. It is harder to get Charlie's attention with other games.

## Teaching children with autism to play

Children with autism can and do learn to enjoy themselves. However, many children 'need to be taught both the desire to play and the skills needed to do so'(Schopler 1995, p.66). But where to begin? How can children with autism be taught to play more effectively? The first stage for many children is teaching them to tolerate other people being near. Placing yourself in their play space, on their level, and watching quietly what they are doing is a start. Once your child has accepted your presence you could start to comment on what she is doing, gradually moving into her world. The final stage is making yourself an important partner in her play, be it by providing missing pieces of a jigsaw puzzle or a bouncy stomach. The time these steps take will vary.

Children best described as socially aloof will need different strategies to one who is passive, or active but odd. For example, a child who is socially aloof is usually content to spend large amounts of time alone, engaged in a solo task. Parental techniques could concentrate on copying the child (playing with a same or similar toy, a small distance away) and then extending the activity in an exciting direction to gain the child's attention. For instance, the child who is lying on the floor gazing through the spokes of a toy car may be interested in joining the parent who initially mirrors him, then comments on what they are both looking at, but then goes on to build a tower of blocks which the car crashes through. Acting in an animated manner emphasises the fun the action is bringing, and is an important way of gaining the child's attention. A passive child may not resist parental attempts to play but does not initiate contact himself. Strategies could focus on using the child's special interests to motivate him into action and playing games that he has to actively contribute to. A child who is active but odd is motivated and interested in playing, but needs to learn how to approach and interact with other children, as well as the rules governing different games.

As well as play techniques there are environmental and organisational factors to consider. The play space your child uses and your approach to play could help increase interactions between you and your child.

## Organising play

The whole household does not need to follow these rules, but certainly having at least one calm room would be an advantage. This will be a space where you can work one-to-one with your child, without the visual and auditory distractions that the rest of your home may contain.

Introduce toys and activities one at a time, and make sure that the child helps you put away previous playthings before embarking on a new activity. It is never too early to teach your child to tidy up after herself. This can be aided by clearly marking the boxes where different toys live. A picture can be pasted on the front to indicate correct places, so that she is clearly instructed as to what goes where. The first stage may just involve the child putting toys in a big box on the floor, as she grows older instructions can become more specific.

Shelves for toy boxes, or roomy cupboards will allow all toys to be removed from sight or reach, to allow a chosen activity to be concentrated on fully. This will also encourage your child to communicate with you in order to request desired toys that she cannot access without your help. Some parents find it useful to have one box of toys available at all times, filled with toys that are rotated each week to prevent the child from becoming too fixated on certain objects.

## Increasing your child's tolerance of touch

Many children with autism love rough-and-tumble play. Parents may be able to embrace their child during this game, which may be something he usually resists. Through this kind of play you can explore what sort of physical contact your child enjoys most and increase his tolerance of being touched. Water play provides another opportunity:

Jack tolerated very little physical contact. His Dad decided to teach him how to swim. Initially Jack was nervous about being in the pool and he clung to his Dad for comfort. He quickly started to enjoy his time in the water. His Dad taught him to swim by physically moving his limbs, and demonstrating the correct moves himself. Jack never objected to being touched when in the water. Jack loves to jump from the side of the pool into his Dad's arms, although previously he had hated being hugged. This game was a great way of improving Jack's eye contact and attention to other people (his Dad would not hold his arms out until Jack was looking at him). I think this physical water play has really improved Jack's relationship with his Dad. It is their special time together that they both look forward to each week.

## Meeting needs through play

Tom was often found squashed into the smallest of spaces. If ever I could not find him, I would look in my washing machine or the tiny cupboard under the stairs. Nine times out of ten he would be in one of these hiding places. I had read about Temple Grandin's squeeze machine, that she used to apply reassuring pressure to her body, and I felt Tom may be squeezing himself away for similar reasons. Although he could never endure soft touches to the body, Tom had always enjoyed firm contact (a strong handed backrub being his favourite).

One day when I was sitting on the sofa, Tom wiggled down the back of the cushions and wedged himself between me and the sofa back. His contentment gave me some ideas for play. I started making 'Tom sandwiches', by putting a big sofa cushion on the floor, next Tom, and then another cushion on top. I then leant on the sandwich to provide a little more pressure. Tom was delighted by this whole idea, and I have now managed to involve his sister in this play too. I now make Tom-and-Elsa sandwiches, squashing them both at the same time, and if I am lucky Tom returns the favour and squashes me. This has proved especially useful when Tom is stressed, this activity calms him right down.

Many children with autism benefit from some kind of regular exercise. Excess energy has to go somewhere, and it is best to provide a positive channel. The next boy found his own solution:

> Jeff loves to count. He also has bundles of excess energy. When his older brother brought an exercise bike home, Jeff was immediately interested. Being quite a new fangled-machine, the display counter digitally registered how many miles have been cycled, how many calories have been burnt, etc. Now, every morning he comes down red in the face and slightly puffing. The other day he proudly told me that he had cycled 88 miles that week! This extra exertion has had a real positive effect on Jeff, his concentration is much better now and he is less prone to meltdowns.

## Making play interesting

Introducing new props into play every so often can prevent your play times from always following the same pattern. Watching other people play with your child can give you new ideas too, as they may find completely new ways of playing with old toys. This mum found inspiration was large and yellow:

> Zena was very hard to engage in social situations. She never listened to any of my suggestions or allowed me to expand her rigid play patterns. I invested in a huge yellow ball from a specialist toy catalogue, which I thought might interest her. I sat her onto the top of the ball and bounced her up and down for a few seconds, before allowing her to escape. I gradually increased the time I bounced Zena before letting her go, and also bounced her enthusiastic younger sister in front of Zena. This combined approach worked well, and soon Zena would approach me and lead me to the cupboard where the ball was kept; this was the first play initiation she ever made. The ball also provided the opportunity to involve Zena's sister in play. They would cling on to each other as I bounced the ball, laughing delightedly.

Zena was reluctant to try new things, but her mum's patience paid off. There may be some activities that you know your child could enjoy if they could just experience it a few times. Demonstrating what fun can be had with a sibling is a good way of introducing new themes.

## Focusing on your child's skills

It is important to focus on all aspects of your child's skill profile – both what she is good at, and what she finds hard. While play can be used to work on areas that are weak, it is also a chance to make your child feel good about her talents. This family found a way to make their son feel important and useful:

> Our family are board game addicts. We have wardrobes full of different games and often spend the evening playing together. James, who has Asperger syndrome, had never really joined in with our family tournaments. He became immensely frustrated whenever he wasn't winning. I thought it would do him good to be included in some way, so decided to make him official referee. James is now in his element. He is a good reader and enjoys telling us the game rules whenever there is a disagreement. He is now socially interacting with us, instead of playing upstairs alone.

## Love of rule-bound play

Sometimes the characteristics found in autism can be capitalised on in certain types of play. In the following example Jonathan's love of rules is complimented:

> Jonathan and Kate love playing together. Although this was not always the case. They used to have very little in common and any play quickly turned to squabbles. Then Kate joined a local board game society and started bringing games home to play. Because the games are rule bound and simple there is no arguing between them – any disagreements are settled by consulting the rule book.

## Simplifying rules to suit your child

The majority of games can be tailored to your child's level of functioning. Games with a simple philosophy, like snakes and ladders, snap, and hide and seek are suitable for most ages:

> My other children are always playing games together, but most of them are too complicated for Denise. So I sat down with her siblings and between us we simplified some of the game rules. Now Denise loves playing the more straightforward versions and spends more time with her brother and sister. Hide-and-seek is a big favourite at the moment. Denise hides with her sister, who reminds her to keep quiet when their brother comes looking. When it is Denise's turn to seek, her brother and sister are given less hiding time, and Denise has her alarm set on her digital watch so she knows when to start hunting. This has proved immensely successful.

## Even up the odds

The following advice helps keep adults on their toes when playing with their children:

> Don't hesitate to enter his world. Join him in his computer or Nintendo games, for example. Try to make the competition exciting. If your child is sluggish and not up to the competition, try to even the playing field by giving him certain advantages until he can beat you at least 55 per cent of the time. It's best to do this by giving yourself certain handicaps or the child some advantage (such as you can play only with your left hand) so that you can be playing your hardest and keeping the competition exciting though he still has the edge. (Greenspan 1995, p.94)

## Building on special interests

Incorporating your child's special interests into play guarantees their attention. By using the familiar topic as a starting point, you can then pair it with a new activity:

Tim's favourite subject is war. He knows huge lists of facts about different battles and colonels, which quickly bore his listener. I have managed to combine his interest with chess. When we are setting up the board I encourage him to recreate a favourite battle. At the moment, the white king is Napoleon and the black is Nelson. To begin with Tim used to insist that the correct victor in history also won in the chess game. However, as he has become better at the game, he has become more flexible, and simply wants his side to win. Chess allows Tim a chance to talk about his obsession in a relevant social situation. My chess skills and historical knowledge have also improved.

## Expanding rigid play themes

It is commonly noted that the play of children with autism is often limited and repetitive in nature. Attempts to expand this repertoire may result in the child refusing to play or ignoring the intrusion. The following mum dealt with this issue by firstly joining her son in his world, and then introducing him to new ideas:

> Connor's pattern of play appeared very mechanical, following the same motions and actions each time. He would line up his toy cars in a particular way, and then lie down on the floor alongside them. From this position, Connor would peer through the spokes of the car wheels and get very excited. Every so often he would sit up and flap his hands. When I tried to join in and move the cars, Connor would get very angry. I decided to try another tactic. I got some similar cars out and lined them up to mirror his formation, a few feet away. For a while I lay beside my cars and looked through the spokes, just like Connor was doing. For the next ten minutes I tried to see what he must be seeing, occasionally I made a comment about the cars. Then I fashioned a ramp and started whizzing my cars down it, so they crashed into the remaining cars at the bottom. Connor stopped flapping and watched me the whole time. I carried on in this way, expanding the basic car lines into more exciting play themes. After a few sessions, Connor left his lines and started joining me. The cars usually start in lines still, but gradually Connor is enjoying playing in different ways.

This parent found that her son would not tolerate his own lines of cars being altered, so she set up a parallel line and used this as her starting point. This new way of interacting was interesting to Connor and he responded well. Your child may not be aware of all the functions different toys are capable of. It is often noted that children with autism can play with toys as if they were just objects (e.g. things to be lined up) rather than realising their true fun potential. Once you have your child's attention you can try and 'sell' a toy to him – by modelling all the possible ways of playing with it.

## Encouraging pretend play

I have used the magic carpet ride with my son Joel to help his pretend play. I spread a colourful sheet onto the floor which we both sit on. I tell him that this is our magic carpet, that can take us anywhere we want to go. Before lift-off I tell him to close his eyes. I then describe the view that I can see below us. Joel likes hearing my stories but found it very hard initially to make up his own. At the beginning he kept saying the whole thing was silly, but he consented to join in because 'mummy enjoys it'. I helped him work on his imagination by asking him to recount trips we had taken to the seaside, on holiday, etc. To begin with, these memories were recounted faithfully but after a few sessions he started mixing them all together and eventually introduced new places and even fantasy lands.

My daughter's pretend play is limited. Through our patience and hard work she has got to the stage where she will act out scenarios that she has seen in real life (e.g. going to the doctor, making a cup of tea). I feel this is an improvement.

The best investment I ever made was a small puppet theatre. There are eight different hand-puppets and my kids love making up stories. My youngest one, Billy, copies his sisters. My girls write endless scripts and one of Billy's puppets always has a role.

My child does not 'get' pretending. When other children are playing in this way and try to include him, he tends to ask them incessantly, 'Are we still pretending?' His teacher hit upon the idea of the imagination hat – a tall wizard's hat with silver stars and moons. Now Oliver knows that when he is wearing the hat, it is pretend play time.

## Encouraging play with other children

Try to provide some activities that peers/siblings can enjoy together. Games that depend on at least two people are a good idea. The notion of turn-taking cannot be introduced too early, and can prevent playtime ending in tears. You may need to be on hand to engineer some success-ful encounters before this catches on. Developing common interests (e.g. computers, horse riding, trampolining, etc.) encourages interac-tion. Rewarding siblings for playing with their brother or sister (token systems can work well here) may be a staged endeavour rather than natural behaviour but can be enjoyable for both parties. Providing basic guidelines for how to play with their brother or sister can encourage some siblings/playmates who may have given up trying in the past.

> The teacher agreed to help introduce Hannah gradually to playing with other children. At first, the teacher would play just with Hannah, rolling a ball to her. Then she brought in another child and served as a 'buffer' between Hannah and the other child by allowing Hannah to roll the ball to her at first instead of to the other child. Soon Hannah and her partner were rolling the ball back and forth directly to each other under the watchful eye of the teacher. (Greenspan 1995, p.78)

## Affordable ways to entertain your child

Forget expensive toys and gadgets. There are many simple and cost-effective ways of engaging your child in play, as the following examples show:

> Water and a sieve keep my son amused for hours. He loves the noise as he lifts the sieve up, allowing the water to flow through the holes.

> My son loves washing up! A big bowl of bubbly water and some of my sturdier glassware is a favourite pastime. Washing the fake

glass drops from my mother's chandeliers is his ultimate treat, and his grandmother is more than happy to indulge his whim.

When Sara was younger she could be amused for hours by a few compact discs threaded onto a shoelace. Finally, I had found a use for all the free trial internet CDs that were posted through my letter box.

Clyde used to drive his older brother mad by 'posting' his rare Beatles records down the back of the radiator. A trip to the local charity shop and a bulk buy of old records solved this problem. Now Clyde has his own collection to play with, and peace is restored to my family.

Contact the National Association of Toy and Leisure Libraries (NATLL – see 'Useful contacts') for factsheets on making toys yourself.

*Play tips*

- Start with your child's special interests. Create interaction that involves whatever your child enjoys and then expand into new directions (e.g. a favourite fire engine could have its wheels dipped in paint and then be wheeled over a sheet of paper).

- Pair an activity that your child already enjoys with a new behaviour, e.g. if you are trying to encourage more eye contact, whenever your child looks at you respond with a favourite activity (like a few minutes' rough-and-tumble play). Verbally making a connection ('Good looking, let's play') will help your child make the connection between what they need to do, and receiving the reinforcer.

- Adjust the activity to meet your child's developmental level. By changing or adapting rules you can increase your child's chance of success, e.g. requesting child rails when bowling (which guides the ball to the pins and prevents it from falling into the funnel). A child who can never win will not be motivated to try the activity again.

- Talk to your child's teacher about starting a 'circle of friends'. The circle is made up of peers who volunteer to help a particular child learn a new skill or adapt her behaviour. Meetings happen on a regular basis, and are used as brainstorming sessions to think of ways to help the target child. Sometimes the changes come from the peers themselves. In one case the children of a class agreed to stop playing mock fighting games, as a fellow pupil with Asperger syndrome often went a bit too far and hurt playmates. The children volunteered to stop playing that particular game, something that they might have resented if asked to do so by a teacher. If solutions are provided by the peer group they are more likely to be followed. A circle of friends can be useful for teaching your child the rules of popular playground games.

- Physical prompting can encourage your child to try new activities that he might not otherwise try, e.g. completing a jigsaw puzzle for the first time can be done hand over hand and parental support can gradually fade as the child gets the hang of the activity. Once established, activities can be prompted with gestures.

- Timers can be used to alert the child to when she needs to clear up/move on to a new activity. This can be a good way of reducing the time your child spends with a particular toy. Over time you could set the timer for a few seconds less each day, so no one activity is monopolising your child's play.

- Free time at home can be structured using visual time tables, see Figure 12.1. Each morning and afternoon you could allow your child to choose two or three activities to occupy himself. The chosen symbols can then be displayed to direct him (a corresponding symbol on the shelf or box that the toy is kept in helps to guide him). This system is especially valuable over holiday periods when your child has more time that he is not accustomed to filling.

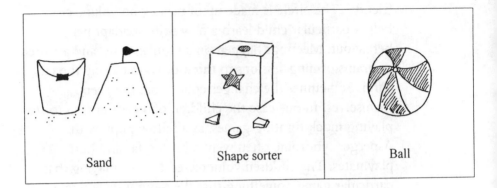

*Figure 12.1 Visual symbols for play activities*

- Children with autism often have problems with free time at school. Playtimes and lunchtimes can be daunting to a child who finds it difficult to entertain herself. Some children may just wander around the perimeter fence, or engage in simple repetitive behaviours to occupy themselves. A few ideas from a teacher, or being able to choose a toy from a box to play with during the break, could make a big difference. For children who need a break from their peers during this time, a few classroom chores that keep them inside can provide a solution.

- Toy libraries can be an excellent resource for parents, allowing a regular turnover of toys, and a chance to try out different products without cluttering up the bedroom. Staff can provide new ideas for play activities, and some toy libraries may have special sections for children with special needs.

- Different games can be used to improve different skills in your child, e.g.:

- ○ attention – stringing wooden beads on to a shoe lace, spot the difference puzzles
  - ○ imitation – follow the leader
  - ○ making choices – art work, palette of paints to work with
  - ○ following commands – Simon says
  - ○ tolerating physical contact – rough-and-tumble play, aeroplanes, whizzes
  - ○ co-ordination – trampolining, swimming, horseriding

- Choose toys that are appropriate to your child's cognitive development rather than her actual age. For example, children at early levels of development may be attracted by simple toys that are brightly coloured, textured or noise makers.

## Useful contacts

### 1. National Association of Toy and Leisure Libraries (NATLL) – Play Matters

*Loans carefully chosen (and sometimes specially adapted) toys to families with young children, including those with special needs. Provides friendship and support for parents and carers. Publishes* The Good Toy Guide *annually.*

68 Churchway
London NW1 1LT
*Tel:* 020 7387 9592
*Fax:* 020 7383 2714
*Email:* admin@natll.ukf.net
*Website:* www.charitynet.org/-NATLL

### 2. STEPS – Special Toys Educational Postal Service

*A small charity that operates a toy loan scheme by post for children with special needs. Toys are usually loaned for 3 months, and the service is free of charge.*

Paul Hames
13 Manor Gardens
Preston
Paignton TQ3 2QU
*Tel:* 01803 552012

### 3. Kids Active – Play and opportunity for disabled children
*Runs fully staffed adventure playgrounds in London for disabled children. Also offers a national information service with advice and resources on all aspects of play.*

Pyror's Bank
Bishop's Park
London SW6 3LA
*Tel*: 020 7731 1435
*Fax*: 020 7731 4426
*Email*: ktis@kidsactive.org.uk
*Website*: www.kidsactive.org.uk

## Toy catalogues

### 1. Krucial Kids
Redburn House
2 Tonbridge Road, Harold Hill
Romford, Essex RM3 8TS
*Tel*: 01708 345123
*Fax*: 01708 345222
*Email*: sales@krucialkids.com

### 2. TFH
76 Barracks Road
Sandy Lane Industrial Estate
Stourport-on-Severn
Worcestershire DY13 9QB
*Tel*: 01299 827820
*Fax*: 01299 827035
*Email*: mail@tfhuk.com
*Website*: www.tfhuk.com

### 3. Special Needs
Hope Education
Unit 14, Carraway Road
Gillmoss Industrial Estate
Liverpool L11 0AY
*Tel*: 0151 5473548

### 4. Nottingham Rehab Supplies (Novara Group Ltd.)
Novara House, Excelsior Road
Ashby Park, Ashby De La Zouch
Leicestershire LE65 1NG
*Tel*: 0870 6000197

*Fax:* 01530 419150

*Website:* www.nrs-uk.co.uk

*This catalogue has an extensive section on toys for pretend play.*

## Suggested reading

Anderson JM. (1998) *Sensorimotor Issues in Autism.* Texas: Therapy Skill Builders.
  *This concise manual addresses specific motor issues. Suggests different activities for working on different skill areas.*

Lear R. (1996) *Play Helps: Toys and Activities for Children with Special Needs.* (Fourth edition.) Oxford: Butterworth Heinemann.
  *A classic practical guide.*

Newson E. and Hipgrave T. (1982) *Getting Through to Your Handicapped Child.* Cambridge: Cambridge University Press.
  *Contains two good chapters on playing with your child.*

*The Good Toy Guide* Published annually by Time Out. Contact NATLL (See 'Useful contacts') for details.
  *For popular and classic toys. NATLL also provides a wide range of publications. Contact the charity directly for an up-to-date list.*

## TOILET TRAINING

> Most children become toilet trained through a combination of imitation, parental pleasure and displeasure, and luck. (Carr 1980, p.157)

Not all families with a child with autism experience difficulties i n toilet training. For some fortunate parents, their child will become clean and dry around the same time as peers. For other families, a more systematic approach combined with greater levels of patience and endurance will be needed. Social factors usually play an important part in a child's becoming toilet trained. When your child has autism they are not usually socially motivated in the same way as other children. This means that pleasing Mum and Dad, or being told they are grown-up, may not be a strong enough reinforcer for your child. If your child has been wearing nappies for several years this may be part of his routine which he sees no need to change.

Success in toilet training your child is influenced by beginning at the right stage, i.e. when he is physically ready and old enough to understand the concept you are teaching. Whitaker (2001) warns against starting too early and lists the following signs of readiness to look for:

- can he remain dry or unsoiled for one or two hours at a time?

- does he notice when he is wet or soiled?

- does he seem to be aware when performing?

- are there any signs of awareness of interest in the toilet and what happens there?

- is there any pattern to wetting or soiling?

The ease with which your child learns will depend on her level of ability; a child with lower functioning autism and/or learning difficulties will take longer to master skills than a more able child. As with all behaviour problems, what works wonders for one family may have no effect in another. This section covers various issues within toilet training, including solutions that have worked for particular children.

## Common problems

*'My daughter has an irrational fear of potties.'*

This mother decided to deal with her daughter's irrational fear by using the flooding method. This entails exposing the child to their fear head on, which enables them to recover from what scares them. As you can imagine, this can be an exhausting process for everyone involved. However, as the family in the following case study demonstrates, flooding can be very effective:

> I held Katy on her potty for a full 30 minutes. She screamed at such a pitch that the sustained note would have done credit to Maria Callas. She survived the trauma. I nearly did not.

The next day I repeated the process once again, and this time the screaming only lasted 20 minutes. Incidentally on neither day had there been any business done. As subsequent days passed by, Katy screamed less and less, until eventually she would sit quietly with eyes screwed tightly shut and her hands clenched into tiny white fists. After a while, the plastic throne lost its sinister side, and it became Katy's favourite place to sit.

Her fear overcome, the next stage was to get Katy performing on the potty:

> To Katy's utter delight, I mixed up a great big jug of Ribena, and complete with jug and cup allowed Katy to drink herself into a state which could be akin to being waterlogged. With Katy sitting on her potty, and the both of us locked into the lounge, so she couldn't escape, we waited. But no, she was not willing to perform. In the end I let her walk around the room, and every 10 minutes sat her back in position. Many times she started to wet the floor and was quickly returned. This had the effect of immediately stopping any further flow. But after two hours, I got the timing just right, and she performed beautifully. At the instant that the job was done an Opal Fruit was popped in her mouth as a reward, and everybody in the house came into the room to congratulate Katy on the outstanding achievement.

> These sessions continued every day, until finally Katie 'twigged' that when she performed, she got a sweet. (From *A Little Potty* by Anne and Peter Ford. This piece first appeared in *Communication* 1986. Reproduced with the permission of the National Autistic Society.)

The success experienced by the Fords was a combination of the flooding technique and their patience and perseverance. Providing an attractive reinforcer and verbal praise were also important elements.

Intensive programmes often get the quickest results. For parents who cannot dedicate a whole day to toilet training, and instead concentrate their efforts into a couple of hours a day, results will be slower. Some families target toilet training over a weekend or during a holiday period. If more than one adult is available, carers could take shifts and share responsibility.

### 'My child doesn't appear to know how to use the toilet.'

> I had tried endlessly to get Jack to pee into the toilet. Despite my efforts, he never seemed able to make the connection between peeing and the toilet. From experience I knew that Jack learned best from being shown exactly what to do. Verbal instructions were sometimes just not enough. After a few days of masterful persuasion I managed to get his Dad to demonstrate for Jack. A week later Jack was successfully urinating in the toilet. It was as if what I was asking him to do, finally made sense.

When dads or other male relatives are reluctant, older siblings or peers could be used as role models.

### 'My child refuses to sit on the toilet.'

A child's fear of sitting on the toilet is understandable. Hard-looking seats with a huge gaping hole and water underneath are not the friendliest looking furniture. Trainer seats reduce the size of the hole but there are other ways of combating your child's fear, as this case shows:

> Fareda was fearful of sitting on the toilet when she was younger. I think it was the fear of slipping through the hole. To begin with I placed some cardboard under the seat, so it completely covered the hole. Fareda readily accepted this. Next I made a small hole in the middle of the card, which I gradually increased in size each day. By the end of the second week the hole in the cardboard was the same size as the hole of the toilet. Fareda did not notice when I slipped the cardboard away and ever since she will happily sit on the toilet. This allowed me to move on to the next stage of getting her to perform whilst on the toilet.

This next mum also found a way to encourage her son to use the toilet:

> My son was using the toilet to urinate but still refused to poo unless he was in a nappy. I knew it was time for him to progress as he soiled the nappy as soon as I put it on, and then came to me immediately so I could change him. I started by making sure he pooed in the nappy, in the bathroom. Next I got him to sit on the toilet whilst he soiled his nappy (the top lid was closed so it was just a seat for him). After he had accepted this stage, I left the toilet lid up, so he was sitting properly on the toilet in his nappy. Over the next week I started putting on his nappy looser and looser, until I could pull it down at the sides just before he soiled the nappy. The final stage was to whisk the nappy away so he pooed into the toilet and strongly praise him. It took almost three weeks to reach this stage, and lots of chocolate buttons. We went a little backwards, as he hated it when the water splashed him. By putting a few sheets of toilet paper into the water first of all, I reduced the noise of the splashing, and the actual splash itself. Now my son regularly uses the toilet.

Some parents find that keeping a particular toy or book for the child to play with when they are sitting on the toilet can be useful. Playing may help your child relax enough to physically perform. However, too many toys may end up distracting him from the task at hand. He needs to concentrate on what he is doing, so use of the toy could be faded out once he is comfortable sitting on the toilet.

### 'My son frequently defecates and urinates around the house.'

One mother was helped to see that her own reaction reinforced her son's behaviour:

> And that was the key to the whole problem. *Reaction*. He enjoyed *reaction*. The day we stopped reacting things started to change. We made a pact: no matter how bad it looks we won't react. We will pretend as if nothing has happened. It was hard, but we managed to do it. Every time he wanted to take off his pants, without reacting we stopped him very coolly, almost without an expression, took him to the toilet and each time he did it in the

pot he was praised profusely. We showed him how overjoyed we were on this perfect act! That was the only reaction he got from us. (Chakravarty 1996)

As Carr (1980) explains, this next mother recognised that she was reinforcing her child for wetting and soiling her pants:

> ...her mother soon realised that this pants-changing was in many ways a very enjoyable time for Julie. She loved attention, and here she had her mother all to herself for ten minutes or so; in addition her mother used at these times to talk to her a great deal, scolding her, commenting on what was going on, praising her for pulling up her pants, and so on. If Julie was soiled her mother often used to give her a warm bath, as this seemed the quickest way to get her cleaned up, and then Julie would play in the water and enjoy being hugged dry in the towel. (Carr 1980, pp.159–160)

Julie's mother decided to change her reaction to pants-changing following accidents. She said little, without praising or scolding her child. If soiled, Julie was cleaned with cool water from a basin. If Julie went for a whole day without soiling her mother rewarded her with an extra long bath and towel-hugging session. In this way, Julie's mother started reinforcing her child's good behaviour.

### 'My daughter is terrified of toilet seats that aren't white.'

> Our bathroom suite at home is white. Sammy is perfectly toilet trained when we are at home. However, if she needs to go to the toilet while we are out, problems begin. Sammy refuses to use bathrooms that have coloured or wooden toilet seats. She does not seem able to generalise her skills from home to different situations. Sammy screams so loudly when I try and use coloured toilets that I usually give up and race home so she can go there.

The solution this mum eventually found was extremely practical. By always carrying hygienic paper seat covers (which were white), she was able to cover any offending toilet seats. Over time Sammy's mum started cutting down the size of the covers, so they covered less and less of the seat. Finally the cover was so small that Sammy was sitting almost directly on the seat. Sammy still likes to put some sheets of toilet paper onto the toilet seat when it is coloured, but this is a demand that her mother is happy to comply with.

### 'My child is afraid of flushing.'

This is not an uncommon problem. Some children with autism have hypersensitive hearing, so the sound of the flush must be deafening to them, especially when they are at such close quarters to the noise.

> My grandson loves playing 'ready, steady, go' with all manner of things. I decided to use this well loved game as a way of overcoming his fear of the toilet flushing. His first impulse was to run to the door as he normally does, but instead of letting him out, I said the magic word 'ready' and Steve automatically shouted out 'steady, go' as I flushed. Giving him warning seemed to make a real difference. He still wasn't happy to be in the same room as the flushing toilet, but at least he knew when to expect it.

> My son is much more tolerant of the flushing toilet since I started encouraging him to press the lever down himself, once he had finished. This very simple thing seems to make a big, big difference, he is now in control.

### 'My child often misses the toilet bowl when he is urinating.'

Ahem, at least a few men out there could benefit from the following tips:

> I add a few drops of green food colouring to the toilet water. This seems to improve Rod's aim.

> We have a small plastic frog in our toilet (too big to be flushed away). It amuses guests and helps Jolyon hit the right spot (and his Dad too!).

### 'My child has begun smearing his faeces.'

This certainly must feature as the most unpleasant toilet training problem for parents to deal with. It is hard to remain neutral when you feel physically disgusted by what your child has done. Dungarees with secure fastenings that fit snugly to your child's body are difficult for him to remove and prevent him from accessing a dirty nappy. Other parents have found success through dressing their children in back-to-front jumpsuits, so that the zipper is only accessible from the back (Schopler 1995). These suggestions are short-term but can be useful while you are toilet training.

If smearing occurs in a particular setting, you could limit the available time your child spends alone there. For example, if your child smears faeces in the bathroom, accompanying her provides the most immediate solution and can help break her habit. Other parents have used simple correction and over-correction to discourage this behaviour. This involves the child clearing up the mess she has made (simple correction) as well as completing other related tasks (over-correction). If you feel that your child is motivated to smear by the texture of the faeces, you could provide activities with materials that offer similar sensations (clay is a good example).

Eating faeces is an alarming problem to deal with. Once again the suggestions already mentioned could be used to prevent the child from getting access to their faeces. Involving the child in lengthy over correction routines each time he eats faeces (e.g. cleaning his teeth and the rest of the bathroom thoroughly) can decrease this behaviour in some cases. If you feel overwhelmed by this or other toiletting problems, you can request a referral by your doctor to a child psychologist. Having a professional on hand to help you devise an intervention programme can make a big difference.

*'My child uses the toilet but refuses to wipe himself clean.'*
Some children are reluctant to get their hands dirty and in certain cases may become constipated to prevent this situation arising. Exposure to play materials can help reduce this fear:

> I talked to my son's teacher about his dislike of getting his hands messy. She had already noticed that Rizwan rarely chose to finger-paint or use clay and play dough. With her help we gradu-

ally introduced activities at home and school that involved getting fingers messy. To begin with the play sessions were only a couple of minutes long, and Rizwan was reinforced immediately with a mini cookie (his favourite) whenever he tolerated substances on his fingers. I allowed Rizwan to clean his hands with liquid soap after we cleared up (he loves using the pump dispenser). Rizwan is still not fond of messy hands but he certainly tolerates it more now. I think knowing that he can clean his hands thoroughly at the end helps a lot.

Teaching a child how to wipe himself clean requires a significant amount of physical co-ordination. The most direct way to teach this skill is by providing physical prompts. Hand over hand teaching lets the child learn the correct movement in the correct direction (from front to back). Most parents encourage their child to continue wiping with a new sheet of paper, until the last piece used wipes clean.

### 'Could my child's problem be physical?'

This is certainly something to investigate with your doctor if toiletting problems are prolonged. Urinary infections can make bladder control more difficult and urinating painful. This could explain the behaviour of a child who avoids going to the toilet until it is physically impossible to delay any longer. In some cases, smearing/playing with faeces could actually be the result of physical discomfort from constipation.

Soiling pants or going to the toilet in inappropriate places could also be traced back to a physical cause. Severe constipation can lead to a bowel blocked by a hard plug of faeces. Some liquid faeces may leak around the blockage, resulting in stained clothes. Laxatives and stool softeners can relieve these problems, although changes to the diet (e.g. more fruit, vegetables and fibre) will help prevent a reccurrence of symptoms. In extreme cases, medical intervention may be necessary to remove the build-up.

Other children produce very loose stools which are difficult to control as they provide no pressure against the bowel wall (which normally alerts the child to the need to defecate). If your child constantly has this problem a diet review may be needed to help adjust their digestive system (your doctor may suggest products to solidify faeces in the short term). Anecdotally, some parents report that one of the benefits of special diets (e.g. gluten- and casein-free) is the alleviation of bowel problems in their child. (See entry in Chapter 13 'Therapies and approaches'.)

*'How can I teach my child to stay dry during the night?'*

The majority of children younger than two years (disabled or otherwise) wet themselves at night. In fact it is unusual for a child at this age to keep dry overnight. Bedwetting tends to occur in the first few hours of sleep. Figures show that boys are more likely to wet their beds, whereas more girls wet themselves during the daytime. If your child has not learnt to wake when he has a full bladder or is unable to sleep through the night without bedwetting you could consider using an enuresis alarm – also referred to as a 'bell and pad'.

The bell in this case is usually a buzzer that sounds whenever drops of urine make contact with a pad placed underneath the child's bedsheet. The noise wakes the child and hopefully the carer. (The bell could be placed in the parents' bedroom to make sure they are alerted.) The aim is that the child can then 'hold on' (this seems to happen automatically) so that he can be taken to the toilet to finish urination. (A potty in easy reach is useful in the early days.)

In theory, this technique teaches the child to wake and use the toilet whenever he feels the sensation of a full bladder. However, as Howlin and Rutter (1987) remark, this method leads to the child sleeping throughout the night without wetting, rather than waking in time to use the toilet successfully. Although the exact learning process of this behaviour is not clear, the results speak for themselves. Success can take weeks, months or sometimes longer, but the use of the bell and pad has proven effective with many children. The use of visual star charts in conjunction with the bell and pad helps to motivate the child to stay dry, i.e. a star can be awarded for each night without bedwetting, and once the child has a certain number of stars he is allowed a favoured treat.

A variation of the enuresis alarm can also be used for children who wet themselves during the day. The pad is small enough to fit into the child's pants (much like a sanitary towel). The buzzer is activated when the child begins to urinate.

### 'Can I loan aids and equipment from anywhere?'

This will vary from area to area. Some local hospitals have arrangements whereby parents can borrow toileting equipment, others will not offer this service. The best way to find out what is available is by speaking to a continence advisor (your doctor can refer you on to this professional). Your health visitor will also be able to offer information and advice and can arrange free incontinence supplies.

Contacts for buying aids and equipment are provided in 'Useful contacts' at the end of the chapter.

### 'Can I receive any financial help to cover the cost of caring for an incontinent child?'

In most areas of the country, there are local charities and trusts that offer subsidies and grants to families with children with special needs. These funds can help parents meet the cost of items like nappies and bedding for children who are incontinent (this can depend on the age of the child and whether the problem is persistent day and night). *A Guide to Grants for Individuals in Need* lists different regional and national charities that parents could approach for help (see 'Useful contacts' at the end of Chapter 8). Once again, a continence advisor will be able to inform you of the polices and guidelines of different trusts.

The Family Fund offers financial assistance to families with a child under 16 years of age. Each year families can make a new application. Money is provided for one-off items like washing machines and tumble dryers (see 'Useful contacts' at the end of this chapter).

The care component of the disability living allowance is a benefit that many families with children with autism are eligible for (a mobility component is also available). The level awarded depends on the amount of care the child needs (see Chapter 8 'Sources of Help' for more information).

*Toilet training tips*

- Stick to a routine. Sit your child on the potty/toilet at regular intervals when she is most likely to need to go. First thing in the morning, shortly after meals and before bed are prime times. Successful toilet training is mainly catching your child at the right moment so that you can reinforce her behaviour.

- Remind your child regularly to use the toilet. If you use timetables with him, build in specific visits to the bathroom. Some children give off visual cues which indicate their need to urinate or defecate. Your child may not associate these physical sensations with the appropriate behaviour. Prompting him to sit on the toilet when you see these signals helps him make the connection, and averts accidents.

- When teaching your child how to tell you when she needs to go to the toilet, use visual information to make the message clear e.g. a photo or symbol for the potty.

- Try to keep calm when accidents occur. However you feel, try to make it appear as though the incident is not a problem.

- Keep your tone of voice neutral. Try not to show your child that you disapprove of what has happened (on the other hand, do not sound cheerful or happy). A stock phrase (e.g. 'Oops, you're dirty/wet') helps you respond more consistently.

- Choose meaningful rewards and reinforcers for when your child performs well.

- If your child wets the bed, invest in a waterproof mattress protector/plastic sheet to minimise damage to bedding. Keep a clean set of sheets in your child's bedroom ready for use, and choose pyjamas and clothes that are easily washed and dried. Avoid giving your child drinks in the hour before they go to bed.

- Consider some aids. Soft trainer seats that fit on top of regular toilet seats can make children feel more secure, and do not feel cold to the touch. Splash guards can be attached to toilet seats to prevent water from splashing your child. Placing a stool next to the toilet encourages independence and makes your child feel more stable (providing a solid surface beneath her feet). Potty seats can be more reassuring than toilets in the early stages as they are child-sized (some have straps to secure the child), and sometimes attractively decorated. (For equipment details see 'Useful contacts' at the end of the chapter.)

- Ask for professional help if you cannot cope with toilet training on your own. You could also consider speaking to someone with specialist knowledge (Enuresis Resource and Information Centre (ERIC) has a helpline; see 'Useful contacts' at the end of this chapter.)

## Useful contacts
*For advice and information*

### 1. ERIC (Enuresis Resource and Information Centre)
*Various products available, including literature, bedding protection, bed pads, seat pads, and enuresis alarms. Parents can also take part in teleconferences with other parents (shared phone calls between three or more callers).*

34 Old School House
Britannia Road, Kingswood
Bristol BS15 8DB
*Tel:* 0117 9603060 (Helpline open 10am – 4pm, Monday – Friday)
*Fax:* 0117 9600401
*Email:* info@eric.org.com
*Website:* www.eric.org.uk

**2. The Continence Foundation**
307 Hatton Square
16 Baldwins Gardens
London EC1N 7RJ
*Tel:* 020 7404 6875
*Helpline:* 020 7831 9831 (Monday-Friday, 9.30am–4.30pm)
*Fax:* 020 7404 6876
*Email:* continence.foundation@dial.pipex.com
*Website:* www.continence-foundation.org.uk

## For financial assistance

*For an application form for the* **Family Fund Trust** *write to:*

The Family Fund Trust
PO Box 50
York YO1 2ZX

## Equipment and aids

*For advice on a whole range of products contact:*

**Disabled Living Foundation (DLF)**
*Helpline:* 0845 130 9177 (10am – 4pm, Monday – Friday)
*Tel text phone:* 020 7432 8009
*Email:* info@dlf.org.uk
*Website:* www.dlf.org.uk

*Please note that the authors are not recommending the following manufacturers, or endorsing the products listed. Contact details are provided as a starting point for parents interested in purchasing equipment. The authors would recommend contacting DLF for any equipment or technology enquiries.*

POTTY CHAIRS

**DCS Joncare Ltd.**
4 Radley Road Industrial Estate
Abingdon, Oxon OX14 3RY
*Tel:* 01235 523353
*Fax:* 01235 531019
*Email:* management@dcsjoncare.freeserve.co.uk
*Website:* www.dcsjoncare.com

*Winnie-the-Pooh (and other designs) novelty potty chairs are available from branches of* **Mothercare.**

CHILD TRAINER TOILET SEATS/PADDED RING REDUCERS/SOFT SPLASH GUARD

**Nottingham Rehab Supplies (Novara Group Ltd.)**
Novara House, Excelsior Road
Ashby Park, Ashby De La Zouch
Leicestershire LE65 1NG
*Tel:* 0870 6000197
*Fax:* 01530 419150
*Website:* www.nrs-uk.co.uk

ENURESIS ALARMS (BELL AND PAD ALARMS)

**Ferraris Medical Ltd.**
Ferraris House
Aden Road, Enfield
Middlesex EN3 7SE
*Tel:* 020 8805 9055
*Fax:* 020 8805 9065
*Email:* ferraris@globalnet.co.uk
*Website:* www.bedwetting.co.uk

*Prices range from £39.95 up to £75 (+ post and packaging and VAT).*

**Nottingham Rehab Supplies** *(as above)*

PAPER TOILET SEAT COVERS
Available from most high street chemists.

## Suggested reading

*The following books are good practical texts covering a range of behaviour issues, including toilet training:*

Carr J. (1980) *Helping your Handicapped Child.* London: Penguin.

Schopler E. (Ed.) (1995) *Parent Survival Manual: A Guide to Crisis Resolution in Autism and Related Developmental Disorders.* New York: Plenum Press.

Whitaker P. (2001) *Challenging Behaviour and Autism: Making Sense – Making Progress.* London: National Autistic Society.

*Staff at the National Autistic Society Helpline can inform parents about various articles on toilet training — Tel. 0870 600 8585 (lines open Monday — Friday 10am — 4pm, all calls will be charged at national rate).*

## SELF-INJURIOUS BEHAVIOUR

Of all the things that Freddy does, without a doubt the thing that upsets me most, is when he sets about hurting himself. I find it unbearable to watch him. If we could successfully reduce his head banging I know life in our family would improve 100 per cent.

Many children with autism do not self-injure. A number of the children who do will engage in milder forms of this behaviour that should pose no long-term health problems. However, for a minority of children, their self-injurious behaviour (SIB) can get to a stage where it is so severe that it has the potential to lead to serious injury. SIB can vary in form and intensity. Some children's behaviour is chronic, whilst others use SIB more sporadically. Types of SIB can range from the 'milder' behaviours of rubbing and scratching to the more severe behaviours of self-biting, head-banging, and eye-poking. The frequency with which SIB occurs often determines the impact it will have on the child's health, as minor behaviours like rubbing can still cause harm if carried out repeatedly. Understandably, of all the behaviours that parents find challenging and stressful, SIB is usually top of the list for most families.

So why do children self-injure? Most explanations focus on the function the SIB serves for the child: the pay-off received. Durand and Carr's (1985) work in this area has had a big influence on the way SIB is tackled. In their functional communication training (FCT), a hypothesis about the function of the behaviour is reached, and carers then work to replace the child's SIB with communication responses. These responses serve the same function for the child as the SIB originally did, and therefore remove the need for the old behaviour pattern. Improving the child's ability to make their needs known in acceptable ways is essential to this process.

The success of FCT depends on carers recognising the function the SIB serves to their child. It may be trial and error until the correct function is discovered. Sometimes this is complicated by a SIB serving several functions to a child at different times (e.g. head-banging may sometimes be used to stop demands being made, and at other times be used to attract attention). Durand and Crimmins (1988) noted that SIB is often a way for the child to gain attention or avoid demands. Donnellan *et al.* (1984) take this further and provide a number of possible messages the individual is giving through their SIB:

- I want it now.

- I don't understand.

- I don't want to do this.

- 'Stop' or 'No'.

- Leave me alone.

- It's all too much.

## Common concerns

*'Could my child's SIB be due to a physical cause?'*

> My child goes through periods of slapping the side of his head. It doesn't seem to be connected to what I am asking him to do. As a toddler he suffered badly with his ears. I often wonder if his behaviour could be because of an ear infection.

Illness, constipation, hunger and thirst have been suggested as possible factors in SIB. Some parents have connected ear infections with SIB (especially head-banging and slapping). As many children with autism are unable to communicate that they feel unwell, parents need to be more vigilant in picking up physical signs of illness. SIB may be your child's way of letting you know she is in pain or discomfort.

If you feel that this explanation could explain your child's SIB, check her ears for redness and inflammation which could indicate earache. Inflamed, sore gums or swelling may suggest toothache, which can also provoke head banging or slapping. Toothache may not have any other symptoms but most ear infections will also cause fever and runny eyes/noses as mucus builds up. Try offering traditional soothers such as a hot water bottle wrapped in a towel to reduce discomfort. A low dose of paracetamol could also help. If your child's SIB or physical symptoms continue, seek medical advice.

Other explanations have looked beyond SIB as an expression of pain or a form of communication. Instead it is considered whether this behaviour is due to a dysfunction of brain biochemistry or alternatively a manifestation of epilepsy (Attwood 1993, pp.52–53). In this later consideration, SIB could be attributed to partial seizures originating in the frontal lobes of the brain. This could account for a person's sudden, unpredictable and intense outbursts of SIB. Parents who feel this may explain their child's behaviour need to be referred on to a neurologist by their family doctor.

### 'How can I prevent my child from using SIB to gain attention?'

Many parents feel placed in a horrible situation when their child self-harms. Some parents have compared SIB with emotional blackmail – because of the situation it can be hard not to give in to demands. The following case involves a ten-year-old boy who regularly slapped his head or regurgitated his food to gain attention. Staff decided to begin daily one-to-one interaction sessions with David, to teach him action rhymes and other routines. An approach to responding to SIB was also agreed upon:

> Whenever the problem behaviour occurred, the adult working with him would immediately stop what she was doing and go limp – head down, face expressionless, shoulders and arms drooping. Only when David stopped the behaviour would she spring back to life. (Whitaker 2001, p.112)

This technique worked very well. David soon understood the connection between his SIB and the dramatic change in the adult he was working with. As David preferred the lively version for his companion he was motivated to use the new ways that he had been taught for gaining attention.

### 'I think my son's SIB is related to his self image.'

Daniel is very able. He attends mainstream school and copes very well. There was a difficult transition period when he first started. I found out that Daniel was being bullied at playtimes. Daniel was not physically hurt, but he was almost continually taunted by an older child. The taunts focused on how Daniel played football 'like a girl' and how nobody wanted him on their team. Sports is not Daniel's forte, and he has never been motivated to play football. However, he was very bothered by this child's comments. Around this time, I noticed red marks on David's arms. I saw him one day digging his fingernails into the soft flesh on his arm with a real force. I could also hear him talking to himself incessantly, 'I am rubbish, I am rubbish,' over and over again. This really distressed me.

I informed the teacher about what was happening and we decided to tackle the problem together. She spoke to the bully, and I started working with my son. We made a 'Pictures of Me' book together, covering all the things Dan is good at, as well as all the things he has problems with. To start with Daniel had nothing positive to say about his talents and needed lots of prompting. I had to remind him how good he is at maths and life drawing, and how kind he is to his little cousin. We quickly made progress, and our list of positives became longer than our negatives. I also taught Dan some positive affirmations to repeat out loud for when he feels low. 'I am rubbish' is now replaced with 'I am good at maths', 'I am generous', etc. Dan's self-injury has reduced significantly, and he is now able to stop himself when he does slip into his old pattern.

This parent was able to make a connection between her son's behaviour and his low self-esteem. Able children are more likely to have problems with negative self image than lower functioning children. By tackling both the bullying and the poor self image, Daniel's SIB was effectively managed. Strategies will be different depending on the child's level of ability. *Pictures of Me* is covered in Chapter 9 'Social ability'.

### 'My son throws himself against windows.'

Window banging prevents two potential risks. First and foremost there is the risk that children who window bang will seriously hurt themselves. Second, there is the risk of costly damage to the property. The next parent used a practical solution to overcome this behaviour in his son:

> There was a period last summer when Simon's window banging noticeably increased. Whereas previously Simon had used window banging on rare occasions during tantrums, he was now engaging in bouts every day whenever he was asked to do any self-care. The sight of Simon flinging himself against the window pane reduced me to tears. His behaviour had become a very successful way of avoiding reasonable demands. I decided to mount a layer of plexi-glass (strong sheets of plastic with the appearance of glass) in front of the glass windows in the lounge. As we have deep-set windows it was easy to attach the extra layer, with a fair gap remaining between the two panes. This adaptation has made a huge difference. When Simon bangs into the window I know he is not going to smash through the glass, which allows me to ignore his behaviour. This in turn has affected Simon's behaviour. He now realises that his old escape route from washing and dressing doesn't work.

This is a good example of the way in which physical adaptations and changing the environment can reduce undesirable behaviours in children with autism. The shatter-proof plastic kept Simon from seriously hurting himself, and enabled his dad to stop reinforcing the SIB. Alterations such as this one can be a useful starting point when introducing behavioural interventions. In this case, Simon was taught to dress himself through backward chaining, where his dad broke down a considerable task into manageable chunks. Simon's dad concentrated on reinforcing his son whenever he complied with self-care tasks.

> There is a multisensory room (a snoezelen) a short drive from our home. Every couple of weeks I take Thomas (who has Asperger syndrome) and his sister for a session. The staff are brilliant, they play with Anna whilst I am with Tom. Following our trip Thomas is noticeably calmer for the next couple of days, and he is able to tolerate things that would normally push all his buttons. We all leave floating on air and feeling completely blissed out.

Some studies have shown multisensory environments/snoezelens can reduce SIB behaviours when part of a programme. Multisensory rooms are designed to appeal to all the senses. Soft music, dimmed lights, slow-moving shapes projected on the walls, are typical features that help to desensitise your child through enjoyable experiences. The room has different sensory-based props and toys to encourage relaxation and learning through play.

Snoezelens are not a common feature in most communities, but some specialist schools and centres are equipped with one. It is possible to incorporate elements of the snoezelen philosophy into your home without huge expense (see suggestions in the section 'What could be changed at home?' in Chapter 6). Many specialist toy manufacturers produce a range of sensory orientated equipment (see 'Useful contacts' at the end of 'Play') but the cost can quickly escalate. Fibre optic lamps, lava lamps, therapy balls, etc., have become more commercially available and can be used to create a stimulating environment.

### 'My daughter pulls out her hair.'

> Miriam is a very attractive little girl, but you probably would not have said that if you met her a year ago. At that time, my grand-daughter had started pulling her hair whenever she was unoccupied, and was in danger of being bald before her sixth birthday. I think her behaviour was a combination of boredom and a dislike of being in unstructured situations. Even if left for a few minutes, I would return to find her with clumps of her beautiful gold hair in

her fists. I had read about another parent who put Vaseline in her child's hair so the child could not get a good enough grip to pull hair out. I tried this, but as Miriam had quite long hair she was still partly successful. Tying Miriam's hair into a bun on the top of her head, secured with a hairnet and lots of pins, worked better. On days when this was not enough I used to put her in an old-fashioned bathing cap with ties under the chin. This was not so tight as to cause discomfort, but it did prevent Miriam gaining access to her hair. When we went out in public, a baseball cap worked well.

A complementary approach would be to teach Miriam how to express her boredom appropriately in order to get her carer's attention. Providing Miriam with a toy when she is otherwise unoccupied and prompting her to play is an appropriate replacement for her SIB. Attaching a stress-ball key-ring to her belt ensures that Miriam always has something to entertain herself with when not in structured play. Ultimately, Miriam's carers have to recognise that she is not skilled at entertaining herself and needs regular activities within a highly structured environment.

### 'How can I minimise my child's injuries?'

My son knocks his knee against the ground, and this has got so bad that he is in danger of reaching bone. This behaviour is most common when change occurs in Omar's routine. My wife has fashioned some protective pads for Omar's knees, which are basically everyday sport knee-pads, extended to cover the shin. We also make sure that Omar plays in the lounge during times of change, where we have thick pile carpet.

My grandson bites his hand when anxious. This is most common when he is at school. The skin on his hand rarely has time to heal before he removes a fresh layer and we realised that he was in danger of being terribly scarred if he continued. His SIB is most intense when the class are asked to complete an exercise by the teacher. We arranged for the classroom assistant to approach Clive directly when instructions were being given. The assistant then broke down the demands into simple steps and prompted Clive to start the next as he completed the previous stage. This has made a big difference. Clive is now given pictorial symbols as well as verbal instructions and he is more independent as a result. If he does start hand-biting, the teacher puts a well fitting leather glove on his hand (it is secured under the wrist with ties rather like a boxing glove). Clive hates wearing this glove so it has proved an effective deterrent.

Both these approaches were effective as the function of the SIB was understood by carers. Omar could also benefit from simple daily timetables that prepared him for any changes to his normal routine.

### 'Could medication reduce my child's SIB?'

In some cases, behavioural approaches to SIB are combined with medication:

> When naltrexone was administered alone (no behavioural intervention), Mark's rate of SIB decreased by 50%. With the addition of the behavioural intervention (FCT), Mark's average rate of SIB was reduced again by approximately 50% during the classroom observations (with the teacher using her typical instructional methods), and self injury rarely occurred during FCT sessions. (Symons *et al.* 1998, p.287)

The theory behind the use of drugs suggests that children who repeatedly engage in SIB may be experiencing an increase in endogenous opiates. The SIB stimulates the production of endorphins resulting in analgesic and euphoric effects. The child is reinforced for their SIB by these opiates, which deaden pain and produce an addictive high. Therefore, opiate antagonists (i.e. drugs like naloxone and naltrexone) that block endogenous opiates, should prevent the child from receiving any benefit from SIB. Most, though not all, clinical trials support this claim. Different forms of SIB and the bodily location targeted, seem to result in different responses to treatment with medication.

Understandably many parents have reservations about resorting to medication to treat behavioural problems. However, in some cases, e.g. where the SIB does not respond to behavioural intervention or when the degree of self injury inflicted by a person is severe, more extreme measures may be justified. It has also been suggested that naltrexone could be useful in situations where there is minimal behavioural intervention (due to limitations in staff and parent time). Families should always seek the opinion of an expert in the field before deciding on a particular treatment. Commonly, families prefer to exhaust all other available options before considering medication.

## Tips for dealing with self-injurious behaviour

- Think about the function of your child's SIB before you try and tackle it. Consider the possible explanations provided at the start of this section if you are stuck.

- Keeping a behaviour diary and noting when SIB occurs will help you pinpoint relevant factors (when, where, with whom SIB occurs etc.). The behaviour chart (see Table 11.1 in Chapter 11) or sleep diary (Table 12.2 in Chapter 12) could be adapted for this purpose.

- SIB is less likely to occur when fewer demands are placed on your child. So try and balance demanding situations like mealtimes with more relaxing periods.

- Teaching your child how to communicate 'I want a break', could prevent information overload. Keep a note of what your child finds stressful, so that you can troubleshoot ahead.

- As always, techniques are more likely to be effective if they are put in place before your child's behaviour becomes an established habit. At the first signs of self-harm in your child, intervene. Your quick action may prevent an occasional problem from becoming an enduring behaviour.

- Don't give into your child's SIB! So much easier to say than to do. But if your child learns that SIB gets him what he wants, you could be faced with severe behaviour problems. If SIBs are maintained as long-term behaviour patterns they could seriously damage your child's health. So use whatever you need to in the short term (adaptations, protection equipment, etc.) to allow you to focus on replacing the SIB with desirable behaviours or improved communication.

## Suggested reading

Attwood T. (1993) *Why Does Chris Do That? Some Suggestions Regarding the Cause and Management of the Unusual Behaviour of Children and Adults with Autism and Asperger Syndrome.* London: The National Autistic Society.
*A compact, informative guide to more unusual behaviours.*

*Chapter 13*

# Therapies and approaches

## Common questions

The range of approaches used to help children with autism can be pretty bewildering, especially for parents having to make choices about what to do for their children. This chapter will look at how you can evaluate the research that supports a particular approach. It will also examine other factors which you need to consider before making up your mind, such as how costly certain approaches are, the impact they can have on your family life, and whether they are likely to benefit your child.

*'You say there are a range of approaches available, what are they?'*

There isn't space to list them all here, instead Part 6 provides an overview of the most widely used approaches. They roughly fall into five categories.

### EDUCATIONAL APPROACHES

This includes teaching strategies such as the TEACCH programme or the use of Picture Exchange Communication System (PECS) symbols. It also includes specific teaching tools, such as the use of computer programmes for teaching social or communication skills.

BEHAVIOURAL APPROACHES

The major behavioural approach used with children with autism is known as Applied Behaviour Analysis (ABA), which includes Lovaas programmes.

BIOMEDICAL APPROACHES

Such as gluten- and casein-free (GF/CF) diets, supplements such as DMG (Dimethylglycine) and Vitamin B6 and drugs such as anti-depressants or stimulants.

PSYCHOTHERAPEUTIC APPROACHES

This may mean traditional psychotherapy but can also include approaches based on a psychodynamic understanding of autism, such as the Son-Rise Programme.

THE 'ANYTHING ELSE THAT DOESN'T FALL INTO THESE CATEGORIES' CATEGORY!

Approaches such as dolphin therapy, riding therapy, aromatherapy. These could also be seen as non-traditional approaches.

Most of these approaches would not claim to have a massive effect in isolation. A medication may help reduce anxiety but the child will still need an appropriate education. Riding therapy may increase the child's self-confidence but it is important to build on this by developing skills in other areas.

It can seem as if every week something new is suggested. Often this is misleading; the press are fond of news stories about spectacular recoveries from autism involving an amazing new therapy. But when you look beneath the surface you discover that the new therapy is simply a variation on an approach that parents have been using for years, and that the 'recovery' amounts only to an improvement in some symptoms.

### 'What is best for my child?'

Only you can know that. A professional may be able to advise on strategies that are worth trying, but the proof of the pudding is in the eating and if you feel an approach isn't working you should trust your own judgement. Keeping a diary over time can help immensely in establishing whether your child's behaviour changes.

### 'How am I to know what will work?'

Examining existing research and finding other families for whom it has worked are probably the best ways to evaluate how effective an approach may be. The next section will look at how to evaluate research. Speaking to other families who have tried the approach is sensible because, even if an approach has shown spectacular results, it may not be right for your child if you do not have the time and resources to implement it in the same way. The families it has worked for may have plenty of money, large amounts of support from extended family or friends, and live in an area where services are readily accessible. If these things don't apply to you, then it's possible that the approach won't work either. Don't despair, there is plenty you can do to help your child, even if you don't plan on re-mortgaging your house to pay for therapies!

### 'Am I doing enough?'

The problem with the endless range of therapies on offer is that there will always be something else you can do for your child. It's always possible to think, 'Well, he's doing well at school and he has speech and language therapy and he's on a gluten- and casein-free diet but imagine how much better he might be if…'

For this reason, it can be a good idea to set yourself some limits both in terms of what you will spend and how much time you'll invest. You could also set some objectives for your child. If she is already making improvements, it may not be worth adding extra ingredients to the pot.

## Research

To find out whether an approach may be suitable for a child, parents often want to examine the research into it. Much debate revolves around different research methodologies. Moreover, when evaluating whether an approach is suitable, research is only one factor to take into account. Not all approaches to autism have a body of research backing them up and those that do are often questioned because of the research methods used. This section will look at how to ensure the research you read is of a good quality and therefore trustworthy.

The question most parents want answered when they look into an approach is 'Does it work?' Good research will identify not only whether an improvement occurs but also whether it is the approach used which causes this improvement. The following are some key questions to ask when reading research.

### Have the children receiving the approach actually improved?

This information needs to be clearly presented, it is possible for researchers to distort findings so that what appears to be a big improvement is actually only slight. It's important to be careful and read between the lines. Tables alone are not convincing unless you are confident that you know what the measurements of improvement used were.

### How much evidence did the researchers collect?

The point of carrying out a research study is to find out whether the approach being tested works on more than one child and to identify which children it is likely to work for. To this end it is vital that research is carried out on a large enough group of children to be convincing. There are no strict rules governing sample size, but it is safe to say that a study which looks at 30 children is more convincing than a study which looks at just three children (provided other elements of the study are well designed).

## HOW WAS THE SAMPLE SELECTED?

Were they picked randomly from a large group of children or carefully picked by the researchers? An approach is likely to get better results if it is only tested on the groups which the researchers believe are most likely to benefit.

## WHO COLLECTED THE EVIDENCE?

It's important to know this because some researchers have particular gains to make out of proving that one treatment works. Someone who runs a company selling equipment for sensory play would be biased if asked to research the use of sensory play for children with autism.

## DO THEY HAVE A BIAS?

Normally, as part of a research report, the researchers will tell the reader what their potential biases might be. For example, if they received funding from the government or from a large pharmaceutical company they would be expected to declare it. Again, research shouldn't be dismissed simply because the study was funded from a particular source. Instead, if you see a research study which you suspect may be biased because of who has funded it, it would be wise to look for other research from other sources and see if their findings are consistent.

## HOW ARE THE RESEARCHERS MEASURING THE CHANGES IN THE CHILDREN BEING TREATED?

In order to measure change effectively researchers need to know what point the child is starting from. To find this out they carry out what is known as baseline assessment. As children with autism often develop unevenly across a range of different skills, it is important that the assessment tool used is designed for children with autism. A study could start by just assessing the IQs of the children involved and then comparing their IQ at the end of the treatment. But this would not take into account important factors such as their behaviour, communication skills or social skills.

## Was the improvement due to the approach used?

Bear in mind that children will grow and develop new skills over time anyway. Research that examines slight improvements made after six months of a treatment may be looking at results that would have occurred anyway.

### IS THERE A CONTROL GROUP?

A control group is a group that doesn't receive the treatment being tested. This is so that the results of the treatment can be compared with the results that would be achieved without it.

### IS A PLACEBO USED?

A placebo is an alternative treatment which is thought unlikely to have an effect. This is given to the control group to give them the impression that they are also receiving treatment when they are not. In a trial of a drug, participants might be given sugar tablets or a solution of flour and water in place of the drug. For an educational or behavioural approach the researchers might spend one-to-one time with children from both the control and experiment groups, but only use the tested approach with one.

### ARE THE CONTROL GROUP AND THE TREATMENT GROUP USING THE APPROACH MATCHED?

It would be possible for researchers to divide a sample of children so that those children who are likely to get the best outcome are placed in the group receiving the approach being tested. To ensure that this doesn't happen, researchers try to match the control and experiment groups as closely as possible. They will try to ensure that both groups have a similar average age and level of functioning. This is known as a matched controlled study. In the research report it is usual to provide quite specific information about the differences between the two groups.

## Could wishful thinking have affected the results?

When children are picked to take part in a research study their own prejudices (or those of their parents) about the approach being tested could influence the results. They may unconsciously try to provide a positive or negative picture of how useful the approach is, depending on their own views on it.

### HAVE THE RESEARCHERS USED A DOUBLE-BLIND TECHNIQUE?

One way to make sure that this problem doesn't occur is for the participants (and their parents) not to know whether they fall in the control group or the group receiving the approach. This is known as a 'single-blind study'. However, it is also possible for the researcher to be biased and therefore to skew the results when measuring them. To avoid this it is vital that the researcher didn't know which patients were receiving which treatment. If this is done, the trial is called a 'double blind-trial'. This is probably the most reliable way to ensure that the expectations of neither the researchers nor the participants are able to affect the findings of a study.

## If an approach hasn't been researched is it still safe to use it?

This depends on the approach. There are some notable strategies which have never been shown to work in an independent research study, and yet many parents swear by them. Social stories, for instance, have never been independently evaluated. But it's fairly safe to assume that the risk involved in trying social stories is not that great. If they don't work, your child is not likely to be seriously damaged.

It's generally easy to guess which approaches are likely to carry the most risks even without research. Anything highly intensive or involving medical treatment should be viewed with caution. Having said that, no progress in autism would be made at all unless some parents and their children weren't prepared to take some of these risks.

The other problem that parents have aside from knowing whether an approach is trustworthy is finding out about it in the first place. The following are some suggestions on how to find out about approaches and how to ensure that your information is accurate.

## Finding out about approaches

### Newspapers, magazines, television and radio

One of the common features of 'flash in the pan' approaches which turn out not to have scientific validity, is that they are widely promoted in the press. This promotion may be genuine, the result of a well-meaning parent wanting to let other parents know what worked for them. Occasionally it is the result of an unscrupulous practitioner trying to drum up custom for a spurious approach.

This means that press stories are just as variable as research reports. Some accurately report breakthroughs in our understanding of autism and point to new approaches and therapies which may help. Some accurately report on the good progress that a number of children are making following a specific treatment plan. But many inaccurately give the impression that what has worked on one occasion will work for many others, even though there is no evidence for this. If you read about an approach that sounds useful, then the next question looks at how to find out more. Similar principles apply to items on the news or other television and radio programmes.

### The internet

The internet is an invaluable resource for finding out more about autism and possible approaches. Mailing lists and talkboards can also be helpful for parents wanting to find other parents facing similar dilemmas. However, the fact that the internet is so easy to access can be both good and bad. It's helpful that information is so accessible but this means that virtually anyone can post information about anything. Urban myths abound and it's hard to know the quality of any information you receive. For this reason it's worth reading what you find with caution. Starting off with a site you trust and then following the links from that is a good but not infallible way of ensuring that you only access high quality information. The new autism portal 'autismconnect' provides links to a wide range of sites which have all been reviewed for you already. Addresses for this and other resources are provided at the end of this section.

### Word of mouth

Understandably, parents who've had a good experience tend to want to go out and shout about it. Equally, those who've had a really bad experience will want to let people know. Either way, the information they give you may be helpful or it may be very subjective (i.e. based on personal experiences) and irrelevant to your circumstances. As with everything else, understanding their particular biases is vital.

### How do I find out more?

If you've only just heard of something but have no pointers as to where to go next, you have a few options. The first is to call the NAS Helpline, or, in the US the ASA Helpline (see 'Useful contacts' at the end of Chapter 1), to ask if they have heard of that particular approach or therapy. If they haven't, they will often try to find out more for you or put you in touch with someone else who might know more.

You can also try the internet; useful websites are given at the end of this chapter.

If you heard about an approach being offered locally, your library may be able to help. They keep comprehensive listings of businesses and service providers in their area.

For questions relating to interventions involving diet and nutrition, the organisation Allergy-induced Autism and the Autism Research Unit at the University of Sunderland are often able to help. However, if something has just received a lot of press attention, staff there can be very busy and you may have to wait a while for a response.

## Choosing a practitioner

As well as knowing how well a therapy has been researched, it is also important to have confidence in the abilities of the practitioners who carry out the therapy. The following are some basic guidelines on how to choose the professionals who work with your child and warning signs to alert you to what to avoid. These suggestions mainly apply to alternative therapies. In the case of some therapies such as the gluten- and casein-free diet, you are likely to be the practitioner, i.e. the person administering the diet. With educational interventions you are unlikely to have any choice about who actually works with your child, as the staff involved will be employed by your child's school.

*Things to look out for...*

- You should expect a good practitioner to explain the theory behind the therapy and what research has been conducted into it. They should also help you feel comfortable asking questions.

- They should tell you what qualifications they hold and what those qualifications mean. You could ask if there is a national body which represents people practising their form of therapy (such as the Society of Homeopaths or the British Association for Counselling and Psychotherapy). If there is, ask them if they are a member of this organisation and whether you can have the organisation's contact details.

- Look for someone who has experience both in their chosen field and also in treating children with autism. Just because someone has no experience of autism, it doesn't necessarily mean that they can't help you. After all, everyone has to start somewhere. Find out what they understand by the term autism. If they honestly don't know much about it they should be prepared to say so. They should still be happy to learn from you about your child's needs even if they have some experience of the condition. Children with autism can vary enormously.

- Ask if they can put you in touch with other parents who have used this approach so that you can get their views.

- Check if they plan to find out about your child's medical history. Will they approach your GP to let him or her know what they are doing? Do they mention whether the therapy is unsuitable for certain people or whether it carries any side-effects?

- They should be upfront about how much (if anything) it is going to cost. There should be an agreed arrangement about what you will pay if you decide to end the treatment halfway through.

- With some therapies your child may get worse before they get better. Does the practitioner warn you about this and offer any support or practical advice on handling it?

*Warning signs*

- Anyone promising a cure should be treated with suspicion. They shouldn't be entirely dismissed. Some effective therapies were initially perceived to be cures. On closer inspection it was found that their impact, though marked, was not actually a cure. At the moment there is no medically recognised 'cure' for autism.

- Anyone charging huge amounts for what they do should be treated with caution. Do not be afraid to ask for a break-down of services offered, so that you can understand exactly what your money will be spent on (e.g. how much is medication, how much are consultancy fees, what is the hourly wage of the practitioner, etc.). This puts you in a better position to decide if the financial cost of the service seems reasonable.

- Try and find out from people who have used this approach without success what the response was. Some practitioners will try to persuade people that if an approach doesn't work it's because they weren't trying hard enough. This puts parents in a no-win situation – unless they carry on with the approach until it works (which may never happen) they will always have the sneaking suspicion that they have failed their child. Practitioners should be honest enough to admit that some children will not benefit from their approach, no matter how hard you try.

- Some parents have been asked to sign disclaimers saying that they will not hold the practitioner responsible for any problems that may arise during or after the therapy. This should naturally ring alarm bells. There are only a handful of circumstances (e.g. if your child is about to undergo surgery) where this is a legitimate thing to do.

### Final considerations

- Don't feel you have to make up your mind straight away. Go away with as much information as you can and think about it. Ask friends, family and teachers what they think as well.

- You can call the National Autistic Society to find out more about an approach if you don't feel you have enough information. They have factsheets on those approaches which are known to be widely used. They also maintain a database of research into autism, which they can search for you.

- Do talk to other parents who have used the approach, if at all possible. Find out what their child was like both before and after the treatment. Ask what impact it had on the family as well. Were the siblings affected by it? Did it take up a lot of space at home? Did their child deteriorate before they improved? How severe was this?

- Think about practical issues as well. Are you going to have long journeys to and fro? Are there going to be problems administering it, and is the therapist aware of these? For example, if your child won't take tablets and the treatment is a course of tablets, has the therapist any suggestions for getting round this?

- Trust your instincts. If you feel that something really isn't right for your child, you are probably right.

## A final note on the therapies

Be realistic. This is the hardest part of all for most parents. It is common for some professionals to dismiss new treatments for autism by saying that 'parents are so desperate they'll try anything', implying that they are a sitting target for peddlers of mad and invalid approaches. However, this apparent dismissal of the lengths parents will go to help their children hides a very sad truth. There are some parents who frantically pursue a long-term cure, but at the cost of helping their child develop in the short term.

Examples of this are rare. The vast majority of parents accept that their child has autism and is likely always to have autism. They then concentrate on helping their child develop to their full potential. The parents who are most desperate tend to be those whose children are most severely affected. They may have anxieties about whether their child will ever be able to cope independently, whether she will ever speak or make friends or be able to attend a mainstream school. They can be very vulnerable to approaches which promise miraculous results, but ignore those strategies which could actually help their children right now.

The hardest thing about being realistic is that no one can really define what realistic means. At a basic level, it is probably safe to assume that if your child has autism he will probably always fall on the autistic spectrum. However, children can move within the spectrum and children are sometimes re-diagnosed as having high-functioning autism when they were originally diagnosed as low functioning.

If your child is nonverbal don't concentrate solely on helping her to speak. The development of a range of communication skills is far more important. In fact, attempts to teach supplementary communication skills, such as pointing, to children with autism may be of more benefit than teaching speech (Potter and Whittaker 2000). Augmentative communication aids such as the Picture Exchange Communication System, while offering an alternative to speech, also seem to promote the child's ability to develop it.

Try and distinguish between secondary symptoms and primary symptoms. It is far easier to treat secondary symptoms, such as anxiety, than primary symptoms, such as difficulties understanding the rules of social interaction. Of course, teaching a child about social rules and providing him with tools he can use to help him understand this, such as social stories, may lead to a reduction in levels of anxiety, so this is not a hard-and-fast rule.

Enjoy the things your child can do. If she is warm and affectionate or has a quirky sense of humour or a natural appreciation of music, then these are great qualities of which you can be justifiably proud. Looking at your child's achievements may also offset some of the pain felt when you see the things she can't do or has difficulty with.

Don't be led astray by people who do not know your child well. Extended family may think it's very sad that your child can't speak, but if they are doing just fine with picture symbols and are beginning to initiate contact with other children, these are far more useful skills than a handful of repeated words. Outsiders are not in a good position to judge your child's skills or deficits.

## Useful contacts

*For more information see* **Autism Connect** *at*

*www.autismconnect.org*

## Suggested reading

Binney C. (2001) 'Ploughing through the jungle of information.' *Communication 35* (2), 25–29.

## A closer look at some therapies

The following section examines in greater depth four of the therapies which are most widely used. The aim is not to tell you which approach to use, but to give an idea of what each approach may entail.

### Applied Behavioural Analysis

ABA is currently an enormously popular approach to improving the skills and adaptability of children with autism. The use of ABA with children with autism was pioneered in 1968 by Dr Ivor Lovaas, who set up the Young Autism Project at the University of California at Los Angeles (UCLA). His work came to be known as the UCLA model for Applied Behavioural Analysis (ABA). Although the Lovaas approach comes under the umbrella of ABA, other models of ABA have been designed for children with autism. Not all of these are as intensive or as closely designed as the Lovaas approach.

> It was great, the first day we started we just felt like we were back in control. (Mother of a four-year-old with autism and epilepsy)

'WHAT IS THE THEORY BEHIND ABA?'

> Applied Behavioral Analysis is a method by which behaviors are observed and measured, and new behaviors are taught. (Richman 2001 p.23)

Put simply, ABA focuses purely on the behavioural or functional aspects of autism. It aims to create improvements in children with autism by continually reinforcing appropriate behaviour. The analysis refers to the need to understand why a behaviour occurs. For example, if your child has a tendency to walk away from an activity very quickly, the first thing a therapist using ABA would want to do would be to seek to understand why. Is it because your child is easily frustrated when he finds something difficult?

Does she find it hard to know why she is doing an activity? Is he very easily distracted? The therapist would then develop a programme which would focus on increasing your child's ability to complete an activity.

> Progress was patchy and sometimes non-existent. It got a bit disheartening, but then Jonny hasn't got a smooth learning curve, some days he'd really get the hang of something quickly and it felt great.

If the therapist felt your child became easily frustrated, then she might start by spending time with him on simple activities that he can already do, offering lots of praise and reinforcement on completion. She would then gradually increase the complexity of the tasks offered, and offer ongoing reinforcement to keep the child engaged and happy during the task. If the child chose to wander away or started to fidget, he would be redirected to the task. If the reason for the behaviour was that he was easily distracted the programme might be slightly different. The child might be encouraged to work on through various distractions and be offered reinforcement whenever he managed this.

> Maia got very annoyed at being asked to repeat tasks to begin with. She'd look at us like we were from another planet. We originally used tickles to reinforce good behaviour but found that we were having to tickle her every other minute to keep her in the room and it was beginning to lose its effect. In the end we switched to giving her jelly tots, which was more effective and meant she wasn't so distracted from what she was meant to do. (Parent of a four-year-old with high functioning autism, private correspondence to the author 2001)

### 'HOW IS THIS DIFFERENT FROM JUST COMMON SENSE BEHAVIOUR THEORY?'

Essentially it isn't. ABA is based on a very long established theoretical understanding of behaviour. However, an ABA programme tends to be far more intensive and formal than anything a parent would normally do with their child. The original programme designed by Lovaas involved 40 hours of therapy a week. The programme is typically carefully designed with input from specialists in ABA.

> It was exhausting to begin with. We had to train lots of therapists and having them troop in and out of the house all day felt invasive and added to the stress. I didn't feel comfortable having them around for several months.

In recent years, while the Lovaas model for behavioural intervention is still used by many, a broader use of ABA has developed (Keenan *et al.* 2000). Some parents felt the long hours involved weren't right for their child so they reduced them. Others objected to the use of aversives (an anti-reinforcer such as saying 'No' loudly or spraying water mist in the child's face to actively discourage a behaviour) and preferred to use entirely positive reinforcement. It is worth saying that the programme used at UCLA no longer allows the use of aversives (Lovaas 2000). Schools have been set up which practise ABA in a classroom environment rather than at home.

> I did a lot of the therapy myself. I had to learn to enjoy being with my son and teaching him otherwise I would have gone mad.

'DOES LOVAAS "CURE" AUTISM?'

A 1987 study of the effectiveness of the UCLA programme carried out by Dr Lovaas made the claim that 47 per cent of participants made such gains in intelligence that they were able to enter mainstream school and appeared to function normally (Lovaas 1987). This caused considerable controversy as it was widely assumed that this meant that children had been 'cured' by the approach. This is not the case, and Lovaas never used the word 'cure', but the word 'recovery' was certainly used in the original research report and it is understandable that people found this misleading.

In fact the jury is still out on just how effective Lovaas is, although it is widely accepted that great results are achieved for some children (McEachin *et al.* 1993). It is still not known whether children who fall within a specific range on the autism spectrum are most likely to benefit (Ozonoff and Cathcart 1998). The optimum amount of therapy hours per week has still not been established/decided upon. The 1987 study mentioned previously used a 40-hours-per week programme. This certainly achieved good results but it is possible that fewer hours would have achieved the same progress. It is also possible that more benefits could have been achieved had the programme been available for longer.

'HOW MUCH DOES IT COST?'

Estimates of the cost for ABA vary and will depend on how intensive a treatment you choose. A full-time programme involving a team of therapists working with supervisors and consultants can cost between £30,000 and £40,000 per year. However, if you decide as parents to act as therapists for part of that time or don't want your child receiving 35–40 hours of therapy a week, the costs can be much lower. Some parents choose to train volunteers rather than employ staff. Views on this vary amongst ABA professionals. Some are concerned that the level of training given to volunteers isn't of a high enough standard and that the programmes offered suffer as a result. Others feel that it is often a necessity, as funding for ABA is hard to attract and paying therapists is beyond many parents' means.

'HOW DO I GET AN ABA PROGRAMME TOGETHER?'

In Britain a number of local education authorities have already funded Lovaas programmes. To get advice on funding it's worth contacting Parents for Early Intervention in Autistic Children (see 'Useful contacts').

In some cases where LEAs have not been supportive, parents have funded programmes either by themselves, or with help from charitable organisations. Some parents follow a less intensive programme with help from ABA professionals and act as therapists themselves.

Unfortunately, ABA provision is patchy and if you want to put a programme together what you will be able to offer your child may depend on where you live. Useful ABA contacts are available from the NAS Helpline, as well as from the ASA Helpline.

Jonny is now at a mainstream school. He still has support in some lessons but he's doing far better than we expected and more importantly he's happy and settled.

## Useful contacts:

### 1. PEACH (Parents for Early Intervention in Autistic Children)
School of Education
Brunel University
300 St Margaret's Road
Twickenham TW1 1PT
*Tel:* 020 8891 0121
*Website:* www.uk.peach.com

### 2. The Lovaas Institute for Early Intervention
2566 Overland Avenue, Suite 530
Los Angeles
CA 90064
USA
*Tel:* 310 840 5983
*Fax:* 310 840 5987
*Email:* info@lovaas.com
*Website:* www.lovaas.com

### 3. Institute for Applied Behavior Analysis (IABA)
5777 W. Century Blvd., Suite 675
Los Angeles
CA 90045
USA
*Tel:* 310 649 0499
*Fax:* 310 649 3109
*Website:* www.iaba.com

## Suggested reading

If you are only going to read one book on ABA, then this is the one to get hold of:

Keenan M., Kerr KP. and Dillenberger K. (2000) *Parents' Education as Autism Therapists: Applied Behavioural Analysis in Context.* London: Jessica Kingsley Publishers.

The research report mentioned earlier was:

Lovaas OI. (1987) 'Behavioural treatment and normal educational and intellectual functioning in young autistic children'. *Journal of Consulting and Clinical Psychology* 55 (1), 3–9. This can be obtained from the NAS.

Comments on this research were made in:

Schopler E., Short A. and Mesibov G. (1989) 'Relation of behavioural treatment to 'Normal functioning': Comment on Lovaas.' *Journal of Consulting and Child Psychology* 57 (1), 162–164.

Lovaas OI., Smith T. and McEachin J. (1989) 'Clarifying comments on the young autism study: reply to Schopler, Short and Mesibov'. *Journal of Consulting and Child Psychology* 57 (1), 165–167.

## Gluten-free and casein-free (GF/CF) diets

The suggestion that a gluten- and casein-free diet can help children with autism was first made in the 1970s by an American bio-chemist called Jak Panksepp (1979). The theory goes like this:

- Gluten is a protein present in wheat, rye, barley and oats.

- Casein is a protein present in all dairy products.

- Both these proteins are broken down in the gut into short chains of amino-acids known as peptides.

- These peptides are known as gluteomorphine and caseomorphine. This is because their structure is similar to morphine. They are also called opioid peptides for this reason. They are highly toxic.

- In most of us, these peptides are pushed through the gut and out of the system without doing any damage. Children with autism have what is known as a 'leaky gut' and these peptides are able to leak through the walls of the gut and into the bloodstream. They then travel round the body and even penetrate the blood–brain barrier, where they cause all sorts of damage. Eventually they are flushed out of the bloodstream by the kidneys and end up coming out in a child's urine.

The science behind this theory is extremely complex and research evidence to back it up is mainly based on small-scale studies. However, there is some evidence that some children with autism have increased levels of peptides in their urine, which suggests that peptides are not being flushed out of their system in the usual way.

In addition to problems digesting gluten and casein, children with autism also have difficulties with monosodium glutamate and aspartame. Monosodium glutamate (MSG) is a flavour enhancer found in many prepared foods and in foods such as prawn-cocktail flavour crisps. Aspartame is an artificial sweetener found commonly in foods such as soft drinks. Both these foods contain chemicals known as excitotoxins. Children with autism seem particularly sensitive to these additives. Advocates of the GF/CF diet also advise parents to remove MSG and aspartame.

'WHAT CAN WE DO ABOUT THIS?'

If the theory is correct, then removing gluten and casein from your child's diet can reduce some of their autistic behaviours. It will not 'cure' the autism but it can help.

Those advocating trying the GF/CF diet recommend that you approach your GP and ask for their support first of all. Even if they aren't supportive, it is important that they know what you are doing. The Autism Research Unit at the University of Sunderland can test urine for levels of peptides. Their contact details are at the end of this section. This test can be useful if you need evidence to convince your GP of the sense of what you are doing.

It may be worth asking to see a dietician for advice on ensuring that your child still receives a balanced diet.

When implementing the diet, take it slowly and eliminate things one at a time to see if the diet is working. This will also give your child time to adjust to the change. Clear guidance on how to implement the diet is available from the charity Allergy-induced Autism (AiA).

'WHAT WILL MY CHILD BE ABLE TO EAT?'

All meat, fish, fruit and vegetables should be fine (although some children have additional problems digesting certain fruits and vegetable). Some grains such as rice, buckwheat and maize are all right, and gluten-free flours can be bought. These are made from gluten-free grains. It is possible to get substitute dairy products made mainly from soya and occasionally from rice though not all are suitable.

Prepared foods can be a problem as many of them contain MSG and aspartame. And substances such as 'modified starch' (often derived from grain containing gluten) and 'whey protein' have a nasty tendency to creep into many prepared foods. Unfortunately MSG and aspartame are known by several different names and it can be hard knowing whether or not a food contains them. AiA provides information on acceptable foods and what to look out for. The book *Diet Intervention and Autism* is a useful guide to take with you when shopping.

Excellent substitutes for things like pasta, icecream and biscuits can be bought or made so that your child's diet does not need to change too dramatically. However, certain foods you will need to make from scratch or rule out altogether. Dairy-free cheese is sometimes not very nice, it is the casein in cheese which gives it a rubbery texture and also makes it melt. If you buy dairy-free cheese which does melt, it probably contains casein. Gluten-free chicken nuggets you'll need to make yourself.

Two books written specifically for parents following this diet are listed at the end of this section. Other gluten-free or dairy-free cookbooks are available. Vegan cookbooks will contain a lot of suitable recipes, as vegans eat no dairy products. Kosher cookbooks may also be useful as Jewish people can't eat dairy produce and meat at the same meal, so have lots of dessert recipes which don't use dairy produce. They also don't eat wheat during Passover and many of their festival recipes are gluten-free.

'HOW MUCH DOES IT COST?'

The urinary tests carried out by the Autism Research Unit cost around £50. However, it is possible that your GP will be prepared to pay for this. Allergy-induced Autism warn against spending money on expensive allergy tests which are largely irrelevant. If in doubt it is probably worth giving them a call.

Shop-bought gluten- and casein-free foods can be expensive. A loaf of gluten-free bread will cost £2–£3. If you make bread at home, however, it does not have to be much more expensive than normal bread, and if you have a sympathetic GP it is possible to get gluten-free foods on prescription.

Casein-free milks such as soya and rice milks can be expensive, but most supermarkets now stock an own brand soya milk which is not particularly different in price to cows' milk. Soya milk also lasts much longer than dairy milk and can be bought in bulk.

On the whole, homemade versions of typically gluten- and casein-free foods tend to be cheaper, tastier and more nutritious. However, if you really don't enjoy baking and cooking, it is important to take into account the cost of prepared products when considering the diet.

## Useful contacts

**1. *Allergy-induced Autism***
  11 Larklands
  Longthorpe
  Peterborough PE3 6LL
  *Tel:* 01733 331771
  *Website:* www.autismmedical.com

*If you send a stamped addressed envelope to the above address, AiA will send you an information pack. Annual membership of the organisation costs £10 and means you will be sent a useful introductory information booklet and a quarterly newsletter.*

**2. *Autism Research Unit***
  School of Health Sciences
  University of Sunderland
  Sunderland SR2 7EE UK
  *Tel:* 0191 510 8922
  *Fax:* 0191 567 0420
  *Website:* osiris.sunderland.ac.uk/autism/index.html

*3. For informaion on the GF / CF diet in North America contact the **Autism Network for Dietary Intervention***

    *www.autismndi.com*

*or go to*

    *www.gfcfdiet.com*

## Suggested reading

Lewis L. (1998) *Special Diets for Special Kids.* Arlington, TX: Future Horizons.

Le Breton M. (2001) *Diet Intervention and Autism* London: Jessica Kingsley Publishers.

## *The Son-Rise Programme for Special Children (Options)*

Barry and Samahria Kaufman, the parents of a son with autism, were the first to use Options Therapy in the 1970s. They didn't actually invent Options, but used the philosophy behind it to design a therapeutic package for their son who had been diagnosed with classic or Kanner-type autism The Kaufmans were convinced that they could help him to recover and were frustrated by the low expectations of existing services. They now train other families in using the Options approach with their children with autism and call this programme Son-Rise.

### 'HOW DOES IT WORK?'

Son-Rise makes the assumption that fear prevents a child with autism from communicating and interacting. It makes no claims about what causes autism; the fear the child experiences is seen as an effect, not a cause. The therapy aims to place the child in an environment which is non-threatening and where the therapists working with them are entirely on their side. It is heavily child-centred. The approach has no general aims, as each child needs to be helped in their own individual way. By offering the child an entirely non-judgmental, warm and accepting environment, the hope is that he will gradually recover from his fear and begin to accept the outside world.

We liked the sound of Son-Rise because it seemed non-judge-mental. They weren't telling us our son was defective, instead they just let him be who he was. (Parent of a six-year-old who did Options therapy for 18 months with her son)

### 'HOW EFFECTIVE IS IT?'

That's hard to say. The original success the Kaufmans had with their son was exceptional. Now an adult, he has recovered to the point where his original diagnosis is scarcely relevant. However, it is hard to assess how many more families have been helped by the training offered at the Options Institute. No independent trials have evaluated their work, and although some independent experts have commented favourably on their work (e.g. Jordan 1991), their approach remains controversial.

Barry Kaufman has written a number of books about the Options approach and the Son-Rise programme. In one he cites a number of successful case studies (Kaufman 1994). We don't know whether these case studies are representative of all the children who have been to the Institute or not.

We probably benefited more than he did. It was a relief to feel that we weren't to blame. That we had done the best we could and we were doing the best we could. I think our increased confidence certainly rubbed off on him though.

### 'SO WHAT DO THE THERAPISTS DO?'

First, an environment needs to be created which is free from anything that could trigger the child's anxiety. Toys and anything else the child enjoys exploring or playing with are allowed in the room. The Options Institute in America provides quite specific guidelines on how to set up a playroom for therapy.

In the time spent with the child, the therapist will follow the child's lead rather than try to direct his activities. They may offer praise or encouragement or just a commentary on what the child is doing, but no negative feedback. For most sessions the therapist will be observed by another therapist. The aim of this is to ensure that therapists stay focused on the child and don't slip into taking the lead and being directional.

The playroom environment is where all the therapy takes place initially. If the child starts to improve and show more confidence and awareness, other places will also be used.

'HOW MUCH DOES IT COST?'

The first step to setting up a Son-Rise programme is for the parents to receive training in the approach themselves. Currently the only permanent centre for training in the Son-Rise programme is in America, but Barry and Samahria Kaufman have run successful training workshops in the UK.

The programmes offered by the centre vary in length and you can go for a week or up to a month. To achieve full training they would advise parents to go out to the US for one month with their child. The child will then start to receive the therapy while the parents begin their training.

The total cost of the initial training (including flights) runs to tens of thousands of dollars.

Therapists will typically be volunteers who won't need payment, but who may need travel expenses. Recruiting volunteers can be costly, depending on your circumstances. Some parents end up having to advertise in local newspapers, others find a team through their own network of friends and family, or by asking at their church or temple.

> Having volunteers not turn up or not be able to continue because of the time commitment was frustrating. In all we used about thirty volunteers over 18 months. You have to add in how much of your time all this recruitment and interviewing and training takes up on top of actually doing the therapy with your child.

To ensure that the volunteers are trustworthy with it's advisable to have their criminal records checked. This is advisable even if you will be supervising the volunteers whenever they are with your child. The police will charge an administrative fee of around £10 for this but the processing can take several months.

Fitting out a playroom for your child is an additional expense. The actual cost depends on how much has already been done, i.e. whether you already have a quiet spare room decorated in soft muted tones.

Some parents have received help with the cost of this approach through charitable trusts, or their local authority. However, this is not funding that can be relied upon. Therefore it is important to be sure that you will be able to finance the whole package before embarking upon training or recruiting volunteers.

## Useful contacts

*The Option Institute and Fellowship*
2080 S. Undermountain Road
Sheffield
MA 01257
USA
*Tel:* 413 229 2100
*Email:* happiness@option.org

## Suggested reading

Kaufman, BN. (1994) *Son-Rise: The Miracle Continues.* California: H.J. Kramer Inc.

## *TEACCH*

TEACCH stands for **T**reatment and **E**ducation of **A**utistic and **R**elated **C**ommunication **H**andicapped **CH**ildren. The approach was first used in 1966 by the Department of Psychiatry of the School of Medicine at the University of North Carolina. The aim of TEACCH is to help people with autism lead effective, happy and productive lives. It uses a variety of approaches to achieve this and is not exclusive. A number of other approaches have been used successfully in conjunction with TEACCH.

'HOW DOES IT WORK?'

TEACCH works in many different ways and at many different levels. In North Carolina where it was pioneered, a complete range of services is offered across the lifespan, are all underpinned by the TEACCH philosophy. Fundamentally, TEACCH believes in a compromise between adaptation to meet the needs of the person with autism and helping the person to adapt their own skills and behaviour to better achieve. In addition to this, emphasis is placed upon the need to involve parents as co-therapists. Services using TEACCH should ensure good communication between parents and staff, as this is vital to ensuring continuity for people with autism.

Because people with autism vary so much, TEACCH places great importance on individual assessment. Regular re-assessment is also necessary to monitor progress and identify new targets.

The core of TEACCH is the need for structured teaching. Over the years it has been found that children with autism need structure in order to learn most effectively. The beauty of TEACCH is that structured teaching need not be confined to specially designed classrooms, elements of it can be incorporated into virtually any environment. For example, it is perfectly possible for a child in a mainstream school to have a clear visual timetable, and for a child in a special school to be given a desk which faces away from any distractions and thus allows her to concentrate more easily.

Like many approaches, TEACCH does not aspire to any one particular outcome but believes in helping all children with autism achieve their full potential.

'WHERE IS TEACCH AVAILABLE?'

TEACCH can be made available in a wide variety of settings. As already mentioned, in North Carolina it is offered in services designed to span the lifetime of a person with autism. In Britain complete packages of TEACCH-based care and support are not available, but the ideas behind this approach can still be incorporated into a variety of different settings. It is widely used in autism specific schools. The SPELL approach used in NAS schools and adult services has many similarities to the TEACCH approach. Elements of it are also offered in many generic special schools, mainstream schools and some special nursery schools. If you are interested in TEACCH for your child it is worth asking local schools whether they use it or whether they would consider using it. Many parents have successfully convinced schools that TEACCH training is worth investing in.

Some parents have had training in TEACCH themselves and have successfully implemented a home-based TEACCH programme.

### 'HOW MUCH DOES IT COST?'

If your child's school offers it, then it shouldn't cost you anything. If this is an approach you want for your child then you should push to have TEACCH-based provision written into Part 3 of her statement to ensure that she has a legal right to it.

Training courses will cost a few hundred pounds, but many of the simpler ideas behind TEACCH can be used without any training. Division TEACCH in the USA has a website which contains a wide range of practical information for parents.

### 'HOW MUCH RESEARCH HAS BEEN CONDUCTED INTO IT?'

As with many other approaches, although research has been done, very little of it is independent (i.e. carried out by people not working at Division TEACCH). Those studies which have been carried out have been largely positive and suggest that children with autism who have received a TEACCH-based education have higher than average attainments in adulthood (compared to other adults with autism) (Mesibov 1997).

## Useful contacts

In Britain training courses in TEACCH are available from the following:

1. *The Training Services Department of the National Autistic Society*
   Castle Heights
   4th Floor
   72 Maid Marian Way
   Nottingham NG1 6BJ
   *Tel:* 0115 911 3363
   *Fax:* 0115 911 3362

**2. Mr K. Lovett**
 Autism (Independent) UK
 199–200 Blandford Avenue
 Kettering
 Northamptonshire NN16 9AT
 *Tel:* 01536 523274
 *Website:* www.autismuk.com

In America information and training in TEACCH is available from:

**3. *Division TEACCH Administration and Research***
 CB7180
 310 Medical School Wing E
 The University of North Carolina
 Chapel Hill
 NC 27599–7180
 USA
 *Tel:* 919 966 2173
 *Website:* www.teacch.com

## Suggested reading

A factsheet on TEACCH is available from the Autism Helpline and is also on the NAS website. Details are given in Chapter 1 'Useful contacts'.

Mesibov G. (1997) 'TEACCH – A Statewide Programme for Serving People with Autism and their Families in North Carolina. *Communication.* (Spring 1997) pp.10–11
 *This article is available from the NAS.*

## Other therapies

The following are some approaches which have also attracted interest among parents.

### Auditory Integration Training (AIT)

AIT is used to help children with autism who have problems with extremely acute hearing – a condition known as hyperacusis. The approach involves listening to specially modified music in order to gradually increase their tolerance of sound. A number of centres now offer AIT around the UK. To find out more contact the Autism Helpline.

### Cranial osteopathy (or cranio-sacral therapy)

Cranial osteopathy involves the manipulation of the head to increase circulation and hopefully improve concentration, attention and eye contact. Anecdotally it seems many parents find this effective and would encourage others to try. However, there haven't been any independent studies evaluating how effective it is for children with autism. You can find local practitioners of cranial osteopathy by looking in your Yellow Pages phone book. The website of the General Osteopathy Council also contains a database of registered osteopaths. This is available at www.osteopathy.org.uk.

### Creative or art-based therapies

Music, art and drama therapies were not designed exclusively for children with autism. They seem to be most successful when used as complementary therapies which try to boost self-confidence, self-esteem and self-expression. They may be best used for addressing the secondary difficulties that autism creates, such as anxiety or depression. Contact details for these therapies are given on pages 279 and 280.

### Daily Life Therapy: Higashi

Daily Life Therapy was pioneered in Japan by the late Dr Kiyo Kitahara. It is an educational approach which aims to help children with autism develop closely to normal as possible. Much emphasis is placed upon physical education to reduce anxiety. There are schools using this approach in Japan, America and the UK. In Britain contact Honormead Schools Ltd. for more information, and in the US contact the Boston Higashi School. Contact details are given on pages 279 and 280.

## Dolphin therapy

Swimming with dolphins is a therapeutic activity offered to people with many different needs. There have been dramatic accounts of the improvements made by children with autism after dolphin therapy, but there has been little independent evaluation of its effectiveness. A range of centres now offer dolphin therapy in Portugal, Israel and Florida. For contacts call the Autism Helpline, or, in the US contact the ASA.

## Megavitamin therapy

The theory that high doses of certain vitamins could help children with autism was first put forward by Bernard Rimland in the 1960s. Again, small-scale studies have shown promising but not universally successful results, but these have not been widely replicated. For the latest information about this approach, contact the Autism Research Institute. Their contact details are:

**Autism Research Institute**
4182 Adams Avenue
San Diego
CA 92116
USA
Fax: 619 563–6840
Website: www.autism.com/ari

## Mifne

Mifne is a child-centred approach to assisting the development of children with autism. The Mifne Centre in Israel uses an approach called reciprocal play therapy. There are some similarities between this and the approach used by the Options Institute. Mifne is based in Israel but the organisation has a website at www.kinneret.co.il/mifne

## Secretin

Secretin is a hormone produced by the body to aid digestion. It has no medical uses but is used in some diagnostic tests. In 1998 a mother in America persuaded her doctor to administer the hormone to her son with autism. The child made dramatic improvements and the story created plenty of media attention. Small-scale studies have not shown secretin to be as effective as was once hoped. A large-scale pharmaceutical trial is ongoing and the results may not be known for some time. Again, the Autism Helpline, or ASA Helpline can provide the most up-to-date information. The Autism Research Unit website may also be helpful, their contact details are given on page 278.

The following organisations can be contacted for further information:

1. *Association of Professional Music Therapists (APMT)*
   Mrs Diana Asbridge
   26 Hamlyn Road
   Glastonbury
   Somerset
   BA6 8HT
   *Tel/Fax:* 01458 834919
   *Email:* APMToffice@aol.com
   *Website:* www.apmt.org

2. *British Association of Art Therapists*
   Mary Ward House
   5 Tavistock House
   London
   WC1N 9SN
   *Tel:* 020 7383 3774
   *Fax:* 020 7387 5513
   *Website:* www.baat.org.uk

3. *The British Association for Dramatherapists (BADTH)*
   41 Broomhouse Lane
   Hurlingham Park
   London
   SW6 3DP
   *Tel:* 020 7731 0161

4. *Honormead Schools Ltd.*
   The Grange
   Hospital Lane
   Mickleover
   Derby
   DE3 5DR

*Tel*: 01332 510951
*Email*: schooladmissions@honormead.btinternet.com

**5. *Society for Auditory Intervention Tecniques***
PO Box 4538
Salem
OR 97302
USA
*Website*: www.sait.org

**6. *The Cranial Academy***
Referrals
8202 Clearvista Parkway #9–D
Indianapolis
IN 46256
USA

*Send a 55¢ stamped addressed envelope to **The Cranial Academy** to find a cranial osteopath in the US. Include the city and state for the referral.*

**7. *Boston Higahsi School***
800 North Main Street
Randolph
MA 02368
USA
*Tel*: 781 961 0800
*Website*: www.bostonhigashi.org

**8. *The American Music Therapy Association***
8455 Colesville Road, Suite 1000
Silver Spring
MD 20910
USA
*Tel*: 301 589 3300
*Fax*: 301 589 5175
*Email*: info@musictherapy.org
*Website*: www.musictherapy.org

**9. *American Art Therapy Association***
1202 Allanson Road
Mundelein
IL 60060-3808
USA
*Tel*: 888 290 0878 or 847 566 4580
*Email*: arttherapy@ntr.net
*Website*: www.arttherapy.org

**10.** *National Association for Drama Therapy*
   733 15th Street, NW, Suite 330
   Washington
   DC 20005
   USA
   *Tel*: 202 966 7409
   *Fax*: 202 638 7895
   *Email*: nadt@danielgrp.com
   *Website*: www.nadt.org

## Suggested reading

Factsheets on many of these approaches can be found on the NAS
website at www.nas.org.uk/factsheet/index.html

National Autistic Society (2001) *Approaches to Autism*. London: NAS Publications.
   *This booklet gives brief introduction to far more approaches than those listed above, parents
   are then signposted on to organisations they can approach for further help.*

## Conclusion

There has not been space here to fully evaluate all of these approaches.
What should be apparent is that the range of approaches used is vast and
this section has still only covered a fraction of those which the author
has heard of. This may suggest one of the key difficulties in helping
children with autism, which is that the right approach may be the pro-
verbial needle in the haystack. Autism is probably caused by a variety of
factors and therefore it is right that a variety of approaches should be
used to treat it. But this doesn't make the parents' job any easier.

   The only advice that is relevant to those parents who are finding it
hard to help their children effectively is: don't be discouraged. If one
approach fails to make any difference, this doesn't tell you that your
child is beyond help. In fact, it doesn't tell you very much about your
child at all. It tells you a lot more about the approach being used.

   The number of approaches available and the intense media interest
in some of them may be misleading. Many children with autism enjoy
healthy and happy childhoods without receiving any autism-specific
therapies at all. Most children need a stable home life, secure attach-

ments and plenty of love and affection more than they need vitamin supplements, injections or 40 hours of one-to-one therapy a week.

# References

## References for chapter 1 – Explaining autism

Asperger H. (1944) '"Autistic pyschopathy" in childhood'. Translated and annotated by Uta Frith in Frith U. (ed.) (1991) *Autism and Asperger Syndrome*. Cambridge: Cambridge University Press.

Attwood T. (1998) *Asperger Syndrome: A Guide for Parents and Professionals*. London: Jessica Kingsley Publishers.

Barron J. and Barron S. (1992) *There's a Boy in Here*. New York: Simon & Schuster.

Elhers S. and Gillberg C. (1993) 'The epidemiology of Asperger syndrome. A total population study.' *Journal of Child Psychology and Psychiatry 34* (8), 327–1350.

Gillberg C. and Steffenburg S. (1986) 'Autism and autism like conditions in Swedish rural and urban areas: a population study.' *British Journal of Psychiatry 148*, 81–87.

Gillberg C., Grufman M., Persson E. and Themner U. (1986) 'Psychiatric disorders in mildly and severely mentally retarded urban children and adolescents: epidemiological aspects.' *British Journal of Psychiatry 149*, 68–74.

Gillberg C. and Rastam M. (1992) 'Do some cases of anorexia nervosa reflect underlying autistic-like conditions?' *Behavioural Neurology 5* (1), 27–32.

Gilpin RW. (ed.) (1993) *Laughing and Loving with Autism*. Texas: Future Horizons.

Goode S., Rutter M. and Howlin P. (1994) 'A twenty-five year follow-up of children with autism.' Paper presented at the 13th Biennial Meeting of the International Society for the Study of Behavioural Development, Amsterdam, The Netherlands.

Grandin T. (1995) *Thinking in Pictures: and Other Reports from my Life with Autism*. New York: Vintage.

Howlin P. (1997) *Autism: Preparing for Adulthood*. London: Routledge.

Howlin P. and Moore A. (1997) 'Diagnosis in autism: a survey of over 1200 patients in the UK.' *Autism: The International Journal of Research and Practice 1* (2), 135–162.

Jolliffe T., Lansdown R. and Robinson C. (1992) 'Autism: a personal account.' *Communication 26* (3), 12–19.

Kanner L. (1943) 'Autistic disturbances of affective contact'. In Donnellan AM. (ed.) (1985) *Classic Readings in Autism*. New York: Teachers College Press.

Kaufman BN. and Kaufman S. (1976) *To Love is to be Happy With*. London: Souvenir Press.

Kopp S. and Gillberg C. (1992) 'Girls with social deficits and learning problems: autism, atypical Asperger syndrome or a variant of these conditions.' *European Child and Adolescent Psychiatry 1* (2), 89–99.

Lord C. and Schopler E. (1985) 'Differences in sex ratios in autism as a function of measured intelligence.' *Journal of Autism and Developmental Disorders 15*, 185–193.

Lotter V. (1966) 'Epidemiology of autistic conditions in young children.' *Social Psychiatry 1* (1), 124–137.

Lovaas, OI. (1987) 'Behavioral treatment and normal educational and intellectual functioning in young autistic children.' *Journal of Consulting and Clinical Psychology 55*, 3–9.

Newson E. (1988) 'PDA syndrome: diagnostic criteria and relationship to autism and other developmental coding disorders.' Available from the National Autistic Society Information Centre.

Park CC. (1990) *The Siege.* London: Little, Brown.

Skuse DH. (2000) 'Imprinting, the X-chromosome, and the male brain: explaining sex differences in liability to autism.' *Pediatric Research 47* (1), 9–16.

Tantam D. (1995*) A Mind of One's Own: A Guide to the Special Difficulties and Needs of the More Able Person with Autism or Asperger Syndrome.* London: NAS.

Taylor B., Miller E., Farrington CP., Petropoulos M., Favot-Mayaud I., Li J. and Waight P. (1999) 'Autism and measles, mumps and rubella vaccine: no epidemiological evidence for a causal association.' *The Lancet 353*, 2026–29.

Turk J. and Zwink L. (1993) 'Autism and the Fragile X syndrome.' *Communication 27* (1), 10–11.

Williams D. (1993) *Nobody Nowhere.* London: Corgi Books.

Wing L. (1995) *Autistic Spectrum Disorders: An Aid to Diagnosis.* London: The National Autistic Society.

Wing L. (1996) *The Autistic Spectrum.* London: Constable.

Wing L. and Gould J. (1979) 'Severe impairments of social interaction and associated abnormalities in children: epidemiology and classification.' *Journal of Autism and Developmental Disorders 9*, 11–29.

Wolff S. (1995) *Loners: The Life Path of Unusual Children.* London: Routledge.

## References for chapter 2 – What causes autism?

Attwood T. (1998) *Asperger Syndrome: A Guide for Parents and Professionals.* London: Jessica Kingsley Publishers.

Baron-Cohen S. (1995) *Mindblindness: An Essay on Autism and Theory of Mind.* Cambridge: MIT Press.

Bettelheim B. (1956) 'Childhood schizophrenia as a reaction to extreme situations.' *Journal of Orthopsychiatry 26*, 507–18.

Bolton P. *et al.* (1994) 'A case-control family history study of autism.' *Journal of Child Psychology and Psychiatry 35*, 877–900.

Cantwell DP., Baker L. and Rutter M. (1979) 'Families of autistic and dysphasic children I: family life and interaction patterns.' *Archives of General Psychiatry 36*, 682–688.

Chess S., Korn SJ. and Fernandez PB. (1971) *Psychiatric Disorders of Children with Congenital Rubella.* New York: Brunner/Mazel.

Deb S. *et al.* (1997) 'A comparison of obstetric and neonatal complications between children with autistic disorder and their siblings.' *Journal of Intellectual Disability Research 41*(1), 81–86.

Frith U. (1989) *Autism: explaining the enigma.* Oxford: Blackwell.

Folstein S. and Rutter M. (1977) 'Infantile autism: a genetic study of 21 twin pairs.' *Journal of Child Psychology and Psychiatry 18*, 297–321.

Gillberg C. and Rastam M. (1992) 'Do some cases of anorexia nervosa reflect underlying autistic-like conditions?' *Behavioural Neurology 5* (1), 27–32.

Green WH., Campbell M., Hardesty AS., Grega D. M., Padron-Gaynor M., Shell J., and Erlenmeyer-Kimling L. (1984) 'A comparison of schizophrenic and autistic children.' *Journal of the American Academy of Child and Adolescent Psychiatry 23*, 399–409.

Happé F. (1994) *Autism: An Introduction to Psychological Theory.* London: UCL Press.

Kanner L. (1943) 'Autistic disturbances of affective contact'. In Donnellan A. M. (ed.) (1985) *Classic Readings in Autism.* New York: Teachers College Press.

LeCouteur A. *et al.* (1996) 'A broader phenotype of autism: the clinical spectrum in twins.' *Journal of Child Psychology and Psychiatry 37*, 785–801.

Nelson KB. *et al.* (2001) 'Neuropeptides and neurotrophins in neonatal blood of children with autism or mental retardation.' *Annals of Neurology 49*, 597–606.

Ozonoff S., Pennington BF. and Rogers SJ. (1991) 'Executive function deficits in high functioning autistic children: relationship to theory of mind.' *Journal of Child Psychology and Psychiatry 32*, 1081–106.

Piven J. and Folstein SE. (1994) 'The genetics of autism.' In Bauman M. and Kemper T. (eds.) *The Neurobiology of Autism.* Baltimore: Johns Hopkins University Press.

Rimland B. (1964) 'The etiology of infantile autism: the problem of biological versus psychological causation.' In Rimland B. *Infantile Autism.* New York: Appleton-Century-Crofts.

Rutter M. and Folstein S. (1977) 'Genetic influences and infantile autism.' *Nature 265*, 726–728.

Rutter M. *et al.* (1993) 'Autism: syndrome definition and possible genetic mechanisms.' In Plomin R. and McClearn GE. (eds.) *Nature, Nurture and Psychology.* Washington DC: American Psychological Association.

Steffenburg S. (1991) 'Neuropsychiatric assessment of children with autism: a population based study.' *Developmental Medicine and Child Neurology 33,* 495–511.

Taylor B., Miller E., Farrington CP., Petropoulos M., Favot-Mayaud I., Li J. and Waight P. (1999) 'Autism and measles, mumps, and rubella vaccine: no epidemiological evidence for a causal association.' *The Lancet 353,* 2026–29.

Wakefield AJ., Murch SH., Antony A. *et al.* (1998) 'Ileal-lymphoid-nodular hyperplasia, non-specific colitis, and pervasive developmental disorder in children'. *The Lancet 351, 637–41.*

# References for chapter 3 – A concise history of autism

Asperger H. (1944) '"Autistic pyschopathy" in childhood'. Translated and annotated by Uta Frith in Frith U. (ed.) (1991) *Autism and Asperger Syndrome.* Cambridge: Cambridge University Press.

Frith U. (1989) *Autism: Explaining the Enigma.* Oxford: Blackwell.

# References for chapter 4 – Diagnosis

American Psychiatric Association (1994) *Diagnostic and Statistical Manual of Mental Disorders.* Fourth edition. Washington, DC: APA.

Baron-Cohen S., Coc A., Baird G., Swettenham J., Nightingale N., Morgan K., Drew A. and Charman T. (1996). 'Psychological markers in the detection of autism in infancy in a large population.' *British Journal of Psychiatry 168,* 158–163.

Elhers S. and Gillberg C. (1993) 'The epidemiology of Asperger syndrome.' *Journal of Child Psychology and Psychiatry 34,* 1327–50.

Filipek PA. *et al.* (1999) 'The screening and diagnosis of autistic spectrum disorders.' *Journal of Autism and Developmental Disorders 29,* 439–484.

Glascoe FP. (1997) 'Parents' concerns about children's development: prescreening technique or screening test?' *Pediatrics 99* (4), 522–528.

Gould J. (1998) 'The Diagnostic Interview for Social and Communication Disorders.' *Communication,* Winter 1998.

Howlin P. and Moore A. (1997) 'Diagnosis in autism: a survey of over 1200 patients in the UK.' *Autism: The International Journal of Research and Practice 1* (2), 135–162.

Jordan R. (1999) *Autistic Spectrum Disorders: An Introductory Handbook for Practitioners.* London: David Fulton Publishers.

Rankin K. (2000) *Growing up Severely Autistic: They Call me Gabriel.* London: Jessica Kingsley Publishers.

Sainsbury C. (2000) *Martian in the Playground: Understanding the Schoolchild with Asperger's Syndrome.* Bristol: Lucky Duck Publishing Ltd.

World Health Organisation. (1992) *International Classification of Diseases.* Tenth edition. WHO: Geneva.

## References for chapter 5 – Accepting the news

DeMyer MK. and Goldberg P. (1979) 'Family needs of the autistic adolescent.' In Schopler E. and Mesibov GB. (eds.) (1983) *Autism in Adolescents and Adults.* New York: Plenum Press.

Fullwood D. and Cronin P. (1989) *Facing the Crowd: Managing Other People's Insensitivities to your Disabled Child.* Melbourne: Royal Victorian Institute for the Blind. Third Printing.

Gray DE. (1993) 'Perceptions of stigma: the parents of autistic children.' *Sociology of Health and Illness 15* (1), 102–120.

Liwag ME. (1989) 'Mothers and fathers of autistic children: an exploratory study of family stress and coping.' *Philippine Journal of Psychology 22,* 3–16.

Meyer DJ. (1986) 'Fathers of handicapped children.' In Fewell RR. and Vadasy PF. (eds.) *Families of Handicapped Children.* Austin, TX: Pro-Ed Inc.

Midence K. and O'Neill M. (1999) 'The experience of parents in the diagnosis of autism: a pilot study.' *Autism: The International Journal of Research and Practice 3* (3), 273–285.

Namak R. (1990) 'Life with Shula: beyond a personal context.' *Journal of Practical Approaches to Developmental Handicap 14* (2),10–13.

Peeters T. (1997) *Autism: From the Theoretical Understanding to Educational Intervention.* England: Whurr Publishers.

Randall P. and Parker J. (1999) *Supporting the Families of Children with Autism.* Chichester: John Wiley & Sons.

Rankin K. (2000) *Growing up Severely Autistic: They Call me Gabriel.* London: Jessica Kingsley Publishers.

Sinclair J. (1993) 'Don't mourn for us.' *Our Voice – The Autism Network International Newsletter 1* (3). www.members.xoom.com/JimSinclair/dontmourn.htm

## References for chapter 6 – Moving forward after diagnosis

Frost LA. and Bondy AS. (1994) *PECS. The Picture Exchange Communication System. Training manual.* Cherry Hill, NJ: Pyramid Educational Consultants Inc.

Grandin T. and Scariano M. (1986) *Emergence: Labelled Autistic.* California: Arena Press.

Moon P. (1996) 'In the mood: can relaxation techniques help create a better learning environment for autistic pupils?' *Special Children,* Nov/Dec issue, 31–33.

Savner JL. and Smith Myles B. (2000*) Making Visual Supports Work in the Home and Community: Strategies for Individuals with Autism and Asperger Syndrome.* Kansas: Autism Asperger Publishing Co.

## References for chapter 7 – Siblings

Folstein SE. and Rutter ML. (1987) 'Autism. Familial aggregation and genetic implications.' In Schopler E. and Mesibov GB. (eds.) *Neurobiological Issues in Autism.* New York: Plenum Press.

Harris SL. (1994) *Siblings of Children with Autism: A Guide for Families.* Bethesda, USA: Woodbine House.

Howlin P. (1988) *Children with Autism and Asperger Syndrome: A Guide for Practitioners and Carers.* Chichester: John Wiley & Sons.

Mates TE. (1990) 'Siblings of autistic children: their adjustment and performance at home and in school.' *Journal of Autism and Developmental Disorders 20* (4), 545–553.

Rodrigue JR., Geffken GR. and Morgan SB. (1993). 'Perceived competence and behavioral adjustment of siblings of children with autism.' *Journal of Autism and Developmental Disorders 23* (4), 665–674.

## References for chapter 8 – Sources of Help

Dobson B. and Middleton S. (1998) *Paying to Care: The Cost of Childood Disability.* York: York Publishing Services.

Harland S. and griffiths D. (2000) *A Guide to Grants for Individuals in Need.* London: Directory of Social Change.

Wright J. and Ruebain D. (2000) *Taking Action! Your Child's Right to Special Education.* Birmingham: Questors Publishing Company.

## References for chapter 9 – Education

Department for Education and Employment (1994) *Code of Practice on the Identification and Assessment of Special Educational Needs.* London: HMSO.

Department for Education and Employment (1999) Circular 10/99. *Social Inclusion: Pupil Support – the Secretary of State's Guidance on Pupil Attendance, Behaviour, Exclusion and Re-integration.* London: DfEE Publications.

Gabbitas Educational Consultants (2000) *The Gabbitas Guide to Schools for Special Needs.* London: Kogan Page.

Jordan R. (1999) *Autistic Spectrum Disorders: An Introductory Handbook for Practitioners.* London: David Fulton Publishers.

Sullivan K. (2000) *The Anti Bullying Handbook.* Melbourne: Oxford University Press.

## References for chapter 10 – Social ability

Akerley MS. (1984) 'Developmental changes in families with autistic children.' In Schopler E. and Mesibov GB. (eds.) *The Effects of Autism on the Family.* New York: Plenum Press.

Attwood T. (1998) *Asperger Syndrome: A Guide for Parents and Professionals.* London: Jessica Kingsley Publishers.

Baron-Cohen S., Leslie AM. and Frith U. (1985) 'Does the autistic child have a "theory of mind?"' *Cognition 21,* 27–43.

Briggs R. (1977) *Fungus the Bogeyman.* London: Hamish Hamilton.

Gerland G. (1997) *A Real Person: Life on the Outside.* London: Souvenir Press.

Gerland G. (2000) *Finding Out about Asperger Syndrome, High Functioning Autism and PDD.* London: Jessica Kingsley Publishers.

Gray C. (1994) *Comic Strip Conversations.* Arlington: Future Horizons.

Gray C. (1994) *The New Social Storybook.* Arlington: Future Horizons.

Gray C. (1997) 'Pictures of me.' In *Communication,* Winter 1997, 22–25.

Howlin P., Baron-Cohen S. and Hadwin J. (1999) *Teaching Children with Autism to Mind-read: A Practical Guide.* Chichester: John Wiley & Sons.

Ives M. (1999) *What is Asperger Syndrome, and How Will it Affect Me?* London: The National Autistic Society. *For young readers with autistic spectrum disorders. (Suitable for nine- to thirteen-year-olds).*

Laushey KM. and Heflin LJ. (2000) 'Enhancing social skills of kindergarten children with autism through the training of multiple peers as tutors.' *Journal of Autism and Developmental Disorders 30* (3), 183–193.

Newson E. (2000) 'Using humour to enable flexibility and social empathy.' In Powell S. (ed.) *Helping Children with Autism to Learn.* London: David Fulton Publishers.

Peeters T. (1997) *Autism: From the Theoretical Understanding to Educational Intervention.* England: Whurr Publishers.

Rinaldi W. (1992) *The Social Use of Language Programme.* Berks: NFER-Nelson.

Roeyers H. (1996) 'The influence of nonhandicapped peers on the social interaction of children with a pervasive developmental disorder.' *Journal of Autism and Developmental Disorders 26* (3), 303–320.

Spence S. (1995) *Social Skills Training: Enhancing Social Competence with Children and Adolescents.* Horsham: NFER-Nelson.

Vermeulen P. (2000) *I am Special: Introducing Children and Young People to their Autistic Spectrum Disorder.* London: Jessica Kingsley Publishers.

Volkmar FR. and Cohen DJ. (1982) 'A hierarchical analysis of patterns of noncompliance in autistic and behavior-disturbed children.' *Journal of Autism and Developmental Disorders 12*, 35–42.

Williams TI. (1989) 'A social skills group for autistic children.' *Journal of Autism and Developmental Disorders 19* (1), 143–155.

Williams MS. and Shellenberger S. (1994) *'How Does Your Engine Run?' A Leader's Guide to the Alert Programme for Self Regulation.* Alburquerque: Therapy Works Inc.

## References for chapter 11 – Understanding behaviour

Carr J. (1980) *Helping your Handicapped Child.* London: Penguin.

Carr J. (1998) 'Children with learning disabilities.' In Howlin P. *Behavioural Approaches to Problems in Childhood.* London: MacKeith Press.

Fouse B. and Wheeler M. (1997) *A Treasure Chest of Behavioral Strategies for Individuals with Autism.* Arlington: Future Horizons.

Howlin P. (ed.) (1998) *Behavioural Approaches to Problems in Childhood.* London: MacKeith Press.

Keenan M., Kerr KP. and Dillenburger K. (2000) *Parents' Education as Autism Therapists: Applied Behaviour Analysis in Context.* London: Jessica Kingsley Publishers.

Park C. (1986) 'Social growth in autism: a parent's perspective.' In Schopler E. and Mesibov G. (eds) *Social Behaviour and Autism.* New York: Plenum Press.

Peeters T. (1997) *Autism: From the Theoretical Understanding to Educational Intervention.* England: Whurr Publishers.

Premack D. (1959) 'Toward empirical behavior laws: 1. Positive reinforcement.' *Psychological Review 66*, 219–233.

Schopler E. (ed) (1995) *Parent Survival Manual: A Guide to Crisis Resolution in Autism and Related Developmental Disorders.* New York: Plenum Press.

# References for chapter 12 – Responding to behaviour

Aarons M. and Gittens T. (1999) *The Handbook of Autism: A Guide for Parents and Professionals*. Second edition. London: Routledge.

Attwood T. (1993) *Why does Chris do That?: Some Suggestions Regarding the Cause and Management of the Unusual Behaviour of Children and Adults with Autism and Asperger Syndrome*. London: The National Autistic Society.

Barron J. and Barron S. (1992) *There's a Boy in Here*. New York: Simon & Schuster.

Carr J. (1980) *Helping your Handicapped Child*. London: Penguin.

Chakravarty I. (1996) 'Neel now.' Delhi: *Autism Network 3* (2), 6.

Donnellan AM., Mirenda PL., Mesaros RA. and Fassbender LL. (1984) 'Analyzing the communicative functions of aberrant behavior.' *Journal of the Association for Persons with Severe Handicaps 9* (3), 201–212.

Durand VM. and Carr J. (1985) 'Functional Communication and Training.' *Journal of Applied Behavioural Analysis 18*, 111–126.

Durand VM. and Crimmins DB. (1988) 'Identifying the variables maintaining self-injurious behavior.' *Journal of Autism and Developmental Disorders 18* (1), 99–117.

Ford A. and Ford P. (1986) 'A little potty.' *Communication 20* (3), 1–2. With kind permission from the National Autistic Society.

Greenspan SI. (1995) *The Challenging Child: Understanding, Raising, and Enjoying the Five 'Difficult' Types of Children*. Reading, MA: Perseus Books.

Howlin P. and Rutter M. (1987) *Treatment of Autistic Children*. Chichester: John Wiley & Sons.

Peeters T. (1997) *Autism: From the Theoretical Understanding to Educational Intervention*. England: Whurr Publishers.

Quine L. (1997) *Solving Children's Sleep Problems: A Step-by-Step Guide for Parents*. Huntingdon, Cambs: Beckett Karlson Publishing.

Schopler E. (ed) (1995) *Parent Survival Manual: A Guide to Crisis Resolution in Autism and Related Developmental Disorders*. New York: Plenum Press.

Symons FJ., Fox ND. and Thompson T. (1998) 'Functional communication training and naltrexone treatment of self-injurious behaviour: an experimental case report.' *Journal of Applied Research in Intellectual Disabilities 11* (3), 273–292.

Whitaker P. (2001) *Challenging Behaviour and Autism: Making Sense – Making Progress*. London: The National Autistic Society.

Williams D. (1994) *Somebody Somewhere*. London: Doubleday.

# References for chapter 13 – Therapies and approaches

Jordan R. (1991) 'The Options approach: an observer-participants account.' (unpublished – available from the National Autistic Society)

Kaufman BN. (1994) *Son-Rise: The Miracle Continues.* California: H.J. Kramer Inc.

Keenan M., Kerr KP. and Dillenberger K. (2000) *Parents' Education as Autism Therapists: Applied Behavioural Analysis in Context.* London: Jessica Kingsley Publishers.

Lovaas OI. (1987) 'Behavioral treatment and normal educational and intellectual functioning in young autistic children.' *Journal of Consulting and Clinical Psychology 55* (1), 3–9.

Lovaas OI., Smith T. and McEachin J. (1989) 'Clarifying comments on the young autism study: reply to Schopler, Short and Mesibov.' *Journal of Consulting and Child Psychology* 57(1), 165–167

Lovaas I. (2000) 'Clarifying comments on the UCLA Young Autism Project.' USA: FEAT. (available online at www.feat.org/lovaas.htm)

McEachin J., Smith T. and Lovaas OI. (1993) 'Long-term outcome for children with autism who received early intensive behavioral treatment.' *American Journal on Mental Retardation 97* (4), 359–372.

Mesibov G. (1997) 'Formal and informal measures on the effectiveness of the TEACCH programme.' *Autism 1* (1), 25–35.

Ozonoff S. and Cathcart K. (1998) 'Effectiveness of a home programme intervention for young children with autism.' *Journal of Autism and Developmental Disorders 28* (1), 25–32.

Panksepp J. (1979) 'A neurochemical theory of autism.' *Trends in Neurosciences 1979*, 175–177.

Potter C. and Whittaker C. (2000) 'A minimal speech approach for children with autism with little or no speech.' *Autism-Asperger's Digest,* Nov-Dec, no. 4–6.

Richman S. (2001) *Raising your Child with Autism.* London: Jessica Kingsley Publishers.

Schopler E., Short A., and Mesibov G.(1989) 'Relation of behavioral treatment to 'Normal Functioning': comment on Lovaas.' *Journal of Consulting and Child Psychology 57* (1), 162–164.

# Index

ABA *see* Applied Behavioural Analysis
ABC approach to behaviour 157, 160
abstract concepts, problems with 19-20
active but odd children 18-19, 208
AD/HD 33
additives, sensitivity to 267, 268
adulthood, planning for 120
advocacy 127
affection, in autistic children 33-4
alarms, for toilet training 230-1, 235
alert programme, for self-regulation 137-8, 152
allergies *see* casein; gluten
aloof children 18, 207
anxiety *see* fear
appeals
  against educational statements 118
  *see also* complaints; legal rights
Applied Behavioural Analysis 261-6
art-based therapies 277, 279, 280
aspartame, sensitivity to 267, 268
Asperger, Hans 46
Asperger syndrome 29
  contacts 35
  and DAMP 32
  diagnostic criteria 51-2
  gender bias 27
  incidence 26
assessment *see* diagnosis; statements of special educational needs
Attention Deficit Hyperactivity Disorder 33
attention deficits *see* DAMP
attention seeking, and self-injurious behaviour 238
atypical autism 30
Auditory Integration Training 276, 279
The Autism Society of America 35
autism specific schools 109
autistic spectrum disorders
  causes
    cognitive deficits 41-3
    environmental 38-40
    genetic 26-7, 40-1
    organic 41
    psychological 33, 37
  characteristics 13-14, 41-3
    *see also* communication impairments; imagination; social interaction
  contacts 34-5, 63
  diagnosis *see* diagnosis
  gender bias 26-7
  history 45-7
  incidence 25-7
  invisibility of 69-70
  myths 33-4
  and other disabilities 31-3

# The National Autistic Society

The National Autistic Society (NAS) was founded in 1962 by a group of parents who were later joined by people with a professional interest in autism. Today, the Society has become the UK's foremost charity for people with autism and Asperger syndrome, and for their parents and carers. The NAS leads national and international initiatives providing a strong voice for autism. The organisation works in many areas to help people with an autistic spectrum disorder live their lives with as much independence as possible.

## The NAS

- runs education and adult centres
- supports local authorities in the development of their own specialist services
- maintains a library available to parents and researchers by appointment
- publishes a range of books and leaflets
- runs the Autism Helpline for parents and carers and people with autistic spectrum disorders
- organises conferences and training programmes
- offers specialist diagnosis and assessment services
- supports local groups and families around the country
- organises members' workshops
- encourages research into the causes of autism
- offers advice and advocacy for special educational needs
- raises awareness and creates a better understanding of autism
- organises volunteering schemes
- provides consultancy to professionals and organisations working in the field of autism
- offers an accreditation programme for autism-specific education and care services
- runs Prospects, a supported employment service for adults with autistic spectrum disorders

### *The National Autistic Society Headquarters*

393 City Road, London EC1V 1NG
Autism Helpline: 0870 600 85 85
Switchboard: 020 7833 2299
Minicom: 020 7903 3597
Fax: 020 7833 9666
Email: nas@nas.org.uk
Website: www.nas.org.uk